"Evan and David are two of the freshest and most impactful thinkers in MBA admissions. Their perspective on taking charge of your career sets the standard for the twenty-first-century model, where leadership comes from within, not from a job title. This book will definitely bring out the best candidate in you."

—Bill Kapler, retired partner of Accenture

"Evan and David are the ultimate authorities on MBA admissions in today's fast-changing business world. They have an uncanny ability to cut straight to the heart of your candidacy and pull out what makes you a compelling and powerful MBA applicant."

—Daniel Zilberman, principal of Warburg Pincus

"No one, and I mean no one, better understands what changes are taking place in MBA admissions better than Evan and David. They have their finger on the pulse of the new-found emphasis on leadership and contribution to community. In this book, they get at the heart of the matter: what applicants need to do to communicate their unique brand and how it fits the wants of the business school. Evan and David don't seek to 'game the system'; rather they teach you how to make the system work for you while discovering yourself and your strengths. You could apply to an MBA program without reading this book, but it would be a costly error. The ROI is incalculable."

—Mark Sklarow, executive director of Independent Educational Consultants Association

"Forster and Thomas have written a compelling book revealing two of the keys to successful business school applications. They stress the art of 'giving back,' distinguishing the doers from the talkers. This is a must-read for anyone who wants to get into business school."

—Lewis B. Cullman, LBO pioneer, philanthropist, and author of *Can't Take It with You*

"When you want a great meal, you hire a chef, not a food critic; when you need to tell a worthy story, you engage an expert storyteller, not an ex-admissions officer. Evan Forster has the uncanny ability to say in a hundred words what others can't say in ten thousand. When I don my admissions hat, there's nothing I value more than a tight, compelling, well written personal essay."

—Professor Richard Walter, UCLA Screenwriting Chairman

"In *The MBA Reality Check*, Evan Forster and David Thomas write extensively about leadership and community service. They practice what they preach. For more than eight years, their work with our students and mentors has helped make the College Bound program at Chess-in-the-Schools the dynamic success it is today."

—Marley Kaplan, CEO of Chess-in-the-Schools

THE MBA REALITY CHECK

Make the School You Want, Want You

WITHDRAWN

Evan Forster and David Thomas

Prentice Hall Press

PRENTICE HALL PRESS
Published by the Penguin Group
Penguin Group (USA) Inc.
375 Hudson Street, New York, New York 10014, USA

Penguin Group (Canada), 90 Eglinton Avenue East, Suite 700, Toronto, Ontario M4P 2Y3, Canada (a division of Pearson Penguin Canada Inc.) • Penguin Books Ltd., 80 Strand, London WC2R 0RL, England • Penguin Group Ireland, 25 St. Stephen's Green, Dublin 2, Ireland (a division of Penguin Books Ltd.) • Penguin Group (Australia), 250 Camberwell Road, Camberwell, Victoria 3124, Australia (a division of Pearson Australia Group Pty. Ltd.) • Penguin Books India Pvt. Ltd., 11 Community Centre, Panchsheel Park, New Delhi—110 017, India • Penguin Group (NZ), 67 Apollo Drive, Rosedale, North Shore 0632, New Zealand (a division of Pearson New Zealand Ltd.) • Penguin Books (South Africa) (Pty.) Ltd., 24 Sturdee Avenue, Rosebank, Johannesburg 2196, South Africa

Penguin Books Ltd., Registered Offices: 80 Strand, London WC2R 0RL, England

While the author has made every effort to provide accurate telephone numbers and Internet addresses at the time of publication, neither the publisher nor the author assumes any responsibility for errors, or for changes that occur after publication. Further, the publisher does not have any control over and does not assume any responsibility for author or third-party websites or their content.

First edition: April 2010

Library of Congress Cataloging-in-Publication Data

Forster, Evan.
  The MBA reality check : make the school you want, want you / Evan Forster and David Thomas.—1st ed.
    p. cm.
  Includes index.
  ISBN 978-0-7352-0448-5 (pbk.)
  1. Master of business administration degree—United States. 2. Business schools—United States.
3. Business education—United States. I. Thomas, David, 1966– II. Title.
  HF1131.F67 2010
  650.071'173—dc22   2009049202

PRINTED IN THE UNITED STATES OF AMERICA
10 9 8 7 6 5 4 3 2 1

Author's note: We have had hundreds of clients and reviewed thousands of essays at Forster-Thomas. The stories and essays in this book are based on the experiences of many clients we have worked with over the years. While they have been fictionalized to protect the individuals' privacy, they are indicative of our actual clients' stories and essays.

Most Prentice Hall Press books are available at special quantity discounts for bulk purchases for sales promotions, premiums, fund-raising, or educational use. Special books, or book excerpts, can also be created to fit specific needs. For details, write: Special Markets, Penguin Group (USA) Inc., 375 Hudson Street, New York, New York 10014.

To Charlee,

who never worried about saying the right thing.

Acknowledgments

We wish to acknowledge the following people for making this book possible: Dan Zilberman, for saying, "Be the best at what you do"; Julie Wong, for taking us to the Street; Kathi Elster, for making us take our own advice; Mark Chimsky, for coaching the coaches; our agent Laura Nolan, for turning us loose; our editor Maria Gagliano, for reigning us in; Julie Cowhey, Bill Kapler, Jim and Christine Ancey, and the rest of the gang at the Little Egg Harbor Yacht Club, for encouraging us to stop talking about what we do and start writing about it; Carter Bales, for teaching us the importance of legacy, and Marley Kaplan and Chess-in-the-Schools, for giving us the opportunity; Leslie Goldberg and Phyllis Steinbrecher, for giving us our start; Cheryl Drasin and Amanda Giroux, for being there; Katie Kennedy, for being our fingers; Pia and Michael Schenk, forever and always; Joe Scalzo and Anne Sullivan, for teaching us to be who we say we are; June and Manny Sweet and Gayle and Gene Thomas, for loving us anyway; and last but not least, all those brave enough to entrust us with their candidacies.

Contents

Prologue
Harvard or Bust

On a Friday night in September 2005, I was being bombarded with questions from the high schoolers and their Wall Street mentors as the college adviser for Chess-in-the-Schools (CIS), the college-bound program that helps New York inner-city kids get into top universities. One of the mentors there that night was Harry, a twentysomething junior-level analyst at an elite private equity firm on Wall Street. It didn't take much to figure out that Harry was volunteering at our program solely to bolster his résumé. When I asked him what prompted him to join CIS, he halfheartedly rolled out the answer he thought I wanted to hear. It had something to do with "world peace" and "hunger." I patted him on the arm and told him I hoped he'd do better in the swimsuit portion of whatever beauty pageant title he was gunning for.

"I'm applying to business school," he answered, with one of those half smiles to let me know he was in on my joke. Problem is, Harry saw the whole b-school admissions process as a joke, as a game he could play and win using the same formula that had gotten him where he was so far. "No, let me take that back," he corrected himself. "I'm applying to *Harvard Business School.*"

Like many highly driven MBA candidates, Harry was on what I call a suicide mission: Harvard or bust. Though he was working with another educational consultant that fall, he continually sought my advice and I repeatedly told him to trust his consultant. Still, he persisted.

Several days before submitting his first-round application he freaked out, phoned me *at home*, and begged me to read his HBS essays. As a courtesy to him for mentoring one of my CIS students, I relented and read his long-term goals essay, which I have long referred to as "$40 million by forty." Afterward, I thought, *Thank God he's working with someone else.* Harry had missed the entire point—long-term goals need to be about something greater than oneself, something transformational. His goals were all about . . . well, Harry. My primary advice was to ditch that "$40 million by forty" theme. "That's the kind of greed that the 1980s flick *Wall Street* was all about," I told him. "Who are you? One of those guys who will run the economy into the ground someday?"

Harry didn't take any of my advice that night. "It's too close to deadline to make those kinds of changes," he said—but I could tell two things: One, he didn't really believe me, and two, he wasn't willing to put that much work into it. He was not accepted to Harvard. He didn't even receive an interview. All three of the CIS volunteer mentors who had worked with me that year were accepted.

I write this not to show off, but because this was Harry's reason for insisting that he work with me the following year on his reapplication. I started with two suggestions: Ditch the "forty by forty" attitude and, at the very least, apply to Wharton and Stanford in addition to Harvard.

He agreed to the first request but not the latter. I told him that even though his essays may be great (and ultimately they were), his "Harvard or bust" attitude would be his undoing. Harry replied, "Without Harvard, I won't be able to return to private equity at the executive/management level." Boy, was he a fool. While many post-MBA hires at private equity shops may come from Harvard Business School (HBS), the best private equity shops hire from all the top five programs. And if you really bring something to the table, they'll hire you from a much lesser school than these. We know; we've seen it happen (when you get to the end of this book, I'll tell you all about the Georgetown grad who got cherry-picked by that medical-device private equity shop and is now running the world (boy, is McDonough getting a donation!).

What separates my candidates from the pack is that they have come to the understanding that, at some level, the MBA program they're applying to must want them as much as they want it. Just like in dating, "Desperate" with a capital *D* never wins. Candidates should, in essence, extend an invitation to b-schools to join *them* in reaching their long-term goals. That's the power of leadership, and the key to "getting in."

There's an old Buddhist saying (that's been appropriated by everyone from Jung to Oprah): "What you resist persists." If your mind is closed to success outside of one particular route, the universe will make sure that that route is closed to you. Great leaders get to where they're going come hell or high water. They don't need plum jobs, great scores, MBAs, or HBS.

This book is about getting into the mind-set of taking risks and building a compelling candidacy from a place of strength, not (as in Harry's case) fear or arrogance. Achieving your long-term goal is not a result of getting into a specific program as much as having a b-school join you on your incredible journey. It's about creating yes in the face of no by pursuing any pathway necessary to realize your dreams. That pathway might be an MBA, and it might even include an MBA from a certain school. But when you decide that that pathway is the *only* pathway, then your commitment is to going to that school, not achieving your goal. Unfortunately, Harry adamantly dismissed this advice from Auntie Evan, and so the universe had to teach him a lesson.

This book is dedicated to Harry, and to all those b-school applicants who did not, and will not, get into Harvard.

PART I

Kick-Starting Your Candidacy

Congratulations! You've decided to take the leap and launch your candidacy to a competitive MBA program. Whether you're six weeks or six months from hitting the "submit" button, you need to understand what makes a candidacy *sing*.

And that comes down to attitude, action, and information; Part 1 of this book addresses all three of those factors. Chapter 1 is all about establishing the framework for a successful mind-set before moving forward. Chapter 2 gives you an admissions overview from thirty thousand feet that will help you understand the parts of your candidacy and how they play out in an admission committee's decision-making process. Chapter 3 lays out the mind-set of a leader and how to tackle your candidacy as a person who has an impact on the world around him or her. The rest of Part 1 takes you into the weeds: building your extracurricular profile, demonstrating leadership, managing your recommenders, and even understanding and dealing with learning differences should they be a part of your candidacy.

As you'll see, your candidacy is expressed through your stats, story, and experience. Grab your number two pencil and get ready to take notes in the margins. I've got a lot to say, and you've got a long way to go—but I promise you'll have fun getting there.

CHAPTER 1

Ready, Set . . . Grow!

This isn't your father's MBA—if you want a degree simply for the skills or the network, you're starting off on the wrong foot. Strap yourself in for an attitude adjustment that lays the foundation for the rest of the book.

This is a book about how to shift into the mind-set of finding the visionary leader in you: the professional whose long-term goal is, no matter what, doing something greater than yourself with the intent to make a difference. More than anything, that is the key to convincing a top MBA program to give you a space in their incoming class. Thirty years ago, business school was just about business, and success was defined by bottom lines and financial analytic skill sets. It was, in fact, the redheaded stepchild of professional schools: If you couldn't get in to medical school or law school, you were going to business school.

But the world has changed. There's been a tectonic plate shift due to the Internet, globalization, and, yes, the sixties. Unless you're following in the footsteps of Jonas Salk, who cured polio, or William Brennan, who defined an activist court, medicine and law are no longer the primary venues for creating change. Business, of all kinds, is. With the advent of true globalization, it's the vehicle through which one can create transformation on its largest scale. It's no longer the redheaded stepchild, but the favorite son. Whether you want to start a nonprofit or make the family business profitable (or some of both—Gandhi, after all, wanted his nation to turn a profit), transformation starts with leadership.

I vividly recall a conversation a number of years ago, when Patty Dowden, a member of the MBA Admissions Board at Harvard Business School, proudly told me, "Harvard has taken the word 'business' out of its mission statement. Now we're about creating transformation." She added, "What we're looking for are exceptional candidates in whom we can create at least one of the following types of transformation: social, personal, or professional."

Focusing on transformation was an idea whose time had come. And having interviewed so many MBA admissions officers, David and I now know that Patty Dowden could have been speaking for any one of them.

This is not a book for people who are looking to game the system or get an MBA to improve their financial modeling skills. You can do that online through the University of Phoenix. Statistics is the same no matter where you take it. People who want to gain nothing more than that out of business school become functionaries. And that's fine; functionaries are a necessary part of every good team. Our clients, past and present, however, are the visionaries and leaders who will hire them.

This book follows different candidates in their personal journeys. Along the way, we'll travel with them while they dig down deep to find truths already inside themselves that they didn't know existed, or learn to see their actions in ways that take the emphasis off their own self-interest, or break out of the "What's in it for me?" mind-set we all have been trained to uphold. In this book, you'll learn to take risks: saying what you want to say, what you believe in, and not what you think people want to hear.

Don't worry; Auntie Evan will still let you talk about how big your deal is. Somewhere in your candidacy belong those facts, figures, metrics that made your merger and acquisition succeed. And you'll still get to show how you delegated responsibility. But what will be emphasized is not your outer Superman but your inner Clark Kent: what you learned about life, leadership, and yourself—how you developed internally, faced your fears, overcame your weaknesses, maximized your strengths.

Each of the chapters tackles the soul-searching inherent in every question asked by top schools, whether it's as obvious as Stanford's "What matters most to you and why?" or hardly apparent, such as Tuck's "How will you contribute to the MBA community?"

The MBA Reality Check will take you through every aspect of the process of applying to top MBA programs. It will cover everything: your long- and short-term goals, why extracurriculars matter, how to research the ways in which you and your desired school are a fit, how to master the essays that prove it, getting the most from your recommenders, and even the interview that will close the deal.

This is not a book that bogs you down in the minutia. I won't even touch the topic of how, say, Harvard is different from Stanford—if you can't figure that out with an hour browsing their websites, then you have no business attending either school in the first place (besides, such information goes out of date as soon as it's published). This book will free you from the old-school checklists that bog you down in "what to do" without showing you how to actually do it. If what you're looking for is a dos and don'ts list, then get on the Internet and search Businessweek.com's forums. Those and other MBA forums and blogs are great—all the checklists you need are already out there.

Instead, I want to set you free, to give you permission to stop worrying about what you think the schools want to hear—by the way, there is no such thing. By the time you finish, you'll know how to invite them to join you in your cutting-edge journey toward your ultimate career goals.

This is a book that unleashes the leadership potential in you—that part of you that takes a right turn down the Back Bowls of Vail onto the black diamond trails, not the part of you that's looking for the fastest route to après-ski.

And finally, this book will help you embrace and welcome the age-old fear: Should I really say this? Am I really about to say this? As you will discover, you've done something wrong if you choose absolutely safe topics and share your essays with a dozen of your closest friends in order to vet your opinions.

Like *Zen and the Art of Motorcycle Maintenance*, not only will you be able to fix your proverbial motorcycle, you might also do the one thing that all the greatest leaders—from Bill Gates to George Soros to Gandhi—have done: Get in touch with who you really are, from the good to the bad, and your own personal Tiananmen Square.

The "reality check" here is that you don't have to be the guy who led the hunger strike in Tiananmen Square to succeed at the top business schools. You don't have his story, and trying to play that game is a losing proposition. I know, because he was my client. The good news is you're not in competition with him or guys like him—*you're only in competition with yourself.*

I'll use that line over and over in this book. It's the most important piece of advice I can give: Comparing yourself to other applicants is a recipe for disaster; I've seen many excellent applicants fail when they file off every interesting aspect of their candidacy by trying to sound as much as possible like their friends who have already gotten accepted. And I've seen candidates at or below the average GMAT and/or GPA succeed at multiple top schools by going out on a limb and letting their proverbial freak flag fly. (How to actually do this is what most of this book is about.)

Appreciating a distinctive story is what I'm all about—and it's how I achieved rapid success as a b-school educational consultant. As a journalist and screenwriter who used my storytelling skills to help students in Beverly Hills write essays to apply to college (I waged a war to end those tired "My Summer in the Holy Land" tales of self-discovery), I was introduced to a young gentleman from Lehman Brothers whom I'll call "Candidate Zero." He had heard about my work with the high school students on Manhattan's Upper East Side and asked if I would be interested in helping him with his seven business school application essay questions.

I sat down to read the MBA application questions. Nearly all that particular year seemed pointedly personal, such as "Tell us about a time in your life when you failed," "Tell us something about yourself to help the committee get to know you better," and five hundred words on a *personal* achievement—right up my alley. Out front in all the applications was this odd question about "a long-term goal" (and I'm all about goals—as long as they go beyond the "what-can-you-do-for-me" and incorporate the "what-I-can-do-for-you").

So I said yes to Candidate Zero. But I told him I had no time for stories about LBOs or M&As, or any other nonsense one could easily locate on his résumé or in the grammar-challenged recommendations. If Candidate Zero wanted my help, he would have to be ready to spill it *all* out—the good, the bad, and the ugly—both professionally and, more important, personally. He agreed to my terms.

And herein lies the birth of Auntie Evan, whom you'll get to know well in these pages: Auntie Evan is that part of me who loves to tell people what to do, who loves a good story, and who lives for the "lean-in"—you know, the juiciest part of the story when your voice drops to a whisper and you're about to get let in on what's *not* being said. And, most important, Auntie Evan is the part of me who gets to help MBA candidates make a difference in their community, industry, and ultimately the world through their participation in a top MBA program.

Candidate Zero is exactly like most of you reading this book: someone who has already decided he's worthy of a top MBA program, but is freaking out about how to convince the admissions committees he's worthy. On the surface he had all the good elements (good undergraduate schooling, GPA, résumé) and one big bad thing (he was a straight white boy who wasn't particularly self-aware). The best thing, however, was that he knew his weakness. And he knew he needed to stand out.

He kept pressing me to help him dig down deep. And there's nothing I'm better at. Eventually, after a grueling, honest search through every aspect of his life, including his family's struggle as Soviet immigrants, we landed on his true desire and reason for going to b-school. He wanted to use private equity as a vehicle to help the then fledgling Russian economy. He transformed his way of thinking from "I want to go from investment banking to private equity" to thinking about the impact he wanted to have in the world, and how private equity was his platform. (By the way, Candidate Zero got a resounding "You're in!" that year from his number one choice, Wharton.)

What I know is how to inspire an Olympic *candidacy*. With my partner David Thomas, or Uncle David, as I fondly refer to him—a man whose encyclopedic knowledge of the most up-to-date admissions trends and statistics could be a book in and of itself—we have spent countless hours building candidacies, from revamping résumés to breathing new life into extracurricular leadership, to counseling where to apply right down to what to wear during the interview.

That said, our success is not rooted in a secret strategy, a gimmick, a technique, a formula . . . I have a simple guiding principle: Dig down deep, find the truth, and tell it—all the while making sure your professional goals are greater than your own personal gain.

So let's get to work.

CHAPTER 2

Stats, Story, and Experience

Understanding the big picture of MBA admissions will help you avoid land mines and leverage each element of your candidacy to its fullest potential.

B-school admissions committees are unexpectedly holistic in the way they review candidacies. Every element matters—from your grades, to your GMAT, to your résumé, recommendations (recs), and essays—but they matter in ways that are often counterintuitive. Getting into business school is a dramatically different ball game than getting into med or law school, which is often just a numbers game (you either have the grades and test scores or you don't).

I'm not going to waste your time describing how to beef up every element of your candidacy, however. This book assumes you're not a high school senior mapping out an extremely farsighted game plan for getting into graduate business school. I'm going to breeze past the fixed elements of your candidacy that you have very little control over: where you went to college, how well you performed, what classes you took, whether you studied abroad. And I'm certainly not going to spend time teaching you GMAT tricks: There are far better-qualified people than I to do that. The rule of thumb is a score of 700 or better if at all possible. There, I said it.

Every admissions committee has its own way of assessing candidacies. Some are rigorously quantitative, rating each element on a scale of 0 to 5 with the highest cumulative scores getting the fat envelope. Others are much more subjective, allowing one or two extremely compelling elements of a candidacy (such as outstanding leadership accomplishments) to overcome other weaknesses (such as a 640 GMAT). What is important for you to understand, however, is how all the elements of your candidacy work together.

No matter what particular process an admissions committee uses, a single simple framework can help you understand the mind-set of the admissions officer—and once you understand the framework, you will find it easier to let go of the candidacy-killing mistakes so many excellent applicants make.

Think of your candidacy as having three broad elements: stats, story, and experience. First, let me lay them out, then I'll get into how they work together.

STATS are the quantitative measurements of your academic ability: your GPA and your GMAT. They answer a specific and distinct question of great concern to the admissions committee: *Is the applicant prepared for the rigorous quantitative curriculum of a graduate MBA education?*

Most of my candidates think about GPA and GMAT in terms of a benchmark: Are my numbers good enough? They compare their GPA and GMAT to the averages of the schools they are applying to. Admissions committees don't cherry-pick the best stats any more than a great basketball coach selects only the tallest guys trying out for the team. Relying only on the criteria of height doesn't account for talent, dexterity, or hand-eye coordination. The same is true for your academic prowess: GPA and GMAT alone don't tell the whole story.

For example, how you performed in certain types of coursework can be more significant than your overall GPA. Admissions committees are most concerned about your performance in quantitative classes such as calculus, microeconomics, and statistics (if you've taken such classes; there is no prerequisite MBA coursework). So a candidate with a 3.3 overall GPA but a 3.6 in a number of quantitative classes may have an advantage over a candidate with a 3.6 cumulative but a 3.2 quantitative GPA.

There's another reason your overall GPA matters, and it has nothing to do with your mathematical prowess: It is an excellent marker of how disciplined you are. (Who would you rather hire into a quantitative job: a math genius who doesn't do her homework or a dedicated student who performs well with a calculator and always turns her homework in on time?) A committed student will usually have a consistent GPA, where a flaky genius is more likely to have peaks and valleys. A consistent 3.4 across four years is better than four years that bounce from 3.0 to 3.8 to 3.2 to 3.6. While the end result is the same, I'm more confident with a reliable student. If you bounce around, you may have some 'splaining to do (see Chapter 18).

Then there is the dreaded GMAT, a standardized assessment of your aptitude in the areas most relevant to an advanced business school education. In three and a half nerve-wracking hours, you demonstrate your basic analytical, verbal, and mathematical skill sets.

The first hour is the least significant portion of the test: the Analytical Writing Assessment (AWA). You're given thirty minutes to analyze an issue and thirty minutes to analyze an argument. The top score is a 6.0. As long as you make a 4.5 or better, you don't need to worry about this score.

The next seventy-five minutes test your quantitative ability through thirty-seven multiple-choice questions divided into two types: Data Sufficiency and Problem-Solving. *Tick tock.* The final seventy-five minutes tests your verbal abilities with forty-one questions on Reading Comprehension, Critical Reasoning, and Sentence Correction. The test is "computer adaptive," meaning that nobody gets the exact same questions: Each answer you give determines what the next question will be. Get your answer right, and the next question is harder; get your answer wrong, and the next question is easier. Doing well at the beginning of each section is very important. You'll score better getting only the first twenty questions correct than you will getting only the last twenty questions correct.

Since nobody gets exactly the same test, what matters to the committee is not your raw score, but how well you perform compared to everyone else who took the test. This is measured by your percentile rank, which is included on your GMAT score report. As a rule of thumb, top b-schools believe that scoring better than 80 percent of all test-takers—referred to as being "eightieth percentile"—qualifies you to handle MBA coursework.

GMAT and GPA combined give an admissions committee a very precise view of how likely you are to excel in an MBA curriculum. If you rank at or above the eightieth percentile on both sections of the GMAT (regardless of your actual score), score a 5.0 on the AWA, and have a GPA of 3.4 or better with no Ds or Fs, you can be confident that any admissions committee will know you are prepared to excel in a rigorous MBA curriculum.

That's the bottom line. Once you've met the bar, everything else is icing on the cake. The more you exceed these minimum expectations, the better—the people with the highest scores will do better than those who simply meet the bar. But remember, stats are just one dimension of your candidacy.

EXPERIENCE refers to what you've been exposed to in your life: your professional background, extracurricular activities, and leadership experiences. They address another issue that's important to admissions committees: *Are you, at this point in your personal and professional development, ready for an MBA program? Do you have something to offer it?*

Some people are ready by the time they graduate from college. If you were a campus leader who created a significant impact in one or more organizations, you may have more experience in group dynamics, teamwork, assessing your strengths and weaknesses, and organizational management than people who graduated five years earlier than you. MBA programs are increasingly friendly to candidates with "zero to two years" professional experience. This is a significant change: As recently as a couple of years ago, few schools seriously considered applicants with fewer than four or even five years' experience. Harvard and Stanford, just like Hollywood studios, seem to keep liking them younger and younger.

Still, extraordinary campus leadership is required to be seriously considered for MBA admissions straight out of college. In 2008, HBS created a novel program designed to lock in outstanding young applicants while they are still in college, yet provide them with professional experience to help them contribute to classroom discussions: the 2+2 program. Applicants apply in the summer after their junior year; if accepted, HBS helps place them in a two-year program (typically in investment banking or management consulting) before they matriculate for the two-year MBA curriculum. The 2+2 program is especially interested in "nontraditional" pre-MBA candidates (liberal arts majors, engineers, artists, etc.).

A candidate's professional background is the source of much angst. There's a common misperception that top MBA programs place a premium on "prestige" applicants: Goldman Sachs applicants are automatically more desirable than Citigroup applicants; strategic consultants are preferred over operations consultants.

This is all nonsense. The truth is that this is really a chicken-and-egg issue. Goldman doesn't get you into HBS as much as what got you into Goldman is likely to also appeal to HBS. What a candidate does in his or her career, however, is much more appealing to a committee than a brand name. A Goldman applicant who merely met expectations can't compare to a Houlihan Lokey applicant who carved out a new client-facing role as an analyst, exceeding all expectations. A candidate who cofounded a start-up company that attracted angel investors—even if the venture failed—probably has a deeper well of experience than Goldman's top-rated analyst. Newsflash: For all you guys and gals coming from advertising, nonprofits, fashion houses, and design and PR firms—or for anyone who doesn't have a traditional undergraduate business background—get over your fear that you are at some kind of disadvantage to those who come from traditional pre-MBA analyst programs at investment banks and consulting firms. You bring a buried treasure that b-schools often find all too lacking in their applicant pools: professional diversity.

Experience is always relative to expectations. Admissions officers don't expect a twenty-five-year-old professional to have had many on-the-job leadership opportunities. It's hard to impact an organization with thousands of employees. Therefore, strong applicants will have created their own leadership opportunities—through community service, for example, or by volunteering for workplace extracurriculars like the social committee, the Women in Business chapter at your company, the peer-review committee, or recruiting efforts. See chapters 4 and 5 for more information about how to beef up your leadership profile.

In addition to your résumé and extracurricular activities, recommendations play an important role in helping a committee understand how you compare to other applicants in the "experience" department. If you don't stand out relative to your peers, you could hold a job for five years and fail to impress in this area. It's not about how long you've worked or how many organizations you've joined, but what kind of impact you've made relative to expectations. See Chapter 6 for getting the most out of your recommenders.

STORY is how I refer to your "intangibles." While stats and experience are concrete—you have a certain GMAT score; you have a certain type of professional experience—story is almost entirely subjective. At the most fundamental level, story refers to how you think, what makes you tick, what you're passionate about, how you relate to others, whether you're proactive and take initiative. In short, it's about how you interpret your stats and experience.

Stats and experience "are what they are." If, like most MBA applicants, you're picking up this book a few weeks to a few months before launching your candidacy, there is very little you can do to change those elements. Don't freak out. Story, the most powerful part of your candidacy, is entirely in your control—and telling your story powerfully and effectively is what the bulk of this book is about.

The "MBA reality check" is that your story plays a much larger role in whether you get accepted than most people ever imagine. At the most extreme positive end of the spectrum, a compelling story can make up for multiple weaknesses in a candidate's stats and/or experience. While your recommenders play a part in communicating your story, this is where your essays take the front seat and play the marquis role.

Three Parts Beat as One

So now we finally get to the fun part: how these elements interact during the admissions process to result in an acceptance. "The idea is that the application is a series of components that comprises a 'real estate of material' that can represent the vast parts of our lives," says Rose Martinelli, associate dean for student recruitment and admissions at the University of Chicago Booth School of Business. "You can't present everything about you, so what do you choose to present in each and every area? And how is that coherent together?"

That is the $64,000 question. The following description of how admissions works is oversimplified and not technically accurate—no one does it exactly this way—but it does create a beautiful framework for helping you understand what goes on behind the scenes.

* * *

LET'S say a school receives ten thousand applications from which to build a class of a thousand—that's a 10 percent success rate.

The first thing the committee worries about is: *Can the applicant do the work?* That's where the stats come in. Applications with GMATs and transcripts that clearly don't demonstrate academic ability—and there are no hard metrics, though GMATs below 600 and transcripts below 3.0 are arguably rules of thumb—may go straight into the trash. BAM! We just weeded out two thousand candidates in one fell swoop. (Don't freak out if you fall into this category—later on I'll explain how other factors can overcome below-average stats.)

The next thing the committee worries about is: *Is this applicant ready for business school? Has she had sufficient professional or organizational experiences to make the most of an advanced business education and be able to contribute to classroom discussions and study groups?* Candidates without any demonstrated leadership potential or thin professional experience, or who have merely met expectations without standing out relative to their peers, get drop-kicked at this stage. Exit another three thousand applications.

At this stage, we have five thousand candidates left on the table—*all of whom have proven their worth*. Let that sink in: 50 percent of the pool is worthy of admission. (Sometimes the percentage is even higher: MIT Sloan Admissions Director Rod Garcia told me it's not unusual for his committee to judge 70 percent of applicants as worthy of a seat at Sloan.)

Our hypothetical committee now has five thousand applicants they'd love to accept, but only a thousand seats available to offer. By what criteria do they cut 80 percent of the remaining applicants? It seems awfully subjective, right?

Yes, it is. That's why story—the most subjective of the three elements—plays such an important role in your candidacy. And hence the "reality check": Your essays are not about proving your worth; they are about creating a lasting impression on the committee by painting an evocative picture of how you think, what you care about, how you make decisions, your personal leadership style, and what you look like in action.

Using the essays to prove your worth is the single biggest mistake you can make. Since the essays don't play a huge role in your candidacy until *after* you've already proven your worth based on stats and experience, you're just spinning your wheels to continue to focus on proving your worth in the essays. Instead, you should focus on being memorable by choosing interesting topics and analyzing your experiences in a compelling, evolved, evocative, sophisticated way. How to actually achieve that vague and abstract goal is what Part 2 of this book, "Zen and the Art of MBA Admissions Essays," is all about.

So, back to our hypothetical admissions committee. Another three thousand applicants just got cut because the committee couldn't find anything remarkable about them subjectively. Now, at the tail end of this process, comes the interview—two thousand lucky souls get invited to sit down with an actual real-life representative of the admissions committee and close the deal. (Some schools have "open interviews" that anyone can sign up for, even before submitting their application—see Chapter 19 for more information on how to use the interview to close the deal.)

These final two thousand candidates are narrowed down to a final one thousand (plus two hundred are given a spot on the waitlist) based on a careful calibration of their entire candidacies. At this point, our hypothetical committee also includes some data completely beyond your control—primarily diversity/demographic issues like gender, industry, geography, ethnicity, etc.—to create a beautifully balanced class.

AS I said, this is an oversimplification. Real admissions committees don't operate in this highly linear style; all of these factors are actually being considered and balanced simultaneously. That's how HBS, for example, ends up accepting some applicants who have low-600 GMAT scores and rejecting quite a few applicants with high-700 GMAT scores. I've turned down many a potential client with 3.8 GPAs and 780 GMAT scores because they were deathly boring, had no self-awareness, never did anything without figuring out what they were getting in return, and/or insisted on emulating the exact same essay topics as their friends who got in last year.

At the opposite end of the spectrum are candidates like Randy. Randy had a 3.8 GPA from a top-tier college—but he majored in classics and placed out of the only math class he needed to earn his degree. So he didn't have a single quantitative class in his transcript by which to judge those abilities. However, his super-high GPA from such a competitive school clearly demonstrated he's both smart and a disciplined student.

A great GMAT quant percentile can easily offset any concerns the committee has about one's math abilities, but Randy's best GMAT score after five attempts was a 640—including a 63 quant percentile. Yet the rest of Randy's candidacy was extraordinarily compelling. His recommendations touted the initiative and interpersonal skills that won him a top 5 percent analyst ranking at his investment bank. His essays were as insightful and witty as he was (I forced him to let go of the dry, business-memo style he initially thought was appropriate), his career vision bold and inventive, and his extracurriculars integrated into his passions rather than randomly selected to pad his résumé. Randy was memorable in every way but his quant ability—and Wharton accepted him on the condition that he take a calculus class and make an A or a B.

There's your MBA reality check. Now, let's talk about leadership.

CHAPTER 3

Leadership

How to Live as a Leader

**This is all any great business school
really wants from you.**

"No" is for functionaries. "Yes" is for leaders.

Business schools love nothing more than people who take things on, who accomplish things, who are continually acting to make things happen, who don't take no for an answer. They refer to this quality as "demonstrated leadership potential," which means you have to demonstrate. This chapter is about how to get into the mind-set of a leader and take on *something* in your life, whether at work or play (yet outside of your job responsibilities), and make it "mo' better." And you need to do so not just like your life depends on it, but as if the future of the planet depends on it. That's the way the best leaders operate: Getting a new watercolor for the office becomes a life-or-death proposition. Such guys are often either despised or adored, sometimes by the same person.

If the past is a great indicator of the future, the present is an even better indicator. So for those of you who have a roster of big-dick accomplishments that ended upon graduation from college—but who are now too busy to do more than work, drink, hammer a nail on an occasional Sunday, or write a check to a charity once a year—you're going to find yourself with a gaping hole in your candidacy.

Nobody wants to know what you *did*. They want to know what you *do*.

And if what you do is *only* about you and how you're able to leap tall buildings in a single bound with no help from anybody, then nobody can help you. Think about it: If I'm a school, my purpose is to help you grow. But you imply strongly that you have no need to grow. The person reading your application may love many things about your candidacy, but since you don't need his or her help, and you already know everything there is to know, then he or she has no incentive to get behind your candidacy. Why should I help someone who doesn't need me? I'd rather give a slot to someone with a great idea who can also identify why he or she needs my business school to achieve those goals.

If admissions officers don't think they can help you, they move on to the next person. Really great athletes understand that to be phenomenal, to win the gold medal, they can't merely have enormous talent, they must be the most coachable. Every book by or about Michael Jordan isolates one main ingredient for his success: He was coachable. Sure, he had major talent, but—barring *Outliers* author Malcolm Gladwell's "right place/right time" theory—coachability is what made Jordan "Jordan." Michael Phelps is "Michael Phelps" because he kept on pushing to get better at what he does, even when he'd already won a gold medal. He wanted to win eight. To play at an Olympic level—that is, the top business schools—you must never rest on your laurels.

About three years ago, I was giving a seminar at a private equity shop on Wall Street. Topic of the day: post-collegiate extracurriculars. That's when Carl—who I would later come to find out had the requisite 710 GMAT, above 3.5 GPA, an economics degree, and who had made his way to Wall Street despite a relatively obscure Georgia State background—boasted (and why not) that he was launching the first-ever Georgia State alumni network in New York City. He had already won verbal commitments from the alumni affairs office back in Georgia to give him the list of New York and tri-state-area members.

You could see the excitement in his face. He saw no reasons why this wouldn't work, nor did he complain about how he couldn't find the time to make it happen. He wanted to make this happen—for himself, not because it looked good. When I rhetorically asked Carl if that's all he's doing, he recited a dashing history of single-handed accomplishments such as making Phi Kappa Phi and winning multiple scholarships.

Carl was really excited when he came to my office. It was as if he had just won a free trip to Disneyland. What he didn't realize though is that the rides were going to be really bumpy. It isn't enough to come up with a great idea or work a lot of hours and just get something done all by your lonesome.

But when he walked in, Carl was feeling great about himself. As he wrote on his Taking Your Inventory workbook (see page 279):

Answering these questions, I feel like I'm signing up for Match.com . . . and so far I feel like I am coming across pretty good. Let's review:

1. Good with kids and worked as a youth counselor.

2. Family guy who helps his parents with their finances.

3. Has French family with a vineyard.

4. Owner of a wine bar in Atlanta (well, investor).

5. Employed.

Now, hopefully, my target schools look at applicants the same way a smart, single woman looks for a man.

Unfortunately, admissions officers don't look at applicants the same way. They want a little something more: They want to see you make a lasting contribution to a community.

Going over Carl's workbook, I began to notice a theme to his accomplishments. His accomplishments included single-handedly putting together the end-of-year dinner for the business fraternity (Carl got the keynote speaker, the food, the volunteers, the liquor, the band . . .). Also single-handedly, he made all of the buy/sell investment decisions in his "by initiation only" portfolio of the student-run investment fund. And this was his proof to me that he would have no problem launching the first-ever New York City alumni organization.

Yet, I kept hearing a song. I thought it was coming from one of the neighboring office buildings, but no—the windows were closed. A strange version of "All by Myself" seemed to be playing—but the lyrics had changed to "I *wanna* be all by myself."

If Carl didn't change that tune fast, he was going to be alone for a long time. Most of his projects either featured him in the single starring role or fell apart eventually. The business fraternity's dinner failed the year after he left—and Carl thought that was a testament to his prior *good* leadership (after all, it didn't fail on *his* watch). By going it alone, Carl had failed to cultivate a leader to take up the gauntlet after him.

So, wrapped in the Serengeti Green walls of our office, Carl and I went through his grand idea to unite Georgia State alumni in New York City. His rationale went something like this: "I'm one of the very few people ever to graduate Georgia State and actually make his way all the way to Wall Street with no help from anyone." Impressive. "The problem is that Career Services in the undergrad business department doesn't really support its graduates," Carl said with an earnest fist-pounding on the arm of my Eames original. "Yet there are so many of us Georgia State grads here in New York. We've clawed our way into careers from design to securities," he barked. "And when I was graduating, there was no one there to mentor me. I intend to change all that and create the first-ever Georgia State alumni mentoring and networking organization here in New York."

In addition to the verbal commitments he received from the heads of the alumni association, he disclosed that the school's online technicians had come up with a plan to create a website, and he also had thought up ideas for three or four of the biggest Saturday night alumni hoedowns this side of the Hudson.

Then I began to ask the hard questions: "Exactly when does the website go up? And who exactly is doing what? And, of course, you have a written commitment from the school?"

"No problem, I'm figuring all that out," he said.

That's when I pulled out our Extracurricular Action Plan (EAP) worksheet and slapped it on the table. "Carl, you need to fill this out."

The EAP is a worksheet we use with our clients to help them organize and develop their extracurricular projects so they can actually make the project a lasting reality—not just a premature ejaculation. It's a week-by-week, month-by-month planner that covers everything from the equipment you will need, the people you need to help you, the location you will require, and the money you will raise, etc. It's a got a place for everything you will need in order to make your project happen—starting with a written commitment to its purpose and the date of completion.

It's not rocket science—a million books and a million groups have used some variation of it—but it is a guide, and it does make you commit and figure out dates, times, and all the particulars. It reminds you of what's done and what needs to be done. But like so many boys and girls who have managed to barrel through and create one-offs one time, just winging it *all by themselves*—only to have their projects never be heard from again except for on a line somewhere below "work experience" and above "conversant in Mandarin"—Carl just looked at the EAP and said, "Don't worry about me getting this done. I have my own way of doing things."

Of course he did. And it was *all* going to get done by the second week of October (that year's first-round deadline).

Choosing dates, making yourself stick to a plan: This turns an idea into a reality.

The real crux of your leadership is how you react when the circumstances and people start saying no. Little things Carl wasn't thinking of in his excitement. Thorny real-world issues like school insurance, privacy issues raised when giving people's names out, your friends who promised to help get a better offer, volunteers who back out when they realize you were asking for help *this* fall.

Still, Carl wasn't having it. He had handled every other successful project in his life 80 percent on his own. And despite the fact that I pointed out that such "lone wolf" achievements don't demonstrate leadership, he had "proof" from his past successes, smaller though they were, that meant he didn't need anyone else's help and could do this—*easy peasy*.

Sometimes a child just has to stick his hand on the burner. I decided not to keep pushing in that moment. Our session ended shortly thereafter.

Ego Versus Mission

Three days later, Carl called me in a panic. Meg, the Georgia State alumni IT director, was suddenly asking him all kinds of probing questions, such as whether he had addressed privacy issues around giving out email addresses and who was going to maintain the website once it was up and running.

"I don't get it!" he wailed. "A week ago she was totally into it."

I began calmly asking Carl if he could answer her questions. He wasn't having it. This revealed the real reason he was panicking: All these issues would take so much time to handle that he couldn't possibly address them all by his round-one application deadline. So I asked him a question—and it's the same question you as a leader should always ask yourself as you make choices: "Is the project about you getting into business school, or is it about the mission?" In Carl's case, the specific question was, "Am I committed to being a hero or am I committed to making a difference for the recent graduates and alumni of Georgia State?"

Leadership is about making a difference. Carl was failing as a leader because the project had become all about his ego, not about the final result. The latter is what it's all about, and if that's what you're committed to, then you are a leader who is going to make a huge difference *despite* people and circumstances saying, "No, it's not possible." If you're committed to looking good, then you're reluctant to fight the battles that all leaders must wage to get something meaningful accomplished. After all, if it's easy, it's not an accomplishment.

And never forget—no matter how many detours your plan takes, no matter how many obstacles you have to work around, as long as you keep your eye on the mission, you will end up somewhere near where you planned to go.

Carl got committed to the mission and, with a well-drawn action plan, and the willingness to—gasp—ask for help from friends and contacts, his project was a success. A solid, written action plan also makes your project more real to others like Meg in IT; it's easy to get others on board with your cause if you can give them precise deliverables and deadlines. In fact, once Carl had a plan, all those intrusive, annoying questions that Meg had asked came into focus as necessary steps to achieve the mission. And as soon as Carl took his ego out of the picture, Meg became a partner instead of an obstacle. Working out privacy issues became a challenge rather than an obstacle, and Carl always loved a challenge.

Carl never ended up having three of four giant hoedowns in Manhattan—he ended up having one, and only 75 alumni showed up. But enough of those alumni got on board with his mission—making it possible for Georgia State alumni to have an easier time of reaching their dreams in the Big Apple—that four newly minted Georgia State grads got Big Apple jobs the next year.

And an even crazier thing happened. By the time Carl left for

Columbia Business School, his posse of New York school buds whom he had groomed for leadership took over the project, and the following year 250 people showed up at the shindig.

Not only do leaders create lasting transformation, but they give birth to other leaders who take over. This is particularly helpful if the original leader gets hit by a bus or goes to business school.

So there's how a leader lives: always in action, with an eye on opportunity. In Chapter 5, I explain step-by-step how to actually build an action plan, get others on board, and create legacy. First, however, let's explore "the extracurricular equation."

CHAPTER 4

Community Service and Extracurriculars

The Extracurricular Equation

Think you work too many hours to get involved in the world around you? First thing you need is an attitude adjustment.

I've said it once and it bears saying again: a 780 GMAT alone is not going to get you into a top MBA program. Neither will a 3.9 GPA. Not even the two of those together is going to raise more than an appreciative eyebrow from the average top-ten admissions committee (in fact, Pete Johnson, director of admissions of Berkeley's Haas School of Business, recently told us with a wry grin that he'd rejected somewhere upward of 80 percent of all candidates with a 760 or better GMAT score).

The slam dunk is extracurriculars. Extracurriculars—whether they're at work, such as being on a recruiting team, or out in Free Willy–land, such as gathering your friends' old suits to donate to homeless people going to job interviews—says a lot about your commitment to something greater than yourself.

Business schools are very interested in what kind of person you are, yet they're very savvy to all the crap that comes out of smooth talkers' mouths; they're like the gal who's been burned by too many silver-tongued douches. Extracurriculars are something you can actually do something about, something you have complete control over, and there's no excuse to do poorly in this department. You need extracurriculars that are not one-offs, but constitute a true commitment to something greater than yourself.

I talk to people all the time who have the most amazing excuses:

- **"I'm in my first year at Houlihan and I'm working hundred-hour weeks!"**

- **"My boss doesn't let me. I don't have any time off."**

- **"What little time off I have, I devote to staying in shape by going to the gym."**

- **"I just started working here. Everybody expects a lot of face time."**

- **"My mother's alone, widowed, and depressed. I leave the city every weekend to go home and spend time with her."**

All of you are right. It's not about lazy. None of you are lazy, and none of you are wrong. Nothing rings truer than my own twenty-six-year-old godson Michael's story. Michael is in his second year at a real estate firm. Talk about a bad market: real estate in Miami. Every other conversation is about how he could lose his job at any minute. So when his mother, my best friend Cheryl, and I kept throwing ideas at him—like spending Wednesday nights at Toastmasters, volunteering as a tour guide at Vizcaya, or at minimum joining the Hillel at University of Miami—Michael just threw the ideas back to us, paralyzed by the fear of not putting in more "face time" at his firm. And he has a winning answer, hands down, especially in a market where real estate has tanked.

All of you have winning answers. But there's an old saying that all successful people understand: "If you want something done, give it to the busiest person in the room." I say three things: Get your work done, do a great job, *and* do a great job at Vizcaya. Doing a great job is certainly impressive. Doing a great job *and* being the guy responsible for helping save Vizcaya is monumental: and that's the guy who gets talked about behind closed doors. So the answer is: If "face time" gets you noticed, Vizcaya gets you promoted. Not to mention into business school.

Which brings me to another note: For months and months and months, I'd been yelling about Michael getting involved. "What if you decide to apply to business school?" I'd say. How could Auntie Evan's own godson not get into a top program? That would be like Jenna Bush not getting into HBS . . . oh well, never mind. So, what's going to really drive getting you in? Is there some sort of equation: grades plus GMAT plus extracurriculars equals a top business school? Hell no. That's not the point.

After months of pressuring Michael and making him crazy about showing up at Toastmasters, I realized that Cheryl and I were pushing him for the wrong reasons. Yes, the equation I mentioned previously is a good one, but here's where it will fall apart. If Michael's going to Toastmasters because Auntie Evan said so, and getting into business school rather than learning to speak publicly is his goal, he's not going to succeed—certainly in no way that's going to make a difference to Toastmasters or to an admissions committee worth its salt.

Once you choose to get involved because you've accepted it's the right thing to do, then your involvement becomes a commitment. When you're committed, you're passionate, and when you're passionate, you're transformational—and *that* is the extracurricular equation. You can't help but be a transformational leader, and everybody begins to see it.

Interestingly, shortly thereafter, Michael started going to Toastmasters without annoying reminders from Mom or me. In short order, he became a leader within Toastmasters, and the people within began to recognize him as a go-to guy; he even won an award for best impromptu speech of the season. And now he's a go-to guy for newcomers who are facing the same fears, the same concerns, and the same complaints that he came in with. He helps them see the possibility of who they could be. And, no shocker to me, I earned a big "you're right again, Auntie Evan" when his direct supervisor mentioned that he not only knows he can depend on Michael to do what he's expected to do, but so much more as well. Michael is, by definition, a transformational leader—period. Inside and outside the office.

PS: Michael's new way of taking on the planet has bled out elsewhere. His boss, along with a few others on the management team, recently offered to write Michael's recs. And, oh yeah, Michael recently turned down a job offer at a major conventional resort. So now that scared little mouse is the guy who's turning down job offers. His new courage is also what will get him into a top business school. *Now that's my boy!*

Admissions Directors on the Role of Extracurriculars in Your Application

We are really looking for people who are going to be as energetic and dynamic and involved and engaged in our community. We're also looking for people who have purpose and passion. Extracurricular activities, whether in the community or in a work environment, show us that the candidate chooses to get involved above and beyond expectations, and wants to make a positive impact. Those kinds of behaviors mean that that person will probably do them not only at Stern, but will also have great potential for leadership success in the future.

—Anika Davis Pratt, Assistant Dean, MBA Admissions and Financial Aid, NYU Stern School of Business

The Wall Street Myth: "I Don't Have Time"

I remember giving a "Kick-Start Your MBA" speech at Morgan Stanley to a room of more than fifty young analysts and a sprinkling of IT guys. The subprime mortgage debacle had recently gone down and the economy was tanking; everyone was freaked out by the presumed tidal wave of applicants. After all, what do twentysomething college grads do in a weak economy? Hide out in grad school. With so many people applying a year earlier than they expected, therefore losing a whole year to pad their résumés, extracurricular involvement would truly separate the wheat from the chaff.

I went through a list of extracurricular "don'ts": one-offs such as a day with Habitat for Humanity, a Breast Cancer 5K, a morning with New York Cares, bringing your housekeeper's son to work, and of course the "I-Climbed-Mount-Kilimanjaro" trope. As I came to the end, I realized that faces were grim.

Extracurriculars show us that a person has more than one dimension. Sometimes you see candidates who have no interest in anything apart from work, and they just don't come across anywhere near as well as someone who is also involved in other things, be it theater or sports or some sort of community work. We're looking at their track record to see whether they have excelled, and to see who is focused on achievement, on delivering results, and who's got the energy and motivation to get things done. Uninvolved people will also come across as more one-dimensional in job interviews, and we're trying to predict how such people are going to come across to recruiters. I think people who are uniquely focused on work are often less open-minded. However, we do take into account cultural factors; people from some countries have more of a habit of being involved in activities, which is encouraged more from an early age than it is in other countries.

—Caroline Diarte-Edwards, MBA Director of Admissions, INSEAD

I thought it best to go around the room and do an ad hoc exercise. I started in the back row on the left side of the room and asked, "What are you involved in extracurricularly?" The first response was, not surprisingly, "Well, I'm a first-year analyst, so I'm really busy all the time. I never leave the office." The second and third responses were similar. The fourth person said something about volunteering at a soup kitchen on Thanksgiving. The fifth, a second-year analyst with a name tag that said something like "Arvind"—but whose ethnicity was less discernable than all the others combined—also defended his busy work schedule. Six, seven, and eight were the same. And so it went, analysts falling like dominoes one after the other after the other, each either sheepishly admitted to their one-offs and/or pleading a busy schedule.

This all went on, a growing rumble in the room, until Denise, a

Extracurriculars are something we look for and we value for a couple of different reasons. One is that it gives us a sense of who the whole person is beyond just what's on your résumé. It also gives us a sense of your ability to commit to something you're passionate about, whether that's related to your job or not. And finally it's a good predictor of whether or not you're going to be involved in our program. If you come to a top MBA program and you just go to class and go home, you will miss at least half of the benefit of being there in the first place.

It's better to get involved late in your application process than never. It encompasses two things: One, is this person serious enough about applying to business school that they're going to go out and put some effort into it? The second thing is a side effect: People who don't have necessarily a history of service discover when they start that it's more stimulating than they guessed—and then they get even more involved. Starting late is not as impressive as having a longer history, but we don't discount it completely.

—Peter Johnson, Executive Director of Admissions, Full-Time MBA Program, University of California Berkeley Haas School of Business second-year analyst, raised her hand and said, "I just launched an elementary school in Botswana."

You could have heard a pin drop. "How is it that she does the same job you do, yet she still found the time to pursue what she really cares about?" Then, to this decidedly athletic group of young professionals, I couldn't help but add, "I guess none of you can find time to make it to the gym, considering how busy you all are."

While many admissions officers understand that some professions, such as investment banking, demand an inordinate amount of time from you, Denise proves that the "I work too many hours" routine is not a game you want to play . . . unless, of course, you're a fan of the roulette wheel. So, if you see yourself as anybody but Denise, take the quiz on the next page.

Extracurriculars are the best example we'll have of how someone's going to impact their community. To be honest with you, extracurriculars also make you more interesting. Most schools don't want people who check in to go to class and then check out and go home. At this time in your life, if you're thinking about going back to business school, it's about more than just getting the grades, it's about making an impact.

—Liz Riley Hargrove, Associate Dean of Admissions, Fuqua School of Business at Duke University

Extracurriculars tells us about the well-roundedness of the candidate. But they could be a lot of different things. If you're a married student with a child or two—that's an extracurricular. I understand that when you live a consultant's or investment banker's life out of undergrad, you're probably not gonna have a lot of extracurriculars unless they're internal—mentoring new consultants or analysts. It does qualify if it's outside your job description but under your company's roof. We'd love you to mentor people.

—Randall Sawyer, Director of Admissions and Financial Aid at Cornell's Johnson School

QUIZ: Do You Suffer from the Wall Street Myth?

1. Is your gym card next to your ATM card?

2. Is *American Idol* a must-see (whether live or on DVR)?

3. Do you have a profile on Match.com? (JDate.com counts as well.)

4. Do you know what "bottle service" is?

5. Do you know when and where the sample sales are?

6. Do you plan your travel around circuit parties?

7. Do you see your parents more than twice a month?

8. Do you play golf recreationally?

9. Do you use Facebook or Twitter?

The biggest mistake applicants make is assuming we're looking for a particular thing from extracurriculars. We hope to get a sense of passion or commitment. And we really look more at quality than quantity. For example, in Russia, where I lived for a few years, they don't have a record for being as involved in extracurriculars as we are. But what we're really trying to assess is somebody's approach to life. So if you're not involved in activities in deed, how about in thought or general approach? Communicate this to us.

—Mae Jennifer Shores, Assistant Dean, Director of MBA Admissions and Financial Aid, UCLA Anderson School of Business

We want you to communicate why you choose to get involved, why you donate energy to a particular activity. Show us the impact you had on other people or an organization. So whether it's an a capella singing group or leading a charitable organization, we want you to articulate what was involved and how it benefited other people.

—Dawna Clarke, Director of MBA Admissions, Tuck School of Business at Dartmouth University

If you answered yes to any of these questions, then you have the time for extracurriculars—you just need to find the commitment.

What You Can Do to "Up Your Extracurricular Game"

What makes launching a school in Botswana more impressive than missing a day with family to ladle soup on Thanksgiving Day? Denise demonstrated organizational skills and leadership as well as commitment to something greater than herself. If you're going to invoke your family to demonstrate such commitment, then tell me about the time you got all

> To me, the first thing about extracurriculars is what it says about the spark of action in a candidate. Why do you do something? When discussing extracurriculars, ask yourself, "Why did I start this organization?" or "Why was it important to me?" What was your role in leading it or influencing the direction of the organization or the people who were involved? Did you bring great people to it? The answers say a lot about you.
>
> —Rose Martinelli, Associate Dean for Student Recruitment and Admissions at the University of Chicago Booth School of Business

> We look at extracurriculars mainly as an indicator of how someone will participate in whatever community or organization they become a part of in the future, including at McCombs. We think that's an important part of sort of the well-rounded student we hope to launch into the world. We are careful, though, to make sure that the student has the opportunity to do extracurriculars. We wouldn't want to ding a consultant who's spending eighty hours a week traveling and who isn't involved in a lot of extracurriculars because they don't have the time.
>
> —Tina Mabley, Director of Admissions at the University of Texas at Austin McCombs School of Business

your cousins together and organized them to do a rotation so that your grandfather was never alone during his battle with cancer. Part of what makes this compelling is that it happened over a period of time. If you write about a one-day event, at least let it be a significant organizational exercise. Anybody who's been through a wedding, for example, knows that it requires a huge amount of commitment, planning, organization, and enrollment of others. Going to the soup kitchen one day, and then painting a school one Saturday through New York Cares, means you're depending on someone else to tell you where to show up. The only organizational challenge that requires overcoming is finding space in your social calendar.

Don't misunderstand—volunteering for Habitat for Humanity is great, but it does not demonstrate vision, leadership, or commitment.

Again, you're not in competition with the girl who started the Botswana school, you're only in competition with yourself. So compete with yourself. Instead of going to one school-painting weekend, call up New York Cares and figure out what you can do to be the guy who uses your skill sets, such as marketing, to get more people than ever to show up to paint more school walls than ever. Pick up *The Idealist.org Handbook to Building a Better World* and figure out what makes you tick. Then go do it in a big way.

Whatever you do, be passionate about it, and make it long-term. Joining a fund-raising committee or a junior board is great, but these by themselves aren't leadership activities. I've worked with many candidates who thought that because they were part of four different fund-raisers, they got to fill out all four extracurricular-activity entries in the application form. But, as one very wealthy philanthropic friend once said to me, "Anybody with enough money can write a check. Talk to me about the guy who, instead of raising money for the homeless, takes the time to bring that homeless guy into the coffee shop, buy him a hot meal, and listen to his life story for a while."

Remember, leadership is a way of being, not a strategy. When you take on service as a way to make a difference in a particular area you care about, you'll be amazed at how easy it is to make time for the weekly meetings despite your busy work schedule. To get in touch with your inner community leader, perhaps you will find inspiration (and see some of yourself) in one of the following three profiles.

Candidate Profile 1: You are involved in an organization (such as one that tutors inner-city kids) once or twice a month. You are not in an organizational or leadership role, but you want to make a difference.

Consider doing what Rudy did: He recruited other mentors.

The story starts before we met Rudy. In early 2002, with Forster-Thomas doing really well, Uncle David and I decided to practice what we preach. What better way to add to our twenty-five-hour days than through a small college-bound program within a larger organization called Chess-in-the-Schools (CIS)? CIS reaches twenty thousand inner-city youth at risk for, among many things, not staying in school and certainly not getting into college. Combining our expertise in college admissions, and our access to a pool of grad-school-bound twentysomethings eager to make a difference, we created what is now the Friday Night Mentor Program, whose purpose is to give low-income students who typically don't venture past local city colleges access to select universities throughout the country. But we didn't do it alone. In fact, we reached out to a number of our clients to see if we could find a group of people who could step in to become ten new Auntie Evans to mentor the CIS kids through the college application process.

We approached several clients, many of whom were at Lehman Brothers (RIP). Fortunately and unfortunately, most of these fourteen-hour-a-day junior investment bankers (also known as worker bees) were already deep into extracurricular activities we'd already helped them discover and/or launch months earlier. But busy people tend to know other busy people. Enter Rudy, who heard through the Lehman grapevine that these two wacky guys who help people get into grad school needed a volunteer coordinator to help launch a really cool program. He wasn't even sure he was going to apply to b-school; after all, he was at the top of his analyst class and the right-hand analyst to a serious big shot in the company.

Being Mr. Big's bitch kept Rudy quite busy. Talk about not being able to tell your boss, "I have to duck out today at six o'clock sharp." (If Rudy could do it, so can you. Don't argue with me unless you're Obama's bitch.) Despite his schedule, Rudy managed not only to make the Friday Night meetings for two school years, but he helped to recruit the first-ever group of mentors who would learn to navigate the college admissions process "the Auntie Evan way" and send CIS's college-bound students to such competitive schools as Trinity College, Union College, University of Virginia, NYU, and Wesleyan.

Rudy's leadership breakthrough was refusing to hear his friends say no when he asked them for help. At first, he was nervous about asking his buddies in the office to spend their Friday nights with surly seventeen-year-olds who were nervous about applying to college. One friend in particular he asked several times to attend, and finally got him there with the promise of going out together afterward. That guy ended up volunteering for two years in a row, and he wasn't even applying to business school. He spread his wings and asked a friend at a different investment bank to start asking his friends as well. They turned it into a competition: Who could get the most mentors there. He kept his mentors inspired, helped them work through trouble spots, and had to deal with *me*. Ultimately, Rudy not only put this group together but also made certain it would exist without him, and because of his work, the mentor arm of this Friday Night mentor program was passed down to other leaders and is now larger than ever.

And by the way: It made for one hell of a leadership essay when he applied to HBS. He got in.

Candidate Profile 2: You're not involved in any organized extracurriculars, but you do spend a lot of time on a hobby or other activity you are passionate about.

Consider doing what Caleb, a Goldman Sachs analyst, did: He brought together two things he cared about and formalized them.

Caleb didn't just answer yes to Quiz Question Number One about gym attendance, he wrote the book on it. He spent two hours a day, from 5:00 a.m. to 7:00 a.m., working out in the gym. And from my vantage point, it was worth every push-up. Now we had to help him sculpt his extracurricular profile. Caleb wasn't willing to give up his gym time—and I agreed; Caleb giving up the gym would have been a loss for everyone. Thank God for Uncle David, who sometimes is just a wee bit more practical: "Why don't you create some kind of awesome leadership activity right there in the gym?" he suggested. While my mind considered what that might look like, Uncle David remembered what Caleb had mentioned he would love to do if he "only had the time": resurrect his involvement in the Big Brothers organization, which he had enjoyed in college.

Do the extracurricular math. Instead of being a Big Brother himself, which required he be available consistently at established hours—something he had difficulty committing to, given his crisis-management role at the office—Caleb leveraged his relationships in his Seattle gym to create a three-month health and wellness program for kids—set right there in his gym. Caleb recruited the gym owner and three trainers (people whose trust he already had) to help with the program, and he wrote a few promotional emails that the organization sent out to members. Instead of writing the curriculum himself, he inspired the trainers to write different aspects of the curriculum, from nutrition to exercise. Caleb then got the whole thing approved by the Big Brothers organization.

The summer event was extremely well attended, and both the Little Brothers and their Big Brothers gave it high marks. And Caleb impacted an entire community, making a difference in the lives of thirty-five kids and the gym itself, without having to barely lift a dumbbell (and sometimes without even leaving his desk or the gym he already went to every day).

You have enough time. Imagination—and the willingness to potentially fall flat on your well-toned ass—is all you need to accomplish something if you know how to wield the resources you already have.

What do you spend time on besides work, eating, and sleeping? Take a look at the Wall Street Myth quiz again: What is your equivalent of Caleb's obsession with working out? You can turn anything into leadership. You love watching *Survivor*? Throw a benefit party for the survivors of the Samoa tsunami (that's where they filmed a season of the show, for those of you who don't watch), and turn it into a quarterly event. Remember, writing checks isn't real leadership: It's organizing the parties that requires a lot of organizational skills, persistence, and charm.

Candidate Profile 3: For those of you whose bosses really do keep you chained to your desk, there are ways to get involved without leaving the office. And you don't even need a gym membership.

"'Extracurricular' doesn't mean that you go down to the soup kitchen Saturdays and help out," says Randall Sawyer, director of admissions and financial aid at Cornell's Johnson School. "Extracurriculars are pretty diverse. I think that when people think 'volunteer,' they automatically attach 'outside of their company.' But especially if they work at a large company, there's a lot that they can do internally."

Indeed, you can have an incredible extracurricular that reveals profound leadership and creates amazing impact by rarely leaving your desk—even while making a difference in your very own company. Let's take Sunshine, for example. She was the first graduate of her Mid-Atlantic liberal arts college to land a job at Goldman Sachs. And she blew them away, working her derriere off in sales and marketing, rolling out project after project, day and night. Sunshine rarely saw the daytime—Sunshine only came out at night. And while she had managed to find her way into this top company, she knew she wasn't the only hot commodity to graduate from her overlooked school.

Yet, bulge-bracket banks and top consulting companies didn't see her college that way. She wanted to change that. So she set out to create a recruiting relationship to open up a pipeline between her school and Goldman.

Just because she didn't have to leave her cubicle didn't mean it was easy. For starters, Goldman wasn't buying it. The HR department thanked her for sharing and sent her back to her desk. They didn't want a new school on their recruiting tour—it was too expensive, too time-consuming, with no proven payoff, etc. But real leaders don't get stopped that easily: When they can't get out, they let their fingers do the walking. She called her college Career Services office, got them excited about the potential of having a recruiting relationship with Goldman, and convinced them to round up thirty of their best résumés to send her for review. Sunshine pared them down to her top five and convinced those five to come to New York. She moved the feast, so to speak. With such a banquet spread before them, HR could not turn down conducting "informational interviews," and two students were hired as summer interns that year. The pipeline had begun its flow.

You can have the same transformational effect on any kind of workplace extracurricular, which is defined as "anything you do at the office you don't get paid for." One guy who was interested in recycling got his office manager to stop buying plastic spoons and forks for the break room. Try doing this yourself—you'll see this requires real leadership. He had to overcome his own fears about people judging him, overcome his boss's fears the project would require too much time away from his daily duties, and overcome the office manager's anxiety that he was trying to do her job. He had to create a cost-benefit analysis to prove that the incremental costs were worth it. This also turned into an amazing thought-leadership essay. The more you hear yourself saying, "This could never work in my office," the more I challenge you take such a project on. Overcoming resistance requires leadership, and I know you've got it in you. Don't take no for an answer.

CHAPTER 5

Gettin' Busy

Beefing Up Your Leadership Legacy

**Three steps to finding your extracurricular passion and creating
legacy—the ultimate sign of leadership.**

"Leadership ties back into passion," says Bruce DelMonico, director of
admissions at Yale School of Management. "The ideal candidate should
be passionate about something and want to make a difference in that
realm, in that field, in that industry, in that sector—a leader finds a problem of significance to him and tries to make a difference in terms of solving it."

You have a passionate leader in you. If you can't figure out where
that leader is hiding, then you haven't really discovered what you're passionate about yet. So, now that I've disabused you of the argument that
you don't have time for extracurriculars, you need to discover some area

in which you care enough to make a change. Perhaps you'll see yourself in Ned, who was full of reasons why he didn't have time to make a difference, followed by reasons why he couldn't do as good a job as the leader who came before him. Ned found his inner leader when he stopped worrying about finding it and, as the commercial goes, just did it.

Ned's story starts with Jeremy, whose claim to extracurricular fame was launching his alma mater's Alumni Mentoring Program in Atlanta in the months after 9/11. While nothing has compared to the finance industry's perfect storm in 2008, the months following 9/11 were nonetheless an out-and-out Hurricane Katrina. Young analysts across the country were losing their jobs right and left, taking cover inside the confines of *U.S. News & World Report*'s top-ten b-schools. Jeremy was one of "the few and the proud" who had managed to keep his job, albeit saddled with twice the work.

So, when his friend Ned, a graduate of the same elite Southwestern liberal arts college, came to me the following year with the opportunity to "take the reins" of Jeremy's mentoring organization, but complained about his workload, I cut to the heart of the matter: "You have an opportunity to be a serious player right here—in an organization you are *already part of* where you can actually *be the guy in charge*. You've already got the leadership role, and you didn't even ask for it."

For me it was a no-brainer. The tutoring organization was in its infancy, and while Jeremy had launched what I call a "First-Ever" (always great for an accomplishment or achievement essay), Ned now had the opportunity to perfect it and make a "Best-Ever" (also great for an accomplishment or achievement essay).

But there Ned was, complaining on the leopard-print love seat in my office, telling me how much work he had to do. I cut him off. I had only this to say: "Your friend Jeremy was just as busy, and now he's packing his bags for Harvard Business School." Ned stopped whining. I believe I now had Ned's attention, and I hope I have yours: "WE SHOULD ALL HAVE A HIGH-CLASS PROBLEM OF THIS NATURE."

Ned continued to look at me as if I were speaking Biafran, or whatever language they speak in that city, so I slowed down.

"Despite how busy your friend Jeremy was during those initial crisis months after 9/11, he managed to pull together his college crew *and* enrolled them in the concept of making a difference in one inner-city high school."

So I walked Ned through the same basic steps that I had walked Jeremy through one year earlier—the same process that everyone can apply to any extracurricular activity they are taking on to up the ante in the leadership game.

Step 1: Choose Something You Care About

(Note: "Something you care about" does not mean that you have to save the planet or even save the cheerleader. It can be anything. You can decide, as one of my candidates did, that fitness was an important issue to him. [What is it about investment bankers and fitness?] He and so many of his first-year analyst class at Morgan Stanley had gained the "freshman fifteen" pounds. So he got some friends together to support each other in their workout efforts at the Morgan gym. The group began to grow in size. He organized the support system into a phone tree and had the organization recognized by the bank.)

If an activity doesn't matter to you on a personal level, not only won't *you* be committed to a great result, no one else will care about it either. And thus you and all of those you are leading will be committed to one thing: mediocrity. More likely, you'll be doomed to failure. And you're certainly not going to be committed to an amazing result.

So, how to avoid mediocrity? Watch and learn.

Once we isolated what was important to Jeremy—helping inner-city kids get into good colleges—we took on the "why." After some poking and prodding, it became clear that Jeremy, originally from Seattle, had a similar set of issues when applying to colleges outside of his hometown.

He neither knew how, nor knew that he *could*, until a family friend mentioned the benefits of small liberal arts colleges with finance-industry connections. Had no one opened his eyes past what he was familiar with, Jeremy might still be singing the Seahawks' fight song.

Step 2: Isolate the "So What!"

What can you expect if nothing is done or no one does anything to change a current circumstance? That's the "So what." In Jeremy's case, the circumstance was as follows: If nothing changes, bright inner-city students from X high school will continue to aim "low and/or local" when applying to college.

With that in mind, Jeremy was fired up and unwilling to sit by and do nothing. As the saying goes, "If not me, then who?" Three months later, all of his friends who had graduated from his alma mater and were living in Atlanta, including Ned, were on board. Six months after that, a significant number of kids from the high school they worked with were going to top schools throughout the United States, and Jeremy saw a new future in which he would have to find someone to take over and continue what he had started.

Step 3: Reinvention

Every leader has to reinvent. Take something that already exists and is doing fairly well, and make it even better. One of my favorite examples is Marley Kaplan, CEO of Chess-in-the-Schools. Marley turned CIS from a one-class, one-room operation to a possibility that now reaches twenty thousand students.

I told Ned to get his feet off the couch and start making a list of things he could do to make an already good organization great: more tutors, more recruiting of students, creating a curriculum. Jeremy started an amazing organization, I told Ned, but it wasn't dishonoring Jeremy's work to take it to the next level and make the program truly great. If Marley had worried about that, tens of thousands of kids might never have graduated from school.

In the weeks that followed, Ned began to see all kinds of possibilities in which he could transform the organization and make it even better. And so he did, and stepped up to the plate. Fast-forward: A year later, Jeremy and Ned's tutoring organization had twice as many tutors, and while Jeremy had made it a First-Ever, Ned got busy and made it a Best-Ever. FYI: Ned ended up at HBS as well.

There's always something you can do to make a mediocre thing better or a good thing great. And if you think there's not, then you need to reconsider who you are and why you're applying to b-school in the first place. *This process cannot be about you.* It's about making something in the world better, be it your office, your industry, or the planet. And the proof that you can do it is usually right at your fingertips.

Step 4: Create Legacy

"Creating legacy" is nothing new. It's what all great leaders do: Give birth to new leaders. If the organization, entity, circumstance, or service you are creating, transforming, or working with is dependent on *you* being there, then as far as any real leader or history is concerned, you failed. A significant part of leadership is making certain that the work you gave birth to lives on without you. Think Gandhi. If he hadn't had Jawaharlal Nehru to take over when he was gone, India would likely be the southwestern suburb of China. Think Alexander the Great, who never had a successor, a son, or a daughter for that matter. He ruled what once was the entire known world, yet when he died with no successor, it completely fell apart. And while Jawaharlal Nehru's vision of a united, free, democratic, and secular India was never to be realized, he did his best and, with his associates and in Gandhi's memory, set the path for India to be the growing success it is today. Somewhere deep down, Jeremy understood this.

Jeremy had created legacy by enrolling Ned, but Ned was nervous about asking someone to take on the program. One factor distinguished the two young professionals from one another: Jeremy embodied the old saying, "If you want to get something done, ask a busy person." In fact,

---

Standout Service in a Nutshell

Step 1: Ask yourself what you are dedicated to.

To find out what you are dedicated to, ask yourself what personal stakes you have in life—what matters to you outside your own survival.

Step 2: Identify what will happen if nothing is done about the issue you are dedicated to.

Answer: "Who will do this if not you?" Make sure you understand why *you* are the right person, right now, to take on this challenge.

Step 3: Reinvent the organization or activity.

Ask yourself what needs fixing. What needs updating? What could be so much better? Again, if nothing is done, what will happen? Will the next group of kids get the same, better, or worse assistance? Will the project or organization fade away, never to be heard of again? Or will you turn it into the most amazing, long-term, mean lean fighting machine for inner-city kids who want to better themselves?

Step 4: Create legacy.

Make sure that someone else is set and ready to "get busy" and take over when you're dead and gone. Otherwise all your work is for nothing and ends up being like a "One-Time-Only Sale."

find the busiest person you know and ask them to get involved. Busy people are *busy* for a reason. Jeremy knew this, and saw in Ned what Ned did not see in himself.

Ned's nervousness about asking someone else to take on the mantle of leadership stemmed from his own nervousness about being a leader. Finding someone to take over for you is insanely difficult for any other number of reasons. You might be worried someone else will do better than you. If they do, be happy! You laid the groundwork. You might be nervous they will let the group fall apart. If so, that's out of your hands. Give them the chance.

That's the bottom line about creating legacy: You have to let go, and you have to let people make their own decisions. Not asking someone to take over for you seems easy to rationalize, because it is asking a lot. But don't take away their choice by not asking in the first place. What's the worst that could happen? They say no. And then you ask the next person.

CHAPTER 6

Rec Creation

Help Your Recommenders Help You

Your recommendations are one of the keystones of your candidacy, yet an area fraught with land mines and potential conflicts.

You've developed your inner leader, beefed up your extracurriculars, and started getting serious about applying to business school. Now it's time to start thinking about your recommenders.

I used to share the same misconceptions that so many of my candidates do: There's not much you can do with recs. *Big mistake.* This is a field of potential land mines that can blow up and destroy your candidacy without your even knowing it if you are not very careful. Yet, you're supposed to have nothing to do with "rec creation," right?

That's just not true. There are many ethical strategies for adding value to the recommendation part of your candidacy. After giving an overview, I will show you the role recommendations play, teach you how to get the most of your recommender and seize as much control of the process as possible, reveal some land mines, and even give you a glimpse into what your recommender is going through, so you can ~~manipulate~~ handle him or her even more effectively.

Recommendations are not a rubber stamp. I break it down into ABCs. Recommenders can:

AUGMENT something you've talked about elsewhere in your candidacy.

BRING NEW INFORMATION to the table that you couldn't fit in anywhere else—an example of your leadership, for example. They can also delineate skills you had no opportunity to mention, such as quantitative skills that are not revealed because you had a low GMAT or limited quantitative coursework as an undergrad.

CORROBORATE what you have said, especially if it seems far-fetched; the rarity of a second-year analyst, for example, closing a deal single-handedly because her boss was on vacation might raise an admissions officer's eyebrow, but the eyebrow falls back into place when her recommender mentions a specific example of leadership from that same accomplishment.

Just as many people wrongly assume that hiring an educational consultant means we'll do the work for you, people mistakenly think that communicating with your recommender somehow taints the process. That's not true. In fact, many of my colleagues who are understandably sensitive about being considered unethical give this topic a wide berth. At most, they may help their clients choose the right people, but they stop right there. It's like giving directions from the Empire State Building in New York City to the Sears Tower in Chicago by saying, "Get on the highway going west and follow the signs."

Uncle David and I have rarely talked to an admissions officer who suggests you should remove yourself entirely from the recommendation process. Tina Mabley of the McCombs School of Business at the University of Texas at Austin told us, "It's fine to prepare your recommenders. They shouldn't be going into the process blind. If you have a draft of some of your essays, especially the career goals essay, share that with your recommenders so they understand what it is you're trying to convey, and so the rec letters can support some of the themes and messages in your application."

J. J. Cutler, Wharton's director of admissions, told us, "I think it's great to speak to your recommender beforehand; I have no problem with that. Take your recommender out to breakfast and get on the same page."

I take that a step further: You *have* to get involved.

Recommenders 101

The first rule of getting fantastic recommendations is to choose recommenders who know you well. So many people make mistakes on this and set mental traps for themselves. So, while it's easy to go astray, the first rule of recommenders couldn't be any simpler: Choose your current direct supervisor as your "primary" recommender.

Even if that person doesn't have a fancy title.

Even if that person didn't go to a great business school.

Even if that person doesn't have an MBA at all.

Read those three lines again, because I mean it. I really mean it. And besides, your current direct supervisor is who all schools demand you choose.

Sometimes, however, you can't ask your current direct supervisor. Schools understand that. For some people, there could be a real and compelling reason to avoid disclosing your MBA application to your supervisor. The rule of thumb is simple: Are you going to lose your job or bonus if, in essence, you give a year's advance notice that you're leaving? If so, then find an alternative recommender—just explain in one simple sentence in the "optional essay" space why you didn't choose your direct boss.

People who make great "secondary" recommenders sometimes also make great alternative primary recommenders, like:

- **A prior direct supervisor (try to avoid going back more than a couple of years)**

- **Your boss's boss (as long as he or she works directly with you on a regular basis . . . if he really likes you on the basis of the great quarterly reviews he's read, avoid him—even if he offers to write a rec)**

- **A client (internal or external)**

- **A counterpart at a partner firm or lateral staffer on a collaborating team (e.g., the project manager of the user interface you are writing the code for)**

For schools like Harvard that want three recommenders, choose two of the above in addition to your current direct supervisor. I recommend a prior direct supervisor as one of the three, when possible.

Stanford is unique in asking for a "peer recommendation"—the person who sits next to you as your equal on the team. If you work at a small firm and don't have a peer in the office, feel free to go back a couple of years or use a peer from an extracurricular activity—as long as you have the analog to a professional relationship. If your extracurricular peer is another volunteer who doesn't actually work with you in a team, he or she is the wrong choice.

Help Them Help You: Create Talking Points

I guarantee your recommender is thinking, "Help me help you." The best
way to do that is by providing talking points after someone agrees to
provide a recommendation. No valuable recommender is going to sit
around and figure out dates, times, and instances. You remember them,
organize them under the questions, and make sure they ABC your recommendation. Believe me, even if you have a recommender with an ego the
size of Texas who claims he or she has done it a million times and has no
need for your assistance, send an email with your talking points or drop

you on development or other teams. Such a colleague can shine light on a whole different aspect of your professional life. For example, while you will have to ensure your direct supervisor does not write a simple endorsement of your technical skills—believe me, admissions officers care about your accomplishments but not a blow-by-blow of how well you know a programming language—a marketing guy on a cross-functional team knows how well you communicate with others who aren't technologists. Such a recommender can vouch for your soft skills (the Kryptonite of many technologist applicants).

FAMILY BUSINESS. Does it get any trickier than, "My father is my direct supervisor—can he write my recommendation?" We've given the thumbs-up to certain candidates whose father was the best person for the job, and in at least one case, the only person for the job. We all know that fathers can be harder on you than a boss could ever possibly be. If you go this route, it's more important than ever that your parent disclose the relationship up front, and use lots of supporting anecdotes to back up his or her assertions. In the end, whether you can use a relative as a recommender varies widely depending on the school and even admissions officer. You need to research this yourself: Call an admissions officer at the MBA programs you're applying to (it's not hard—most will take your call) and ask.

them off in person. He or she might toss it into the garbage in front of you, but somehow, magically and mysteriously, your examples will find their way into a kick-ass recommendation.

It is tacitly unfair to ask a very busy person to remember that in May 2007 you were the person who made that presentation that helped break the logjam that was holding up the year's biggest deal. It's even more unfair to expect the recommender to realize that doing so marked a pivotal point in your development as a leader because it was the first time you ever spoke up at a board meeting. Yet, that level of detail is exactly what makes a recommendation persuasive.

To ensure your recommender remembers your "great moments in history," prepare a talking-points memo. All talking points should include the following:

- **Names of projects, companies, colleagues**
- **Description of what you accomplished (for example, you built a chair out of plastic cups, you created the first telecom primer, you developed your company's first weekend retreat, you created the first recruiting relationship between your college and your company)**
- **Dates for everything mentioned above**
- **Metrics (that is, percentage growth created, number of people impacted)**
- **When possible, legacy (the impact your leadership had on the team, company, culture, or performance after you left)**

Each point should be five words or less. And if you've got a subject and a verb, you're tempting your recommender to go to a dark place: lifting the recommendation straight from your talking points. Overly scripted points quash the potential for your recommender to come up with really great ideas in his or her own voice—*not yours*—that make the recommendation a value-added, discreet element of your candidacy, rather than just an extension of your own message.

Another great thing about talking points is that they can steer your recommender toward information you couldn't fit elsewhere in your essays or application data (many schools limit the number of extracurriculars you can include to three or four, and if a workplace extracurricular had to get dropped, a recommender can mention it for you). This technique is called "integration." You get to help your recommender answer the school's questions, but you also get to tie together and confirm things you've mentioned elsewhere in your application's short answers, essays, and résumé. This is the cherry on top of your application. The recommender tells the admission committee what others think about you, while also corroborating details you've chose to mention yourself.

Six Surefire Rec Killers—and How to Avoid Them

GLOSSING OVER THE FIRST QUESTION, "DESCRIBE YOUR RELATIONSHIP TO THE APPLICANT." While the exact wording differs, the first question often has many corners that recommenders leave unexplored—to your detriment. This question is vital because it establishes the writer's credibility by laying clear the exact nature of your relationship. Ask your recommender to elaborate on the following:

- How long he or she has known you
- The exact reporting relationship
- His or her role in the organization
- Did he or she hire you or inherit you?
- How many hours a day do you work together, and how many days a week, and/or for how many months/years?
- The different types of exposure he or she has had to you: on teams, as a leader, during business trips, in staff meetings, presenting at conferences, etc.

GIVING A BULLSHIT WEAKNESS. You already know the two biggest bogus weaknesses: "He is a workaholic" (with its sisters "He needs to develop work/life balance" and "She takes on too much") and "She is too detail-oriented." These are not weaknesses; they're backhanded compliments about annoying yet still positive professional characteristics. They render your entire rec as nothing more than a giant commercial—something your mother could have written. Put yourself in the shoes of an admissions officer. There's only a few ways to interpret such pablum: (1) Your recommender doesn't know you that well; (2) Your recommender is trying to do you a favor by covering up a real weakness (which just makes the reader wonder what the hell could be the problem, and this never helps your candidacy); (3) You wrote your own recommendation. Real leaders, whether you or your boss, are not afraid of the truth. The weakness question not only establishes credibility, but also helps the school understand your development as a professional.

NOT CONNECTING THE WEAKNESS TO AN OPPORTUNITY FOR GROWTH. While a weakness that has been completely overcome or compensated for is no longer a weakness and therefore falls into the "bullshit" category, your recommender must absolutely include that you are aware of the weakness and include a detail of how you are addressing it. A nice additional detail is your reaction to hearing the weakness: "When I mentioned to John my concern that he wears his heart too much on his sleeve—for example, that he needed to control his reactions better when he heard an idea he didn't like—he agreed. At the next team meeting, when a staffer mentioned that we should take out ads on Facebook, John did not roll his eyes but nodded pensively and suggested we hash out the pros and cons of the idea. I appreciated the effort he made and continues to make." If your recommender understands the b-school curriculum, he or she can go on to get specific about how an MBA education will help you overcome a weakness once and for all.

GIVING A FATAL WEAKNESS. As much as we are advocates for honesty and transparency in this process, there is such a thing as Too Much Information. Recommenders should avoid weaknesses involving lack of leadership potential and poor verbal communication skills (especially for schools that rely on the case method).

FORGETTING THAT LENGTH MATTERS. HBS restricts answers to each rec question to 250 words. Excellent guideline. While your boss may want to wax eloquent—or, more likely, plow hastily through—let him know the admissions committee is full of Goldilocks: They don't want answers too long or too short, but just right. We say follow HBS's lead for every rec question at every school.

CUTTING-AND-PASTING YOUR TALKING POINTS. Your recommender is very busy. As much as he wants to see you succeed, and as much as he's honored to help you get there by writing you a rec, on the list of priorities you're not only below finishing the annual report but you're also below ordering the inflatable castle for his son's birthday party. Until the last minute, however, when he can no longer put it off. And there they are . . . your beautifully written, elaborate, anecdote-filled talking points. Next thing you know, your recommender has simply cut-and-pasted your memo—bullet points and all—into the online rec system. Don't think the admissions committee won't notice. Reading thousands of applications has given them strange and mysterious powers, and they read your application enough times to notice similarities in wording, thought, and structure. That's why we don't recommend writing talking points in complete sentences. If you think you shouldn't be judged for a recommender's sloppy mistake, don't tell that to Randall Sawyer, director of admissions and financial aid at Cornell's Johnson School: "Errors like that reflect poorly on you for making a bad choice of recommender," he says.

Prepping Your Recommender: The Meeting

Once you've prepared your talking points, it's time to prepare any recommender for what he or she needs to do and how you can make it easy on him or her.

STEP 1: CALL A MEETING. Go to lunch together, have a sit-down in his office, have drinks; whatever feels right and appropriate for your relationship. Make your request formal. If you don't take the rec seriously, neither will your recommender. Don't ask someone while you pass him in the hallway. In the meeting, disclose that you're applying to business school, and that you would be honored if he would consider taking the time to recommend you. Let the person know that, before securing the commitment, you'd like to ask a few questions and describe in detail what you're expecting.

No matter what, don't wait until the last minute. Timing is every-thing. Get the ball rolling early—at least four weeks in advance, and prefer-ably eight. I cannot tell you how many candidates—and I'm talking about those who have finished the rest of their applications weeks in advance—have called me the night before a deadline, screaming, "John still hasn't submitted his rec—and now he's glacier skiing in Montana!" And now not even the "can you hear me now?" guy can get a hold of him.

STEP 2: ASK ABOUT THE RECOMMENDER'S EXPERIENCE. If you've got a very touchy recommender, you may want to skip this step. But if you have a good relationship, it's well worth asking, "Have you written a business school recommendation before?" If the person wants to know why you ask, just explain that it's a lot of work, and you want to make sure the recommender knows what he or she is getting into.

If the recommender has written recs before (as is likely to be the case for you finance people and consultants), ask about his or her track record: "How many have you written? What schools did you write recs for? Did your recommendees get in?" Again, use your judgment, but beware of most recommenders who get defensive at this point. If it's your current direct supervisor, you don't have much choice, but when you've got a choice (as you would for your secondary recommender), it might be time to move down the list. Tell them that you'll let them know if you're going to need the recommendation or not. I guarantee that if you don't follow up, they won't follow up.

STEP 3: DISH OUT THE DETAILS. If you feel comfortable with the answers so far, move on to some details: how many schools you're applying to, which schools you're applying to, when you need the recommendation by (give at least a month). Read your potential recommender's reaction as you lay out these details. If a look of horror spreads behind her eyes, use your judgment: Is this the expected reaction to a lot of work, or a clear signal that she is not going to come through for you without a lot of kick-ing and screaming, not matter how "delighted" she pretends to be? Ask them if they'd like talking points and let them know you've already pre-pared some just in case. Whip them right out and slide them across the table. It's a gift too good to refuse. You also want to ask if it's okay for you to glance over the rec after it's written and provide some feedback.

If you aren't already getting a feel for how open your recommender is to being your partner in this process, what we recommend happen next will make everything clear.

STEP 4: DESCRIBE HOW YOU CAN MAKE YOUR RECOMMENDER'S JOB EASIER. Tell your recommender that when you input her name into the online application as one of your recommenders, she's going to get an email that says you selected her to be one of your recommenders. To complete the recommendation, just click the link to access the recommendation site, and use the password provided to log in. Then tell her that when she gets that email, she should just forward it to you. You'll gather all the questions from the different schools, sort them by type, and give her a customized list of questions to answer. Then you'll take her answers, cut-and-paste them into the relevant fields in the application, and let her know when you've finished. Then she can review the work, make any changes she wants, and hit "submit."

At this point, your recommender is probably going to be thrilled, at which point you've got a clear green light to move forward together, bound by the eternal bonds of recommender and recommendee. You've also got an opening for providing some gentle feedback on the recommender's wording, if your recommender already said that was acceptable. However, if your recommender is balking at this point, evaluate whether you believe in your heart of hearts that your recommender will do the "heavy lifting" required to make your case enthusiastically and in detail at each school you're applying to.

DISCLAIMER: Don't interpret this strategy as giving you permission to write your own recs; I dare you to find that actual phrase in this book "write your own recs." DO NOT WRITE YOUR OWN RECS. Admissions officers can see right through that. Even if you got straight As in creative writing, there's a fat chance you can truly distinguish what you say in your essays from what you write in your recommendation. Read the box on page 70 to hear straight from the horses' mouths all the things that can go wrong when you write your own recs. Notice some of the admissions directors give advice almost identical to mine, whereas others contradict me completely. Find your own comfort level using what you know of your recommenders. And if you don't know them well enough to use such judgment, you've chosen the wrong person to begin with.

The Ominous Rec Waiver

I often get asked, "Should I sign the waiver?" The waiver is that box you check that generally says something like, "I wish to waive my right of access to the letter of recommendation and the material recorded on this recommendation form."

Of course you sign the waiver. Underneath all that legalese is a simple idea: If you get accepted to the school and therefore earn the right to review your application file, not included in that review is the right to see your recommendations. This is intended to give skittish recommenders or recommenders who, for whatever reason, feel they cannot write honestly without hiding this from you, the freedom to be honest. The schools believe this feeling of freedom is vital to getting an honest recommendation, so they like it when you sign the waiver.

Forget the myth that signing the waiver means you never saw or never will see the recommendation or that seeing it taints the rec or gives you an edge over others who did not see their rec. Even if you sign the waiver (and you better!), don't turn down an opportunity to see your recs. It's just stupid.

It's Only Okay Not to See the Rec If:

1. You've done your homework and know that your recommender has experience writing recs.

2. You've done your research like any leader would when, say, buying a house or hiring a consultant: What's your recommender's track

record? What percentage of his recommendees actually got into the school of their choice? If you hear phrases like, "Everyone John recommends gets in; John knows what he's doing," you're in good shape. If your recommender is in finance or consulting, he probably knows what he's doing. He or she probably also went to business school.

3. Your recommender isn't a good writer. If your recommender meets these qualifications but you've seen emails from him that read like he didn't graduate eighth grade—you know, he commonly writes "your" when he means "you're"—don't worry about it. Content trumps style when it comes to recommendations. Unless you're Uncle David and you have a journalism degree, nobody expects all the commas to be in the right place or even knows where the right place is (are we talking *AP Style* or the *Chicago Manual*?).

Exception Alerts! When You *Have* to See the Rec:

1. Recommenders from nonprofit organizations can be a great second or third choice (if you a play a leadership role in the organization), but be careful. Not all nonprofit recommenders have a successful business background so they may not know what they're doing. Some nonprofit-based recommenders have a tendency to be overly vague and complimentary, and use irrelevant, soft adjectives like "compassionate" and "loving." I've even seen a rec in which someone described an HBS applicant as "sweet." Who takes you seriously if you're described like Miss America? This doesn't mean you don't use the recommender, but make sure you can see the rec and are able to steer that ship if necessary.

2. The tech recommender can also be troublesome. Just the opposite of the nonprofit recommender, he tends to describe leadership in terms of your ability to design a user interface anyone can use. Of course, you might be the last person to realize there's a problem, given that you're a techie too. So ask yourself, which "Bones" is my recommender more like: the one from *Star Trek* (a famously emotional intergalactic doctor) or the one from the TV show *Bones*

Letters of Recommendation Versus Letters of Support

Confusing a letter of recommendation with a letter of support is like mixing up *The New York Times* and *The Onion*: the former is required reading, while the latter can be brilliant but has no intrinsic value. In short, letters of support can play a role in drawing some attention to your candidacy. If George W. Bush really does want to write you a rec to HBS—where he got his own MBA from, of course—but hasn't seen you since the Bush Family Barbecue of 1999, then ask him instead to write a letter of support.

Letters of support should be no more than a page, and they should get no more specific than two points: (a) the writer vouches for your character, and (b) you're a great fit with the school's personality and community.

Letters of support are *extremely* hit or miss when it comes to how much influence they exert—especially when coming from a faculty member, current student, or alumnus without an active record of involvement with the MBA program. "We're always happy to hear from Yale SOM community members or others who have an opinion. More information is better," says Bruce DelMonico of the Yale School of Management.

But be careful. Considering a letter of support from an alumni of the university-at-large? *Forgettaboutit*. Dartmouth College and Tuck are not the same thing. Neither are Harvard College and Harvard Business School. Unless the writer donates several million a year, don't expect the letter to pull too much weight, and even then, it may be the development team (rather than the admissions office) that is most impressed.

Final note of caution: Know that, if you get accepted after someone has gone to bat for you with a letter of support, you *must* attend or you will burn some serious bridge.

(an unnervingly rational forensic anthropologist)? If your answer is the latter, then make sure you give talking points that include qualitative aspects of your skills and abilities: how you handle conflict, how you inspire others on a team, and how you otherwise (dare I say it) think outside the chip.

Two Types of Recommenders to Avoid

Now that I've laid down the basics, I'd like to point out two very common mistakes people make: choosing recommenders based on their status rather than their relationship to you, and choosing a recommender solely because he or she earned an MBA from the school you're applying to. Both scenarios are worth elaborating on, because I find so many people refuse to believe they actually are mistakes—I have to wear them down with reasons and examples of all the failed candidates who wouldn't listen to me.

Mistake 1: "My Recommender the Senator"

If I had a ten-spot for every recommendation strategy conversation I have had that began with a candidate saying, "I worked on the campaign of the senator from the Great State of So-and-So," or "I know Goldman Sachs CEO Lloyd Blankfein" or, last but never least, "Why don't I ask the managing director of my Energy Group?" I'd be as wealthy as those potential recommenders are.

Let me do for you now what I've done for everyone who's on the edge of this particular cliff and nip this in the bud. There's a rule of thumb: If you are not now working for or have not specifically worked with an individual on a regular basis (and by "regular" I mean for a few hours at least twice a week for a minimum of three to four months), move on to another choice. Even if they're willing to write the rec, these people cannot possibly give an insightful/thorough assessment of your abilities. They add nothing to your candidacy—at best they might be able to vouch for your character (see Letters of Recommendation Versus Letters of Support, page 64).

Here's a quiz: It's 1997. You are applying to business school and you are Monica Lewinsky. Do you:

(A) Get a recommendation from Bill Clinton (then president of the United States)

or

(B) Get a recommendation from Bettie Curry, personal assistant to the president (then Clinton's intern supervisor)

While Monica certainly knew Bill, and his name was known by everyone on the planet, he was not her supervisor and he did not staff her on projects. Conversely, she reported to Bettie Currie on a daily basis. Bill could not, in a business school recommendation, respond to questions like "Please describe an instance when the applicant demonstrated unexpected leadership in a team setting." One simply cannot get away with platitudes about how generally awesome your leadership skills are in that question. The recommender needs a specific story. And the only story Bill Clinton had about Monica's leadership is not something he would want later surfacing in the Starr Report.

Choose a recommender who can support his or her opinions with specific on-the-job examples. If you don't believe me, perhaps Randall Sawyer of Cornell will convince you: "Some people think, 'Well, I've run into the CEO in the hall three times, maybe he'll write me a letter.' I don't care about the title after the name. I care about what this person's working relationship to the applicant is, how well they know each other. If your recommender's going to write one sentence for each question or have his secretary write it, move on. Wrong choice."

Mistake 2: The Alma Mater Recommender

Let me be clear: Playing "matchy-matchy" (aligning your recommender's diploma with his or her alma mater and the school you're applying to) is a fool's game. It seems like the natural way to go, it's easy, but all too obvious a ploy. The mileage you will gain by employing this strategy is zero, especially when compared to the mileage you gain when you play it straight. (Of course, it helps when the recommender is a fan.)

Pablo absolutely refused to believe me. Pablo was a determined blond, blue-eyed middle-class Spaniard who had pulled himself up by his bootstraps and reached a mid-level executive position at a reinsurance company in Zurich. From the day he came to me, after just about every top-ten school had rejected him the prior year, it was clear that name-dropping and status symbols (like "I just returned from skiing in Zermatt") were of grave importance to him. I managed successfully to rid his candidacy of all traces of *Town & Country*, *Vanity Fair*, and *Hello!* magazines. And in stripping them away, what we were left with was actually a lean, mean candidacy—a great story of a boy who didn't let his "station" in Switzerland's strictly stratified social and professional hierarchy "keep him down," as we say in the 'hood.

But what I didn't catch was the presence of an obvious candidacy killer. Frankly, given his 700-plus GMAT, excellent liberal arts background from Berkeley, and strong professional and social experience, I was shocked to find out that Harvard had not even so much as given him an interview . . . until I dug deeper during that overseas phone call in which we desperately tried to diagnose what had gone wrong.

With Pablo on speakerphone, I stood at my whiteboard running through possible scenarios of where his candidacy might have derailed:

ESSAYS—insightful, visionary

INTERVIEW—charming, clear, had quick answers to all questions

SCHOOL VISITS—that, and info sessions too

NETWORKING—he had reached out to club presidents

LEADERSHIP, EXTRACURRICULARS—check, check

Then Pablo sheepishly suggested that "Michael's rec" might have had something to do with it.

"Who's Michael?" I asked warily.

"I chose him as my second recommender," Pablo explained, as he tiptoed into a troublesome story of office drama. Apparently Michael was not a Pablo fan. Michael was a year ahead of Pablo in the analyst program. As the story unraveled, Pablo explained that the boys had had one or two run-ins during their tenure together in reinsurance. "We eventually worked it out, although I'm not sure we ever really became friends. But he is a graduate of Harvard Business School, so naturally I sought him out!" At several other top schools, Pablo had employed the same misguided tactic.

My system went haywire. I will tell you now what I told him then. Beyond the fact that they had a history of tumultuous, treacherous, and troublesome tension (*duh!*), choosing your recommender based on his or her alma mater is *absurd*—particularly when they're one of your main recommenders. Forget about the fact that Pablo and Michael didn't get along, and focus on the fact that, as I stated earlier, schools are truly looking to get a new perspective and a clear understanding of who you are, particularly from the point of view of someone you have worked for, unless otherwise specifically stated.

Never again have I allowed our candidates at Forster-Thomas to choose recommenders without our guidance. When the notion of "recommender by alma mater" rears its magnetic head, we are there to chop it off. I understood why Pablo would make this choice, and have understood this inclination by others time and time again, but it is the *ultimate* mistake in style over substance.

The following year, with our help, Pablo shored up that mess, chose recommenders based on the strength of their relationship (including some who had not even gone to business school). That season, Pablo was accepted to MIT Sloan.

The Illustrated Rec: Alanna's Story

Dealing with recommenders can be thorny. I think it's time for a story to illustrate the whole process so you can see how easy it is for the "rec ship" to capsize—and how easy it is to right it again.

Going over the first draft of Alanna's rec was like going to a summer art fair. It doesn't matter which one you go to; the same "one-of-a-kind" papier-mâché masterpiece you purchased at the Port Clinton Art Fair in Illinois pops up the following year at the Festival of Fine Craft in Millville, New Jersey. Like these art-fair-circuit paintings, Alanna's recommender's critique began to read like Any Rec, USA.

Imagine you are an admissions officer at Wharton trying to figure out what a candidate brings to the table, and you get the following: "Alanna's greatest strengths are her analytic skills, tireless work ethic, and great leadership skills."

Wow. All great attributes, but what do these old standards really teach me about Alanna as an individual? Especially considering that eight out of ten of the applicants to follow will sound quite the same. Furthermore, I do need to ask a few questions: What exactly is a "tireless work ethic"? What exactly does "great leadership skills" mean?

If you answered this with things like "It means inspirational, motivational, thinks on her feet" or even "fearless," then you are also what I like to refer to as a platitude machine.

The way Auntie Evan thinks about it is not "what does X *mean*?" but "what does X *look like*?" For example, what does "beautiful" look like? To some, "beautiful" implies long brown hair, almond eyes, thin lips. To someone else, "beautiful" implies big hips, small waist, green eyes. So, the word "beautiful" doesn't equal a set of physical characteristics; instead, it's whatever the reader decides it is. So, here comes my UCLA screenwriting professor Richard Walter's immortal words: *Show, don't tell!*

To be clear, when a recommender writes "great leadership skills," he's not describing anything in particular, simply making a judgment that your skills are good. But what do those skills look like: Are you a lone-wolf leader? A leader by consensus? Are you a supportive leader or someone who foments internal competition? These descriptions are good. But to get to great, the recommender needs to write brief anecdotes.

So I called up Alanna and explained to her that while I was more than impressed, these wonderful platitudes are just opinions; worse, in the absence of *actual examples*, they are meaningless opinions. Without examples, not only does your recommender look like the artist who hops from art fair to art fair, but worse, he looks like the artist who replaces the impressionist lighthouse you just bought with an identical one after you've left his stall fifty dollars poorer.

But Alanna was in mortal fear of her recommender. She did not want to question him and/or ask for any kind of rewrite, despite the fact that it was only a first draft. At this I rolled my eyes and thought of the countless recs I've been asked to write for my CIS mentors. WRITING RECOMMENDATIONS SUCKS—NO ONE WANTS TO DO IT.

So I asked Alanna what she was more afraid of: annoying her recommender, or submitting a rec that reads like it came from the "Recs 'R'

Admissions Directors on Recommendation Dos and Don'ts

My primary advice about recommenders is, choose the people who know you well in a daily work context, rather than because the person is the CEO of your company. That means a current supervisor, a former supervisor, or as well as maybe someone above that supervisor. The ideal student we would like to have here is someone who has more than one relationship in an office; if that person only has one person who can recommend him, then there's a problem here.

—Rod Garcia, Director of Admissions at the Sloan School of Management at MIT

Us" file that his secretary keeps in the back of the locked filing cabinet. "Alanna, trust me, the last thing your recommender wants to do is write this rec while he's on vacation skiing in Telluride with his mistress. He won't be annoyed; he'll be thrilled that you've given him talking points, because he'll get back in the hot tub that much faster."

That's when she finally relented and we created "talking points" for every question (and remember, talking points are phrases, not sentences). Mindful of these common factors, I grilled Alanna about her "great moments in history" until we came up with specifics that included accomplishments she had yet to even mention anywhere else in her application.

So, to be sure, while Alanna didn't write the recommendation for her supervisor, she did provide him with specific dates and examples of great moments in her history that she had mentioned in one of her essays. Her talking points for that went something like this: (1) worked in March 2005 on the Mortgage Capital restructuring, (2) supervisor found herself in a tight spot, (3) associate had just quit—no time to hire replacement.

That part of the recommendation ended up looking like this: "When our associate quit, Alanna recognized the situation, and without hesita-

---

Prepping your recommenders is perfectly alright. It makes sense to sit down with your recommenders and tell them why you're applying to business school, what you hope to get out of it, what you plan to do afterwards. They're off on their own and they write it all by themselves. I would hope that there wasn't any sort of additional interaction. I would avoid giving them something written, but not because I'm worried about something nefarious happening. Rather, if you give your recommenders something written, it's very easy for them to take what you wrote and incorporate that into what they're submitting verbatim—and if we see a recommendation and an essay that has the same language, we're not going to draw a very benign conclusion based on that.

—Bruce DelMonico, Director of Admissions at the Yale School of Management

tion took on the job with the ease and expertise of one far superior to those with the normal analyst-level skill set. She made sure production did not falter during this period, doing the work of two analysts with little supervision. I was able to completely rely on her organization of other analysts, her work and the team's numbers, allowing me to focus on the big picture aspects of the deal." Now it's clear how Alanna "took charge" and had "leadership capabilities and a tireless work ethic."

The point is, without examples, a rec is just a thirty-second commercial. Not only did Alanna's recommender transform his entire recommendation after she gave him her talking points/great moments in history, he was able to get back to his mistress on the slopes.

I think it helps to prepare your recommender. Take them out to lunch, take them for coffee, give them an updated copy of your résumé, and just remind them about some of the great things you've done over the past couple of years. Just like your standard performance review, the boss never remembers all the great things you did . . . he has other things to focus on. By refreshing their memory, I don't think that's an untoward way of making it more likely that the specifics you mention will find their way into the letter of recommendation. I actually think if you don't do that you're missing an opportunity.

Regarding weaknesses, an applicant's awareness that there's an issue and his willingness to confront it are always very impressive. Don't skirt the issue. I'd much rather see an actual weakness and, more importantly, the applicant's plan for dealing with it. Figuring out what the letters of recommendation say about weaknesses is often an exercise in figuring out what's *not* said. It's rare that a recommender actually says something bad. However, if you look at the pattern of what they omit, you can figure out what's really going on with the applicant.

—Peter Johnson, Executive Director of Admissions, Full-Time MBA Program, University of California Berkeley Haas School of Business

Postscript: I Feel Your Pain

One of the most excruciating experiences I've ever had was asking for my own recommendation. Perhaps my own story will help you find your own way to get the most out of your recommenders.

In 2002, I recognized the value of being part of an exclusive community of well-respected educational consultants who pledge to uphold a certain ethical standard and hold each other to it. That's when I decided to join the Independent Educational Consulting Association (IECA). To join, I needed recommendations. Following my own advice, I asked for a rec from my then-current direct supervisor, Marley Kaplan of CIS, where

> We're reading between the lines very often, so obviously, having someone who knows you in a work situation is far better than asking the CEO of the company because you met him in the elevator. It is the applicants' responsibility to really be insightful about whom they ask. You're being evaluated not just on the recommendation, but on your judgment regarding who you selected.
>
> —Linda Meehan, Assistant Dean and Executive Director for MBA Admissions, Columbia Business School

> One surefire recommendation killer is when people take the bullet points you give them about your candidacy, and then they take that a little too far—you can see that the recommender has cut-and-pasted examples from those bullets directly into the recommendation letter. Then you know that the applicant potentially helped their recommenders a little too much.
>
> Many people are scared of the question about where you have room for improvement or areas of challenges for you. When the recommendation actually honestly answers that question, it gives the whole rec more credibility, more authenticity—including the glowing things.
>
> —Liz Riley Hargrove, Associate Dean of Admissions, Fuqua School of Business at Duke University

I am the college adviser for a group of inner-city chess players. When Marley said, "Let's get together next week to talk about it," I didn't know what to expect. Was she going to ask me to write the rec myself? Was she going to expect something of me? It was kind of embarrassing.

On one of my daily chats with one of my girlfriends, Barbie, while we traded anxieties over our careers, I mentioned my concern about this lunch and the recommendation to Barbie (then VH1's director of talent development and soon-to-be founder of Barbara Barna Casting; she would later cast *Queer Eye for the Straight Guy* and become one of my company's best interview-skills coaches).

Barbie didn't understand why I was stumped by the meeting. I recognized in her voice that same slightly incredulous edge that my own voice so often takes on when the answer seems self-evident. "Evan, this woman is really busy. She's running a nonprofit with fifty employees that

The best recommendations—whether they come from your boss, or in the case of the second recommender, from your boss's boss or a prior supervisor—are the ones that can bring your candidacy to life a bit. So, instead of making a comment like, "Evan is a strong team player," it says, "Evan is a strong team player. For example, last month, he volunteered to work extra on a team he was not staffed on for two weeks in a row because he had some skills that the team lacked." Broad, sweeping, grandiose comments don't give me a sense of what this applicant is like. I'd rather have one or two stories that cover less ground but go into more detail.

We do prefer work-related recommendations, as opposed to academic recommendations and the ones from your college best friend's dad.

—Dawna Clarke, Director of MBA Admissions, Tuck School of Business at Dartmouth University affects thousands of students. Simply put, and it may be difficult to hear—you're not the center of her universe. The reason she said yes to writing it is because you're doing an amazing job and she supports you and doesn't have to follow your every move. She just sees the results. So give the lady some specific talking points already and be done with it."

What Barbie—that's Mrs. Abel to the rest of you—said made so much sense that I immediately adopted it into our *mode d'emploi*, the very fabric of who we are today. And that is: Help them help you. And there's nothing unethical about that. In fact, it's simply the right thing to do for someone who not only is helping your career, but has also agreed to "stay late" to do so.

Since I got that clear myself, I have consistently told my candidates to bring on those talking points! Just walk into the office, hand over the talking points, and say, "If this is helpful, here you are. If not, feel free to

I have different expectations of different recommenders. For example, I expect less from the person who's written one rec in thirty years compared to the managing director of a group at Goldman or McKinsey who's probably written a lot. For example, how someone who has helped dozens of applicants ranks you relative to others means something different than how an entrepreneur might rank you relative to others. So it's all about context and some relativity.

I don't expect anything in particular before I read a recommendation. For example, should a rec reinforce what you've said elsewhere in the application or bring a new piece of information to the table? In general I like the recommendation to do both.

—J. J. Cutler, Director of MBA Admissions and Financial Aid at the Wharton School, University of Pennsylvania drop them in the trash." The busiest people are just going to thank you, and we all know what I say about the busiest people.

In my capacity as college adviser for CIS, I have written numerous recommendations for mentors and helped my coworkers write numerous recommendations for college-bound students. And let me tell you, there's nothing worse than being asked to write a rec. You really, really want to do it. You even feel honored for being asked. But then you have to do it. Writing a rec is the most energy-draining, thankless task that one can be expected to do. It's almost as horrible, but not quite, as having to be the best man at a wedding: You're honored to have been asked, and once it's done you're so glad you did it, but in the meantime you have this thing looming overhead—you have to write a toast. The pressure is bone-crushing.

So I know, having sat on both sides of the table, how difficult the whole subject of recommendations can be. It cuts straight to your fears

I don't believe in coaching the recommender other than giving the recommender several key points. But do make sure your recommenders know you well. I remember a recommendation from a former president of the United States who basically ended the recommendation with: "I don't personally know the applicant, but what I hear is terrific."
—Mae Jennifer Shores, Assistant Dean, Director of MBA Admissions and Financial Aid, UCLA Anderson School of Business

One recommendation killer is when questions are raised about how ethical the person is being—where the recommender feels that the applicant has manipulated people or they haven't been very honest in their dealings. So that would be a big red flag. Another problem is when about whether a valued boss or mentor values you back, and it's asking a lot of someone for whom the dynamic of asking usually goes the other direction. But stop worrying: You really are amazing, and your recommenders—given the proper guidance and handled correctly, as described previously—will help you shine.

we hear, "He's very quiet or shy." If this is inhibiting their performance at work, and then we see in the interview that the person can't communicate very well, then that's going to be a problem.
—Caroline Diarte-Edwards, MBA Director of Admissions, INSEAD

If we ask for commentary and the recommender is too succinct in that commentary, then we may assume they had nothing more or nothing better to say. If the recommender doesn't have the time to do it, the person asking for the recommendation needs to know that so that they go to somebody else.
—Kelly Wilson, Director of MBA Admissions, Georgetown University's McDonough School of Business

CHAPTER 7

Learning Differences

You're Not Stoopid, the System Is

If you keep doing poorly on the GMAT, despite your best efforts,
don't discount the possibility that you may have a learning
disability or its less-obvious cousin, a "learning difference."

Warning: Auntie Evan's law prohibits using any of the following
information to drum up or create a false diagnosis of a learning disability
or learning difference in order to increase your chances of getting into
a desired MBA program. Let me be perfectly clear: We take learning
differences and learning disabilities very seriously—as do GMAC and
those who actually suffer from them. A learning disability is not
something people with lower standardized test results get to create
as a backdoor acceptance strategy. Learning disabilities and differences
are real. Don't fake them. And for those of you looking for information
to go hunt down your own brand of disability, skip this chapter. Ignore
this warning and I hereby put a pox on you and everybody from your
ancestors to future generations of your family.

This book makes no effort to teach you how to do well on the GMAT. For that, hire a test-prep company, take private lessons to target your weaknesses, read the prep books, take practice tests, and be prepared to take the actual test more than once to earn a score commensurate with your abilities. Admissions committees don't care how many times you've taken the test, and they don't care about your range of scores. They look at your highest score as an indicator of your ability to handle the rigors of an MBA education.

For some, however, the GMAT is *not* an indicator of ability—and if you've got an A average in quantitative coursework but can't seem to score at least a 650 on the test, despite hard work and genuine effort, you may have a learning disability or learning difference. This chapter will help you determine if you should be tested and how to handle this element of your candidacy.

So what's a learning disability (LD)? According to Cindy L. Breitman, PhD, founder and partner of Behavioral and Neuropsychological Consultants, LLP, a private practice in New York City, a learning disability is "when a significant discrepancy occurs between a person's potential abilities (intellect) and their actual skill level in regard to academics (reading, writing, math)." With respect to reading, "the underlying deficit is almost always relayed to a phonological dysfunction, that is, the ability to decode letter and word sounds. Often, pure word recognition takes place and the person is unable to sound out unfamiliar or irregularly spelled words. This is related to language skills. In regard to measurement and testing, significant differences are identified by being two standard deviations below intellect; this means that the variance is not chance related but instead indicates a learning deficit. For instance, the average measure for intellect is considered to be a standard score of 100 with a standard deviation of 15. When evaluating for an LD, if the person's skill levels fall at a standard score of 70 for reading ability, that indicates a learning disability."

While a learning disability is a neurodevelopmental disorder that occurs from early childhood, some individuals are not identified until adulthood. Why? Dr. Breitman explains, "If in college the student took pass/fail classes, had unofficial accommodations like extra time on a test, or [like many of us] took a class format which allowed them to excel (for example, grades based on class discussion rather than tests, essays rather than multiple choice, or, for those strong in math, multiple choice rather than essays), they may have circumvented their weaknesses. In elementary school, an extremely bright individual may be passed along due to his or her class contributions or personality. Teachers think they are being kind, when they are truly hurting the individual. And, of course, those who grew up in other countries where it is taboo to be diagnosed with a learning disability may never have been assessed at all." The latter is true for so many people, foreign and U.S. born.

A learning "difference" is what we will focus on in this chapter. It's the more elusive problem, and the one that many people suffer, often without even realizing it. Think of a learning difference as a weakness. "This would mean that the person struggles in an academic area and their skills are not as strong as would be expected based on their intellectual abilities," says Dr. Breitman. Essentially, your skills do not test far away enough from "normal" to be considered a disability. What does this mean to you if you fall into this category? It means GMAC is most likely not giving you extra time or any other extra accommodation on the exam. So why bother to discuss this learning difference? Because while GMAC might not give you extra time on the exam, most of the top schools, particularly those interviewed for this book, understand the concept of a learning difference and, when it is documented, will take it into consideration when examining your candidacy. So, if you've got a really low GMAT but a strong GPA, and did not get accommodations on the GMAT, being tested and getting a documentation or a letter from a reputable psychologist stating, for example, that your learning difference rears its ugly head during a standardized exam like the GMAT but does not affect you in class, can be very helpful in explaining the discrepancy between your grades and your GMAT score to an admission committee.

Many people don't even realize they have a problem until they are faced with the GMAT. That's what Uncle David and I are faced with all the time. To clarify what we are dealing with, we asked the expert opinion of Dr. Sue Quinlan, a Connecticut psychologist who has worked success-fully with several of our candidates. She explained, "The two things that people with learning differences face—that most people do not—are the way they use their intellect (what I call 'horsepower') and the coping strat-egies they have developed over the years. [When faced with the GMAT] they come up against a wall and realize they can no longer cope, one of the legs is getting a little wobbly, and they can no longer compete without some sort of leverage." Almost monthly, someone calls or comes into the Forster-Thomas office with the following complaint: "I've been an A stu-dent from elementary school through college and I currently excel in my job as a financial analyst. Now what happened? Did I hit my head before taking the exam . . . three times?!" Sound remotely familiar? This chapter is, most of all, for you. See if Amy's story hits home.

Amy, What You Gonna Do?

No matter how hard she tried, how much she studied, or how many courses she took, Amy, a straight-A marketing student at Northwestern University, could not crack that GMAT. Despite her practice scores—650 and above—Amy could not break a 540 during an actual exam. She came to me frustrated, ready to throw in the towel. She was at her wits' end, despite the fact that her college transcripts, both in qualitative and quan-titative coursework, said otherwise. "I have high-level quantitative coursework, macro- and microeconomics, A and A–. For God's sake I got an A in calculus for accounting." Lord knows, I didn't even take that class—and I won't even discuss the reasons for econ being my lowest grade at Northwestern.

I glanced at Amy, glanced at her transcripts, glanced at her again when she interrupted the candidacy assessment touting her excellent SAT scores. Sound familiar to those of you who are struggling with the

GMAT yet flourishing in your competitive Wall Street/Silicon Valley/ McKinsey Consulting careers? It was clear to me, but shocking to her, when I suggested the following: "Have you ever been diagnosed with any sort of learning difference?" You would've thought I had asked her if she was a crack addict.

Once again, there I was, faced with the all-too-common ego versus reality check. The truth is that according to the National Institute of Mental Health, up to 8 percent of U.S. elementary schoolchildren have some sort of a learning *disability*, including a reading or math disorder. Because a learning *difference* is not a clinical disorder but represents weaknesses in particular areas of functioning, there are no percentages on what we refer to as learning differences. So they often go undetected until the student is faced with a test like the GMAT.

Back to Amy, who, like so many, slipped by for years without ever noticing her learning difference because it was not severe. But just because you do well in class does not mean you're going to do well on a standardized, timed exam.

Amy couldn't accept that she might have a learning difference, and she rattled off a number of reasons why, including her recent promotion and her top 10 percent standing as an undergrad. She left my office on that afternoon in early February insisting I didn't know what I was talking about—but not before snatching the piece of paper out of my assistant Katie's already-proffered hand with two top psychologists' phone numbers on it. Amy wasn't the kind of person who took no for an answer, and I knew she ultimately wouldn't let the GMAT slap her in the face.

"Multiple Intelligences"

What Amy did not get is that we all don't learn or process information in the same way. As such, certain circumstances present different challenges— different struggles, so to speak, when it comes to getting over an academic- based hurdle. In this case, I am talking about the ability to master the

GMAT. Our ability or inability to master the "learning" of one subject or skill is described as something called multiple intelligences. Breitman explains this concept as follows: "People have individual strengths and weaknesses, which stand out from others. For instance, a person may be extremely emotionally perceptive but have average verbal abilities." So, not doing well on the quantitative areas of the GMAT, for example, doesn't mean you're not smart, and it doesn't mean you can't get to the answer. It simply means that for some, it may take a little longer. In this case, it's a "processing speed" issue. So, computer geeks, tech nerds, and those of you who were put through college by owners of nail salons and restaurants in Curry Hill may have an edge quantitatively. Others of us may be faster in the area of reading comprehension.

"Information processing speed is an ability that varies like any other ability," Dr. Breitman goes on to explain. "Some individuals are extremely fast and others are slow. Reading comprehension not only involves speed of reading but interpretation and understanding of concept, concept formation, attention, and working memory skills and visual imagery of the material." Problems in any one of these areas will slow down reading speed, for example. Or, you might read quickly without actually grasping what you read. Think CPUs and gigasomethings. While many of us come to the table with the latest Pentium chip, most of us operate with DOS, and a significant number of us come to the table with punch cards. If you come to the table with a punch card, it doesn't mean you can't calculate the value of pi to the hundredth decimal, it just means it's going to take you a little longer to get there. It doesn't mean you're not smart. (I mean, hello, although unconfirmed, many historians say Einstein was dyslexic. And look at the impact he had on nuclear energy!) The point is that if you have some sort of learning difference like this, it's going to impact the outcome of your GMAT score.

So, GET OVER IT. You're not *stoopid*. You just may have some kind of learning difference—and getting it checked out is exactly what Amy finally did.

Lo and behold, she had a learning difference. It was slight, almost imperceptible. Specifically, her psychologist labeled it "divergent thinking." What that essentially meant with respect to the GMAT was that when faced with multiple-choice questions, Amy's high intellect gave her the reasoning ability to consider why more than one answer could be correct. You can see how that would slow her down on the exam and/or make her susceptible to choosing the wrong answer, thereby negatively impacting her overall score. Conversely, her learning difference made her an asset when it came to "in-class" performance and to being a leader. You know, she was able to see numerous points of view and could easily and deftly consider alternative solutions to puzzles, problems, and challenges she and any team she would be a part of faced.

The Lesson

I won the bet. To be sure, Amy not only contacted the psychologist and got evaluated, but also took the GMAT three more times. In the end, however, GMAC did not grant her extended time on the GMAT because she did not have a legal LD. However, she did have a learning difference and because Amy set her ego aside and got the help and the information she needed—and got it early—she knew what she was dealing with. And knowing that she had a learning difference, accepting it, and knowing what it was meant several key things that made her a successful candidate:

1. **Amy could practice for her GMAT in a more effective, intelligent, and decisive way. And yes, she raised her score each time she took the test (four times in total, so yes, I won that bet). By the time she applied, Amy had raised her score to a 660.**

2. **Understanding the nature of her learning difference gave her the ability to effectively write a targeted, clear optional/additional information essay response. She was able to articulate, in layman's terms, what her issues with the GMAT were. She was able to explain how and why her learning difference would not be a problem**

in class, and give the admissions office insight into why it should not give unnecessary weight to her GMAT score, but instead, why it should feel confident in placing greater value on her grades and experience when considering her candidacy.

3.   Having been formally tested, Amy was able to utilize her psychologist to write a brief, official letter that backed up the claims she made about her strengths in her optional essay. Because Amy put her ego aside and got the neuropsychological testing done, she had another tool in her arsenal, something she never could have gotten if she had not received a proper evaluation from a reputable psychologist. A short but powerful letter from her psychologist explained the negative impact of her learning difference when taking a standardized exam, as well as the benefit it would have when she was an actual student in class.

Amy was accepted to two top-five schools, including Kellogg; graduated at the top of her class; and has gone on to have a stellar career in marketing. And that's what not taking no for an answer does. In sum, admissions officers know that low GMATs don't always correlate to your ability to contribute powerfully to their MBA program. Tina Mabley, director of admissions of the University of Texas at Austin McCombs School of Business, says, "Many of our students who become very successful class student leaders are the ones who come in with the lowest score, who had the most stacked against them at the outset. But there was something that we saw that sort of pulled them through the process." By not letting your score define you, you can create the sort of powerful candidacy that clear-eyed admissions officers like Mabley can respond to.

Come Out, Come Out

Embrace who you are—the good and the not so good. Embrace your strengths and your weaknesses. This is what smart leaders do. They don't whine, and they don't get proud. They get busy. People who don't have legs and can't swim don't jump into the water and hope for the best, and if they do jump in, they certainly don't complain when they start drowning. They ask for help.

I could go on and on about successful candidates who found out about, revealed, and dealt with their learning differences. Recently, Jerry with a 600 was accepted to University of Michigan's Ross School of Business. We taught him to be fearless and proud, and instead of being the guy who hides that he has one of the lowest GMAT scores in the class, he is out, proud, and loud. He is much more than just a GMAT score. After all, it's *Ross*, for God's sake, and obviously they saw that despite his score, he was worth it. (I remember being told once while pursuing my

---

Take Your GMAT Well in Advance

Standardized tests are all "takable" tests. You can actually learn how to take them. While many star-studded standardized test tutors tout their secrets to success, pretty much the secret to standardized test mastery—with or without an LD—is simple: Study your ass off, take plenty of practice tests, and don't wait till the last minute to begin studying. Also, conventional wisdom says that the longer you've been out of college, the poorer you do on standardized tests. Certainly, you want to take a course, and if there are still areas you are having specific trouble in, consider getting a few sessions with a private tutor. Let a test-prep tutor tell you what and what not to answer and how to approach your answers wisely.

Furthermore, if you try to get extended time on the test, you need a lot of lead time. No, it's not easy, especially if you have no history of receiving accommodations. But yes, it can be done. It's going to be easier, although it's no guarantee, for those of you who have had neuropsychological tests done on a regular basis from high school through college.

screenwriting MFA at UCLA, "You don't actually think it was your GRE score that got you in, do you?") So compared to those people who have a 700-plus GMAT and the great grades in college, Ross saw that Jerry must have something pretty special going for him.

But the story that comes to my mind and consistently blows it, is the following. Two years ago, I had a candidate who made me look like focus personified. Having a conversation with Mickey was like having a conversation with a fly endowed with Ben Franklin's brain. So you can imagine how difficult it was for this genius to fare well on a GMAT. When we talked to him about getting tested and seeing a psychologist, his waspish background went at first into "DANGER, WILL ROBINSON!" mode, à la the robot in *Lost in Space*. But when he finally let go of his ego and got the testing and the help he needed, he wrote what is unequivocally the most spectacular, most honest, optional essay I have ever seen. In this essay he basically said, "Every school's gotta have one out-of-control ADD genius, and I'm your man." Harvard agreed.

PART II

Zen and the Art of MBA Admissions Essays

Essays are the ultimate expression of "story"—the topics you pick aren't nearly as important as the way you spin them. Essays allow the admissions committee to get a glimpse into how your mind works, so focusing on the facts and results of a situation you write about is a waste of word count. Instead, you need to push your analysis to a higher level of sophistication. Knock the committee off its feet by how transparent you are about your fears, your obstacles, how you create strategies for action, and how you assess your own and others' strengths and weaknesses to create results.

Uncle David often says, "An admissions committee is going to be more impressed by sophisticated analysis, evolved-beyond-your-years insight, and 'realness,' even if the essay is written in lipstick on a napkin, than it will be impressed by a beautifully written essay that spews empty platitudes." This is the ultimate substance over style.

Yeah, it's a lot easier to say "be sophisticated" than it is to, well, be sophisticated. In the following chapters, I'll introduce you to a number of clients who faced the same wall you're up against now—and by showing you how we pushed their thinking into a new level of insight, you can draw parallels to your own experience.

CHAPTER 8

The Career Goals Essay

The goals essay is the heart of your candidacy. Here's how to get real, defy expectations, and have "the vision thing."

"Vision is making people see what they have not seen, and making them follow you," says MIT Sloan's Rod Garcia. Our success at Forster-Thomas is, in large part, predicated on helping each of our candidates dig down deep to determine his or her long-term vision. It is the central theme of your candidacy around which every other part hinges. One thing is certain: Until you know your long-term goal, you cannot possibly know why you and the school(s) you're applying to are a "fit." And your long-term goal must be as specific as possible. "Private equity" by itself is about as vague as it gets. Your goal is to get the admissions officer on board, so your task is to *enroll* him or her in your goal. And you cannot do that when you don't really know exactly what you want to do. And you certainly can't get specific until you get passionate. The sections that follow will help you identify and leverage passion and specificity in your own candidacy and, indeed, career.

Ask yourself this: Why should the admissions officer care when I don't?

When push comes to shove, many people have no trouble *being* visionary, but they do have trouble giving themselves *permission* to be visionary. We all have those critics running through our head, making us worry about "what would my mother say?" "What would my girlfriend think?" "What would my coworkers, or worse, my boss or mentor, say?"

So what do we all do? We end up killing off transformational goals—the very thing that most top business schools want. Can you imagine if whoever invented the wheel had paid attention to the rest of the tribe: "You want us to chip away at some rock for a month just because you've got this ridiculous idea that somehow it will make it easier to bring water down the mountain? What's wrong with the womenfolk carrying it down by hand? They've got nothing better to do while we hunt!"

You're supposed to be in the 5 percent that's going to lead the world, not the 95 percent that's going to agree with the world. So, the barometer for a visionary goal is really simple: If at least one person looks at you like Scooby Doo and says, "Rhat?" like you've lost your mind, you're probably on the right track.

But don't take me too literally: Just because everyone agrees with you doesn't mean you have a boring idea. It's just that when one or two people disagree with you—especially if that person is someone like your mother who fears for your security—you might be onto something exciting. Remember, Gandhi's own mother must have been horrified when her son put on a lungi and started agitating for a free India. After all, he had a law degree from Oxford!

"No Essays by Committee"

One of our most stringent rules is "no essays by committee." That is, don't share your essays with friends, lovers, colleagues, MBA-program alumni . . . not even recommenders (there's nothing in your essays you can't communicate in person or in talking points). This is because:

1. Opinions are like assholes—everybody has one. You end up driving yourself crazy.

2. People want to help—we assume you're going to ask smart people, your most respected friends and advisers, and such people don't like to come up empty. They'll find problems where none exist to feel like they've contributed to your success.

3. You'll spin your wheels—once you start playing the "tweaking" game, it never ends. It's like a multiple-choice quiz: Usually your first impulse is correct.

4. You can get the same result from a single well-chosen friend. Pick that one friend who isn't afraid to tell you that you look awful in that outfit (you know the one).

Goals Essay 1: "OPE"—Other People's Expectations

At twenty-five, Jared was the whole "stats" package with his 720 GMAT and 3.7 in economics from a good Mid-Atlantic college. His résumé boasted an associate's role in the retail group at a prominent French investment bank, and Columbia Business School was his number one choice. When he walked in the room, he flashed me a confident smile that, when combined with his stellar résumé, revealed how he had earned his promotion. I knew this kind of guy well. He wasn't a charmer, although he had lots of charm. He wasn't a genius, although he had worked very hard at school and on the job. He was his own Rocky Horror, a perfect creation meant for one thing: getting accepted into b-school. I was certain his closet hosted a Brioni, a Zegna, or an Abboud, and a requisite pair of bench-made Allen Edmonds.

Gazing at the intake form we give all prospective candidates, I wondered why I would bother reading it: Just as I knew what was in his closet, I knew what it was going to say. Jared was going to be one of those candidates with excellent stats and experience—but who risked blowing his candidacy in the story department by playing it safe.

He sat down across from me at my intake table. Wordlessly, I grabbed my trusty Magic Eight Ball and held it up the way a magician holds up a top hat before pulling a rabbit out of it. "You have stood high atop Mount Kilimanjaro's Uru Peak!"

I shook the ball. "Yes, definitely," it read.

"You venture out into a faraway land called Brooklyn to spend time with underprivileged children."

I shook the ball again. "Yes, sometimes," it read.

Jared couldn't tell if I was mocking him or praising him.

"What are you getting at, dude?" he said. "I know so many people just like me who've gotten into Columbia."

"That's the problem, *dude*," I began to explain. "You've got all the stats and extracurriculars, but that's not enough. There're more than enough guys like you to fill Columbia's next class—even if you were the only type of guy they took. You know, the kind of guy who wants an MBA to go from investment banking to private equity."

Jared stared at me. I stared back. I slid my Magic Eight Ball over to him and said, "Do you even wanna bother to shake it? At this rate, you know what it's going to say."

Jared squirmed in his seat and mumbled something.

"We can play the game this way—with the Magic Eight Ball and a pair of dice, because that's the game you're playing, Jared—or we could do what you came to me for, and that's get real and find a way to let the true you come out."

I knew I had to put this in terms he could understand: "Jared, there are two kinds of girls who go out with you. At your age, you probably can't tell the difference, but your Auntie Evan can. There's the type who go out with you because you're wearing Brioni and work at Lazard Frères, and there's the type for whom that's not enough: They demand the whole package, and that includes your killer smile and your charming personality, not just your earning potential. Columbia's like that second type of girl. But in your application, all you're showing her is the suit. Where's the *smile*? Writing 'I want to go into private equity' is just pulling out another suit."

Then I asked him to tell me what made him so passionate about private equity. His response was even less audible. He was getting my point.

Jared simply did not care about private equity—at least, not specifically. When pressed—because he's not the kind of guy who quits easily—he started throwing out jargon like "returns," "growth," "developing businesses," "skill sets I need."

After I came to, I snatched my Magic Eight Ball back, folded my hands, leaned forward, and asked, "Tell me again—why would Columbia's Dean Hubbard—who's all about the entrepreneurial mind-set and making a difference wherever you are—care that you want to go into private equity? I'm sure all that financial jargon are things he expects you'll learn in some class somewhere, but I'm not sure that's why he would want you to be part of his program. After all, those are things you can pick up in *The Ten-Day MBA*. Somehow, I'm thinking he's going to expect . . . let's see . . . *vision*? You know, that thing that distinguishes why you'd go to Columbia over an online MBA?"

I could see I had my work cut out for me. Jared needed to play a little game I call Three Blind Mice, where we add vision to three vision-impaired goals.

Three Blind Mice

By the time most people graduate college, they tend to stop being great. They tend to stop thinking they can do anything, and replace "sky's the limit" goals (like inventing a new energy source or landing on Mars) with cautious, "sensible" goals that first and foremost include paying their rent, second doing something—anything—in a field of their choice, and then one day, when they have "enough," that's when they will pursue what they really want (and maybe even help out their fellow man with a check).

There's nothing wrong with this guy; the problem is that he's not who Dean Hubbard is looking for. He's what none of the deans of the great MBA programs are looking for. He's just what 95 percent of the world is. And that's okay, it's just not competitive.

If I just described you, you can make a choice. Close this book now and try to get your money back, or get back in touch with the guy or gal in you who was determined to go to Mars.

How do you take that second option? That's where Three Blind Mice comes in.

It's as simple as this: Come up with at least three goals, one for each of the following categories (you'll find a worksheet for this in Workbook 4):

The first is the one where b-school will help you return to your current industry at a level via which you can make a difference in that industry. The second, and most common, is a career shift wherein b-school will be the lynchpin to the new industry in which you hope to make a difference. The third, and usually the most visionary, is what I like to call "The dream goal" or "I want to be a rock star." You know, it's the one you generally don't tell people because you are afraid they'll laugh at you. (Think about one well-known visionary: "Mom, Dad, I want to quit school and make a program that allows everyone to run a computer even without a computer science degree." Or here's an example I like a lot: "I want to create an amusement park place where everyone can experience the future." Thank God Bill Gates and Walt Disney ignored the laughter, the confused stares, and the closed minds they surely received when they first had their ideas for Microsoft and Disneyland.)

Now, being in private equity in and of itself is not a "bad" long-term goal. It's just so abstract and so overdone that no one's getting on board with that one. It's like trying to sell ice to an Inuit sitting in an igloo: "*Next.*" That's what I'd be saying if I were on the admissions committee at Columbia Business School. At the risk of launching a thousand ships, I'll describe what one transformational private equity goal that Stanford loved looks like: "I want to invest in companies that modernize the electrical grid infrastructure of Third World countries." That's a simple, elegant, private equity–oriented goal that would be beautiful, as it somehow ties into your professional background or personal story. Don't think your goals needs to be set in the developing world either: That Stanford guy's essay would have been just as compelling if he'd been referring to America's own outdated power infrastructure.

But all too often we find ourselves in Jared's position. He thought private equity was the "right" thing to say given his professional and academic background. But did he really want to do it? If you glanced at his workbook, he had practically written a treatise on finance and why he had the right background, and on and on and on. To this day I cannot tell you what the hell he was talking about, and not just because I can't add or because I couldn't care less about buy/sell, or LBO, M&A, or any other financial acronym. I didn't care because *Jared* didn't care. I didn't care because he could not get specific about what he wanted to do in private equity.

One acronym that did catch my eye, however, was scribbled at the bottom of the goals page, below the dream goal: WWE. World Wrestling Entertainment. All it said was, "I've been watching the WWE since I was a kid, when it was the WWF. It's my favorite waste of time—mine and X-thousand Americans who watch it daily. But the company's going under, the P/E ratio is out of whack, and they've been telling the same old story since Mr. T was on *The A-Team*. I want to take over Vince McMahon's role as CEO of this publicly traded company and turn it around financially and creatively."

Three things I assure you of: (1) I do not give a rat's ass about fake wrestling, let alone that it was a publicly traded $500 million-a-year business (if you want to talk about the potential for *Legally Blonde 3*, on the other hand, count me in); (2) I wasn't convinced that the actual wrestler stories had *ever* been good; and (3) What I thought about it didn't matter.

Jared loved wrestling. His excitement was palpable both on the page and when I asked him about it. He went on for an hour about the winners and the losers, the fights and the medals. He was so into it that he got me excited about it as well. To top it off, he was able to discuss it from a financial point of view. After all, he had a whole new skill set—finance—plus a lifetime of knowledge about the world of ersatz wrestling. It was a perfect fit. He was the right guy—and I was suddenly enrolled. The only problem was that when I brought the conversation back around to his long-term professional goal and an MBA, Jared shut down. It was a no-go. "How could I write that?" he asked me. We were right back to private equity.

Again, I slumped into my chair. I had more work cut out for me.

When I asked Jared why he could not write about it, he mumbled a few reasons, something about what the admissions committee would think. But I'd been here many a time—there was always something else at play when they tried to hide behind the admissions committee. Let's dispose of the myth that the "admissions committee is out to get you" right now: They're not like the Harvard Law admissions committee in *Legally Blonde* (clearly one of my favorite movies)—a bunch of grimacing white-haired old men sitting around an enormous oak table in a room with dark paneling. They're real people who respond to real stories and real passion. In fact, over my years of meeting admissions officers, I'm afraid *I'm* closer to meeting that stereotype than the actual admissions officers I've met.

Still, you can never be too sure. On the spot, I dialed up a former admissions officer friend of mine at Columbia. I broke it down quickly. "Oh, please," she said, "give me the WWE goal!"

Still, Jared refused, concerned about his managing director's opinion. After all, one of Columbia's traditional rec questions had been, "What do you think motivates the candidate's application to the MBA program at Columbia Business School?" He was afraid that making his goal outside finance would burn a bridge with his managing director.

"So you're going to decrease your chance of getting into Columbia on the off chance that your WWE goal would keep you from returning to basically the same job you have now in an industry where you already have connections and you've already proven your value?" I said skeptically.

"You don't understand, Evan. My managing director has really been there for me, guiding me every step of the way. I really value his opinion."

The phrase "I really value his opinion" rang a bell . . . Where had I heard that before? Flipping through Jared's workbook, there it was: In the Friends and Family section of the workbook, Jared had written about how his father was a role model and a mentor, and he wanted to "make him proud."

And so I asked the big question: "Okay, Jared, is this about your dad?" A silence filled my office and finally, sheepishly, Jared admitted it: "Dad would kill me if I wrote a business school essay about the WWE."

Let's Make a Deal

So, I made Jared an offer he couldn't refuse. "Let's do it both your way and my way. You'll write two goals essays, we'll show both of them to your father, and see which one he likes."

This whole deal sent a shiver down my spine. It went against one of my most fundamental tenets as a consultant: "No essays by committee." Almost without fail, it ends up diluting the purity of your idea and the power of your essay—you end up sounding just like everyone else (which isn't surprising, since everyone else had a hand in your essay). But Jared's resistance was so intense I knew I had to take a walk on the wild side.

And so we did. Jared completed both versions of the essay. But by the time he finished writing about returning WWE to its glory days, I could tell that his father's approval was no longer a match for his own excitement. I had won the war without having to go to battle. Ironically enough, however, Jared was wrong about his dad in the first place (as sons and daughters generally are): Jared's dad loved the essay and chose it over the generic private equity goal. After all, he was a successful businessman himself, and he knew a value proposition when he saw it.

With or without Dad's approval, Jared was now going to be the man who would bring back the golden age of wrestling. When he saw an intelligent version of the WWE essay and had it in his hands, Jared finally got on board. The moral of the story is: "You know you're telling the right story and choosing the right topic when you have enrolled yourself."

And, by the way, Jared got the fat envelope from Columbia.

JARED'S GOALS ESSAY

Over a recent lunch, I told my boss I wanted to pursue an MBA. He was shocked; he thought I was at the bank for life. None of them knows that I have a secret, kept from everyone but my best friends: I love pro wrestling. The fake and funny kind, with soap operatic storylines where the bad guy cheats. Not that any of my friends know this; I stopped mentioning it when it became uncool. Yet, I have found that wrestling is not even fun to watch in secret anymore. No, it's not because I'm getting older. The stories are tired and recycled, no longer even loopy enough to laugh at.

My boss thinks I am pursuing an MBA just to return to Lazard Frères with a better title. While that may well be a short-term goal, my long-term career objective is to revitalize pro wrestling. Don't laugh: I have done my research. From WWE to TNA on Spike!, pro wrestling is proliferating into companies worth hundreds of millions.

As a banker, I have watched the marketing, the strategic investments, and the growth story of pro wrestling. Cable television has invested deeply in it, and competitors rise and fall. But none of the "federations" match the glory days of good versus evil; the more sophisticated the companies try to make their storylines, the more boring it gets. Someone needs to tell the writers to have fun again. As a banker, investor, and wrestling fan, I have the vision to pump blood back into this industry.

What I need are business-strategy skills, marketing concepts, and a transformational community of like-minded thinkers. Columbia Business School has both the community and curriculum I am looking for. Columbia prides itself on its premier network of students, faculty, and alumni that I will be part of for a lifetime. The cluster approach and Integrated Project will allow me to work closely with a subgroup of talented and diverse students. Within these groups, some of the individuals may be exploring their own secret dreams, too. As my former roommate Adam, a Columbia graduate, told me, "The people here will help you explore anything that interests you." Of course, he does not know about my secret.

Columbia will allow me to polish my finance skills at the institution that leads the way in finance while I also develop a new mind-set to analyze industries from the ground up through core coursework such as Strategic Formulation. Advanced courses such as Economics of Strategic Behavior and Turnaround Management will help me further explore business strategy and the possibility of my vision. My particular industry I can always learn.

I plan to be a member of the Columbia Entrepreneurs

Organization to work closely with other visionaries and together take advantage of the Lang Center for Entrepreneurship. The institute is appealing because, as the Lang website says, its focus is not only on how to launch a new venture, but also on identifying, valuing, and capturing opportunity with an emphasis on individual initiative, uncertainty, and tight resources.

Then there is the appeal of New York, the global capital of business. Columbia has the authority to access what New York has to offer, such as the established leaders who come to speak. Furthermore, internships in media are available on every corner. I

The Archetypal Goals-Essay Structure: A Sonata in Six Beats

While almost every MBA program requires a career-goals essay, the information these essays require varies somewhat. Some schools want a brief description of your career progress; others ask why now is the right time for you to receive an MBA. Harvard doesn't ask why you want to go to Harvard, but most schools require a detailed description of exactly how their program fits your development needs. If you're applying to a number of MBA programs, start your process by writing an "archetypal" goals essay: one that contains every element that any business school could ask for. Once you've written that, you can cut-and-paste the different sections as necessary for the different schools: All you need to do to complete the essay is smooth transitions and add on the "why your school" supplement to the end. Here are the six elements and a suggested word count, assuming the school allows a thousand words for the total essay. Berkeley's question typifies the standard wording: "What are your post-MBA short-term and long-term career goals? How do your professional experiences relate to these goals? How will an MBA from Berkeley help you achieve these specific career goals?"

would love to work at Spike!, which manages TNA. As I look at
my secret business from a different point of view, Columbia is the
perfect setting.

As someone who has a background in finance and a passion
for New York City, I will be able to add value to my cluster and
the rest of Columbia. I will guide other students through the core
corporate finance class and other advanced finance classes. In any
group, I will be able to offer a perspective on the way companies
evaluate their capital structure. In addition, I will want to be
involved in the Investment Banking Club and help with the annual

Beat One (100 Words)

■ A narrative paragraph that describes the moment that inspired or clarified your vision.

Beat Two (150 Words)

■ A description of your long-term goal.

■ Followed with your short-term, post-MBA transitional goal. Feel free to include statistics that back up your idea, such as the available market size, lack of/nature of competition and how that creates an opportunity, trends, etc.

Beat Three (300 Words)

■ A brief survey of your career thus far. Only include data that illustrates how your professional experience has:

• Prepared you for an MBA education (emphasize leadership development).

• Given you unique insight into your industry of choice that will drive your success.

• Unusual experiences that truly distinguish you from your peer group.

Investment Banking Conference. I have the contacts and the background. Beyond that, I will also encourage others to explore their dream. Once they hear what I am thinking about, anybody who feels nervous about what they want to do will always have me as their example.

Most importantly, especially with its Master Class structure, Columbia will teach me to think in a new way. These new skills will guide me no matter what I do. Even if I decide to go back to Lazard Frères for a while, no matter what I do, I am going to be out and proud about my goal to transform professional wrestling. Wow—it's so much easier the second time you say it.

Beat Four (50 Words)

- Why *now* is the right time to leave your job and begin an MBA degree.
  - For example: "With four years of finance experience, I can no longer grow in my job."
- An overview of what you expect to gain from an MBA program.
  - Be specific about your development needs vis-à-vis your background.

Beat Five (300 Words)

- A detailed, sophisticated explanation of why "X" program is right for you.
  - See page 112 for details about researching schools and campus visits.
  - As a general guideline, think of beat five as three paragraphs: First paragraph describes how you will tailor your first year to your needs (be specific with a couple of classes; include why the core curriculum is important to you, what you will place out of); second paragraph describes the same thing, only for electives in your second year; paragraph three describes noncurriculum resources you look forward to ("The X Institute," a speakers series, a field project, etc.).

Goals Essay 2: Passion—Finding Your P-Spot

Vinod, an Indian national born and raised in Mumbai, came to me through the Internet. He shared the same goal as so many South Asians and almost all techies applying to business school: He wanted to transition from backroom to the boardroom. In Vinod's case, he was a project manager at a telecom company, though he did have a relatively sexy position in the entertainment-software division.

When Vinod first came to me as a round-one candidate for his top-five choices including Harvard and Kellogg, I was concerned for several reasons. One, he had a relatively low GMAT (relative to the pool of ap-

---

- **DO NOT describe classes in a generic way.** ("I want to take the Social Enterprise class so I can learn about social enterprise.") Rather, describe how that class gives you a new skill set required for your goals in the context of what you already do or don't know. ("The class Social Enterprise will complement my existing finance background by teaching me how to evaluate...")
- **DO relate how specific elements of the program align directly to YOUR needs/interests/background.** ("I want to take the Social Enterprise class because, as an equities researcher, I have a practical understanding of how operational variables impact a company's valuation, but I do not understand how to make strategic decisions in an operations context, particularly when the bottom line is not the sole imperative.")

Beat Six (100 Words)

- A one-paragraph description of what you bring to the table: skills you can contribute, perspectives you bring to classroom discussions, clubs you want to join or start, etc. Then end with a summary—if you have room left.

---

plicants he was competing against; he "only" had a 710). He also had the requisite graduate degree in engineering from Somewhere USA State University, which had allowed him to earn his U.S. visa in the first place.

Finally, he came across as a typical high-waters-wearing guy you might find at a *Star Trek* convention. So it was of no surprise when he came to us after four other consultants had already told him he had no chance of getting into any of his top-five choices and to lower his expectations.

On face value, I shared their concerns. After all, Vinod seemed to have no "dazzle." What he did have, however, was tenacity, and an infectious, goofy good spirit that made me want to help him. The challenge would be finding a concrete way to infuse his candidacy with that same off-kilter charm. I was mostly nervous because if we failed, I would have to contend with my own Jewish guilt. It's not as if he made a Wall Street salary, and he had made it clear that a large part of what he did make went back home to India to help his family.

And so I said to him, "There's only one way I'll take you: You have to be ready to go against all your cultural and professional instincts, be completely honest and confessional, and let me operate like Toto to pull back the curtain and reveal the little man behind the Great and Powerful Oz." I sent him off to think about that.

Shortly after the first-round deadline passed, I received a second call. Apparently, Vinod knew enough to know that he needed creative help, and thus had never submitted a first-round application. I found that very interesting. Clearly, he knew that he needed "something extra" to succeed in his candidacy, which called all my assumptions about his being your run-of-the-mill tech applicant into question. Even though he didn't know how to give his candidacy "spirit fingers," he knew enough to recognize their absence. So, he showed back up on my proverbial doorstep, ready to do battle the Auntie Evan way: Since the possibility of rejection is scary, you have to be scarier.

To get Vinod to let go of his boring, bland tech-management goal was going to be difficult. His story was better than I thought (although still not the most unusual to come out of India). After all, engineering and the struggle to rise from poverty seemed to run together in India like chocolate and peanut butter. As open as Vinod was, he couldn't shake the idea that his goals had to be engineering-related.

After peeling the onion away a little bit more, I found in his work something that only four of his American friends knew. In Mumbai, he was quite well-known as a top jazz guitarist. His band, The Peacocks, played at the Blue Frog, the swankiest jazz club in Mumbai, and had a fan base.

The farther away our conversation got from the wireless company, the more excited Vinod got. He stopped being just another South Asian technologist and became his own unique individual personality who was a master of the guitar riff in Van Halen's "Jump"—which Vinod told me was the most difficult riff in rock music—and had scraped together enough money to buy a guitar previously owned by jazz master Thelonius Monk.

I had found what I needed to make his goofy charm concrete. The forum would be his goals essay. Instead of relying on his background as a technologist, we would move to his background as a jazz guitarist.

Once I made that decision, the pieces just started falling into place. It turned out that he made an attempt to make a foray into the music industry in India. But in a world where Channel V (India's homegrown MTV) rules, and every song has the same Hindi Pop structure (girls on the left, boys on the right, and dance moves clearly influenced by Paula Abdul and her animated cat paramour in the "Opposites Attract" video), jazz music was non grata, and The Peacocks had received a series of door slams from every recording studio in Mumbai.

I knew Vinod was getting close when he finally understood that a country of a billion people should be able to support more than four genres of music: Hindu classical, Hindi Pop, Western pop, and Western classical. "In a country of more than a billion people," Vinod complained, his voice unusually sad, "there is as big a market for jazz there as there is in America. Yet the music industry shuts it out. Somebody should do something about that."

Do you, gentle reader, see the huge flashing sign over Vinod's head as easily as I did?

"Yes, somebody should do something about that," I said. "And that somebody is you."

I suddenly looked at him and said, "It is your responsibility to break the stranglehold that the producers of its three monopolistic genres had on the music industry by bringing webcast radio to India." His music goals now incorporated his technology background, instead of having to deny one or the other. In fact, he'd never need to ask anyone again to keep the door open to jazz. India already had technology covered. They didn't need more technology managers. And, considering his music background, he had much more than that to offer.

PS: He was accepted to both Harvard and Kellogg.

The Lesson

Look for the idiosyncratic aspect of your life: Make sure your goal is something that drives your passions and makes you want to get up for work every day. This does not mean you have to be a classical jazz guitarist. You don't have to be a closet prima ballerina or Division I college baseball player. What you have to do is consider taking your professional and practical skill set and combining them with something you care about—a lot. Something where you can change and transform some community: Be it, as one Harvard admissions officer said, the PTA or the world.

VINOD'S GOALS ESSAY

What is your career vision and why is this choice meaningful to you?
—Harvard Business School

In 1998, just after my 21st birthday, Suchit Kumar, a talent executive with Staccato Records, became the ninth label rep to tell me my demo was "brilliant," followed by, "but it's neither Hindi nor pop—sorry." As he pointed me to the door, I began to realize that it did not matter that I was a classically-trained, award-winning session musician.

No music company in India dares challenge the 50-year-old domination of Hindi film-based pop. Despite having the second-largest music market in the world, growing 18% a year, the industry supports only three genres: 60% film music, 35% Hindi-pop, 5% classical. I knew that some day, I would change this system of assembly-line music production.

I did not know how I would pull this off, but my gut told me that my other love, technology, would play a huge role. The last thing I wanted to become was a stereotypical Indian engineer. But I discovered that the philosophy of jazz—creating a framework of open dialog and encouraging improvisation—worked perfectly well in software development.

Now, my accumulated insights as a successful software entrepreneur and a lead designer of my firm's audio and video content catalog have converged into a well-defined vision of how to revolutionize India's $840-million music industry.

In America, I have seen innovations such as iTunes shatter the industry's monopoly on production and distribution. In India, however—even as growth in Internet usage has jumped 296% since 2000—no parallel transformation exists. My career aspiration is to build India's first online music company, which will not only provide a mouthpiece to its creative voices, but create an entire "ecosystem" that will help upcoming Indian artists hone their talent, produce their albums, and organize their concerts.

My music career and technology expertise alone are not sufficient to achieve my goals. An MBA education's core curriculum will extend my skill set into crucial areas such as marketing, organizational behavior, and finance. HBS also will position me to refine my skills in the short-term by working in the A&R division of a niche company such as Blue Note records or the operations division of a larger music company to gain exposure to global music promotion and distribution. Ultimately, an MBA will enable me to transform into an exemplary manager and leader, capable of opening up India's stagnant music industry to a multitude of new genres, voices, and marginalized talents.

FOR comparison, here is the same essay expanded to Kellogg's two-page limit (recently reduced slightly to six hundred words):

Briefly assess your career progress to date. Elaborate on your future career plans and your motivation for pursuing a graduate degree at Kellogg.

Just after my 21st birthday, Suchit Kumar, a talent executive with Staccato Records, became the ninth label rep to tell me my demo was "brilliant," followed by, "but it's neither Hindi nor pop— sorry." As he pointed me to the door, I began to realize that it did not matter that I was a classically-trained, award-winning session musician. No music company in India dares challenge the 50-year-old domination of Hindi film-based pop. Despite having the world's second-largest music market, the industry supports only three genres: 60% film music, 35% Hindi-pop, 5% classical. I knew that someday, I would change this assembly-line system of music production.

I did not know how I would pull this off, but my gut told me that my other love, technology, would play a huge role. The last thing I wanted to become was a stereotypical Indian engineer. But I discovered that the philosophy of jazz—creating a framework of open dialog and encouraging improvisation—worked perfectly well in software development. It was the time of the Internet boom, and I saw a great opportunity for building regional-language websites. After putting a business plan together, I created Codaphone, a software program that empowers small businesses to create and maintain Indian-language e-commerce Web sites. To market it, I also created Netbiz.

The success of both ventures emboldened me to pursue a career in the United States. Although it was difficult to leave my friends and family, I accepted an offer by Harisoft, a wireless consulting company, to lead a team of ten programmers to build my firm's first wireless Web portal. When the project ended, I was asked to lead the nationwide launch of its broadband service. I accepted. Most recently, I authored a software solution that lets media companies securely sell games and ringtones to subscribers. Furthermore, I designed its architecture so that independent musicians and game developers could also distribute content—and get paid for it.

Now, my accumulated insights as a successful software entrepreneur and lead designer of audio and video content catalog have converged into a well-defined vision of how to revolutionize India's $840-million music industry. In America, innovations like iTunes shattered the industry's monopoly on production and distribution, but in India, no parallel transformation exists. My long-term career goal is to build India's first online music company, which will not only provide a mouthpiece to its creative voices, but create an entire "ecosystem" that will help upcoming Indian artists hone their talent, produce their albums, and organize their concerts.

My music career and technology expertise alone are not sufficient to achieve these goals, which is why I am pursuing an MBA at the Kellogg School. The core curriculum will extend my skill set into crucial areas such as marketing, organizational behavior, and finance, in an atmosphere that encourages visionary thinking and emphasizes leadership, communication, and ethics.

At Kellogg, I can tailor the curriculum perfectly to fit my unique goal. Through Kellogg's Media Management major, regarded as the industry's best, I can deepen my skills in courses such as "Entertainment Culture & Marketing" and "Media Strategy & Implementation" and learn the complex decision-making processes of the industry. Prof. John Lavine's insight and research on the challenges facing media will prove invaluable when I set up my own company. The International Business major will help me understand the success factors of operating a global organization from India. And I may use the Independent Studies program to cross-register with the School of Music.

The more I researched Kellogg's MBA program, the more I gained an appreciation of its integrated approach towards leadership development, such as LEAP, and experiential learning opportunities that "go beyond the classroom." TechVentures will give me an opportunity to evaluate real-world approaches for my ideas. The Global Initiatives in Management program will open my eyes to new cultures and perspectives in a place I know little about, such as South America.

Kellogg's collaborative philosophy and open, friendly community was proven when I contacted Jane Smith, co-chair of the Entertainment and Media club. I was surprised when she replied immediately, furnishing me with all the information I needed. Jane corresponded several times with me and gave me

Tip Sheet: School Research and Visits

Your Research Checklist

If you need to buy a "school guide" to learn about a top MBA program, then you're probably not what that program is looking for in the first place. (You wouldn't buy a research paper from a learning team member, would you?) For a decision of this caliber—where you're going to spend two years of your life and almost $200,000—you should accept nothing less than firsthand research.

personal insight into what Kellogg has to offer. She was thrilled to hear about my music background and encouraged me to learn more about the Special K music revue club.

Kellogg will prepare me for my short-term goal, working in the artist & repertoire division of a niche market music company such as Blue Note records, before moving to the operations division of a global music company to gain exposure to music promotion and distribution. Ultimately, a Kellogg MBA will enable me to transform into an exemplary manager and leader, capable of opening up India's stagnant music industry to a multitude of new genres, voices, and marginalized talents.

NOTICE the differences. The additional length of the Kellogg essay comes almost entirely from two areas: a brief assessment of the candidate's career progress, and a detailed description of how Kellogg will help you reach your goals. Harvard neither asks for either of these specifics, nor requires them. Vinod included a brief mention of his career because it answered questions about how a studio musician ended up at a technology company. Rather than focusing on his accomplishments, he puts it directly into a context that teaches you something about what matters to

Research even a quarter of the following questions for each school you're considering applying to, and you'll be able to write your own study guide. Select the three or four things that excited you the most, and include them in the "why I want to go to your MBA program" part of your goals essay. You'll really stand out from the guys and gals who relied on a study guide. When writing your "why school" section, include a standout attribute from the core or first-year curriculum, as well as at least one standout from the second year or elective curriculum. About 20 percent of your "why school" section should be devoted to how you'll contribute to the program outside of class: which him—"The last thing I wanted to become was a stereotypical Indian engineer"—and implies that he's no longer willing to settle for anything less than what is truly meaningful to him in his professional life.

Goals Essay 3: Get Real—Leveraging Your Personal Story

Pia was a typical overachieving beautiful white girl (not to be confused with a White Boy—see Chapter 13—although she was a bit of that as well). After graduating from Bryn Mawr with honors, she continued her upward mobility with a position at an engineering-consulting concern. Currently, she was doing product packaging. While working with Susan, one of my coaches, she hit a roadblock in her long-term career goal. She was doing great work, but Pia's resistance—this appropriate girl wanted an appropriate goal, not a visionary one—required an Auntie Evan intervention. (Imagine the love child of Judge Judy and Barbara Walters: Hit

clubs are attractive to you, and how you could contribute to that club (leading a panel, organizing a conference, bringing in speakers from your network).

- Core curriculum
  - Can you place out?
  - Do you even want to? There's something to be said about having a former director of marketing in your marketing-class study group.
  - What majors/concentrations are available?
  - What are the program's strongest department(s)?

- Flexibility
  - How many electives can you take?
  - How broad are the electives offerings?
  - Can you take classes outside the b-school?

'em hard with the facts, then make 'em cry when the truth sets them free.) So I gathered all of Susan's notes and began to examine the disparate parts of Pia's life.

Rummaging through Pia's file felt like being in an episode of *Cold Case*: She was the daughter of a single dad, who raised her to be a die-hard feminist and encouraged her to break through the glass ceiling; she had grown up in Los Angeles and attended an all-girl, private day school, which gave her the mathematical confidence to study engineering; she was a young muckety-muck in a women's engineering society.

And then there was the non sequitur in the workbook that was originally overlooked: the tattoo. Pia didn't like talking about this two-inch-long dragon beneath her right collarbone, the last testimony of a crazy girlhood and former rebellious nature. But she wouldn't get it removed: something about honoring a friend and promises made for life. But nowadays, Pia was a respectable young consultant who would never straddle a Harley! As much as she loved the tattoo, she was also deeply ashamed. She never wore open-collared shirts in an effort to hide it. In short, she

- ■ **Learning method**
  - • **Case study versus lecture versus practicums: What's the difference?**
  - • **What kind of grading system does the program use?**
  - • **How important are these to you?**
- ■ **Learning environment**
  - • **Study groups, cohorts, or both?**
  - • **Collaborative, competitive, team-based?**
  - • **Life on campus (or do you prefer a commuter school?)**
  - • **Variety of clubs, leadership opportunities**
- ■ **Class size**
  - • **Does school create ways to commingle the classes?**
- ■ **Placement statistics and career center**
  - • **What is their placement rate?**
  - • **What recruiting relationships does the school have?**

viewed the tattoo as a necessary burden, like the needlepoint pillow my best friend made for my living room.

When I asked Pia if she really needed to cover up the tattoo or was she just being insecure, the floodgates opened. She *had* to cover it up—it was completely inappropriate in her workplace, and what would all the linemen in the packaging plants she worked in think of her (I think she feared getting asked out most of all). The tattoo was big enough to be noticeable when she wore a V-neck, so she either had to limit her wardrobe to grandma's casual or cover it up with concealer.

Apparently makeup was a big issue. Pia began to talk about her experiences at cosmetics counters looking for the perfect concealer. One brand wasn't thick enough. Another ruined a Theory blouse, and the rest, in one form or another, had destroyed her best clothes; it was a runway massacre.

Before we knew it, our conversation had strayed far from her firm. The whole thing became a classic bitch session about how nobody was doing anything effective about heavy-duty concealers.

When you catch yourself thinking or saying the complaint, "Why hasn't anybody . . . ," insert yourself there. Be that somebody. Ask not what anybody can do for you, but what you can do for everybody. That's transformational leadership in a bottle (or a cosmetics tube, if you will).

Just by doing a little digging, I put my finger on something Pia cared

Campus Visits: What to Do

- Attend information session, meet admissions staff
- Go to the student union and chat up students
  - Most love to talk about their experiences
  - Ask what surprised them most after arriving
  - Ask what disappointed them most
- Stay in a campus dorm

deeply about. Her professional passion had been staring at her in the makeup mirror the whole time.

Suddenly Pia got that Elle Woods glint in her eye. "I could dominate the cover-up market with a concealer that *actually* works. I wouldn't even have to go on late-night TV to sell it. But QVC is the natural outlet! I could get an endorsement from Dr. 90210!" She grabbed my arm. "What about Sanjay Gupta? Do you think he's big enough?"

Wow. Pia had gone from an obsession with appropriateness to outside-the-box visionary in just one quick session. Her fire was real, not manufactured, because she was her own customer. She knew the market and knew how to address it.

Then I saw her crash back to earth. "But I'm not an entrepreneur. Do you know how much money it would take to get a product like this off the ground? The manufacturing costs alone would require a huge capital investment. Who's going to give me that kind of money? How do I even ask for that kind of money?"

I finally interrupted her litany of self-minimizing concerns to ask a rhetorical question: "Isn't that what business school is for? To learn how to write a business plan? To understand capital investment? To become an effective entrepreneur? To master persuasive leadership so you can enroll anyone to do anything for you? I mean, you've not only discovered the difference you can make on the planet, you've expressed your ratio-

- ■ Attend at least one class
  - • Take detailed notes: Did the professor encourage questions? Did students seem intelligent and engaged?
  - • Talk to the professor after class about research projects, his teaching philosophy, other interests
- ■ Check out the surrounding community and city
  - • Can you see yourself thriving there?

nale for needing an MBA education! I couldn't have made this up if I tried!" She had practically written her goals essay already.

But Pia was going to need a little more than that. I knew from experience that it never works to tell somebody what her long-term goal should be (don't you just hate it every time cousin Horace shows up and tells you how to renovate your apartment?), but in looking at all of Pia's success, personally and professionally, I had enough belief in her for both of us.

I could see self-belief start to take root. "If you don't believe in yourself," I told Pia, "nobody else will believe in you. And if you don't believe you can do something like revolutionize the concealer industry, why do you think you belong at a top business school?"

We ended that conversation with a piece of homework: "Go surf the Internet and get me some facts. How many people have tattoos? What is the annual revenue for those useless products you've gone through? Are they all made by big cosmetics companies or by specialty providers? And is Alyssa Milano hawking one on late-night TV?"

A couple of days later, Pia reported her findings to me with an excitement that neither Susan nor I had yet to hear in her voice. Suddenly, the tattoo turned from a burden to a blessing—and a great basis for a successful company. Making a difference in seven million lives is big— and certainly a more visionary long-term goal than being some kind of manager in some kind of consulting firm.

PS: With this goal, Pia got accepted to the Triple Crown—Harvard, Stanford, and Wharton. At the risk of sounding like Madonna during the Blonde Ambition Tour, I later told Pia, "Go on, girl. Show me what you can do!"

The Lesson

If you're not sure what you're passionate about, do a little inner-view— an interview with yourself—and objectively put the pieces of your life together. And I don't really care what color you want your parachute to be. Somewhere inside your life is an unmet need, or an unrealized objective, a plan you put on the shelf when you were a kid. And then ask yourself this: If something isn't done about this issue, how many people am I willing to let go unserved? And for how long? And if the answer is "not one more day," then you probably have a long-term professional goal right there.

For those of you who are reading this and saying, "I don't have an embarrassing tattoo," and you're bummed out because the most exciting thing in your life is turnarounds or semiconductors, be careful not to play the "is my goal catchy enough?" game. Your goal doesn't have to be catchy, cool, or involve a near miss with death. If it's real, if you can really get behind it, then that will come through—no matter what.

Here's how you know for sure: Are you behind it enough to go after it even if you *don't* get accepted to business school? Full stop. Admissions officers will get on board even if you're talking about semiconductors when it's obvious that your goals have your full faith and credit (that is, if you don't get into business school and learn how to get financing, you'll *still get* financing) even if it means maxing out your credit card to get the ball rolling.

Note: A goals essay is not a business plan. It's a vision kicked off by an action (that would be your short-term goal). And, oh yes, a reason to go to business school (after all, you need certain skills to realize your vision). By the way, if you already know how to write a business plan, you may not need to go to business school. And you've seriously missed the point of this chapter.

CHAPTER 9

The Accomplishments Essay

Accomplishments essays are not about measuring your worth, but determining whether you act on your values.

From Harvard's infamous "What are your three most substantial accomplishments and why do you view them as such?" to Yale's "What achievement are you most proud of and why?" accomplishments essays come in many shapes and sizes. Some are really obvious and some are incredibly elusive. The purpose of the accomplishment essay is not simply to show off. That's one of the mistakes candidates make when answering this topic. Conversely, people also get into trouble thinking they have nothing to say. You don't have to climb Mount Everest with one arm to have a great topic.

At the end of the day, it's all about the insight you show when writing about the accomplishment. What's an accomplishment to *me* may not be an accomplishment to *you*, and that cuts to the heart of this question: What do you value?

Unlike leadership essays, which should always contain a description of who or what you led—show versus tell—such a word-count-consuming narrative can't always fit into an accomplishment essay. In this genre of essay, storytelling is often less important than a meaty analysis of why the accomplishment is important to you, as well what it says about how you think and what experiences you believe define you. Accomplishments essays are often short and need to cut to the chase. HBS, for example, asks for three accomplishments in only six hundred words, which is two hundred words per achievement. Good luck. In such tight real estate, a narrative "you are there" introduction has to go.

Regardless of word count, a healthy portion of the essay needs to be allocated to the "why," not the "what" or the "how." It goes like this: a little bit of what, even more how, and a whole lot of why. Most of the accomplishments I've read are written in the exact reverse—we have to fight this tendency constantly in our applicants. If your response has a lot of "what" or "how," and only one or two sentences about why it is significant to you, you have pretty much failed.

And I don't care how amazing the accomplishment is. It no longer matters to me that you invented the Internet if you can't articulate its significance to two things: the world and to you. That's the home run. Focusing on the significance, not the substance, reveals not only that you understand who you are and the work that you do, but also that you can spot and seize opportunities. And that spells l-e-a-d-e-r. It's easy to *locate* greatness. Articulating what makes something great is what's difficult. Having that talent marks leadership potential, and it's why schools like Harvard, Michigan, MIT Sloan, and Emory consistently ask questions that require you to define, not just describe, accomplishments. To describe is to list facts about something. To define is to give those facts context and meaning.

You are probably dismissing some of the most substantial, significant, and moving accomplishments in your life. After all, when the shackles fell off Forrest Gump's legs, all he was doing was running. Almost everybody can run, so why does everyone remember that scene? Because in that moment, Forrest Gump was redefined. And those unique little moments make up who we are and what matters to us—all any admissions committee is trying to get out of you in the first place.

This doesn't mean you should only look for the simplest accomplishment. It means dig down deep and figure out why your accomplishments matter to you, be they large or small, whether you swam across a pool or the English Channel.

Of course, picking the right story is also crucial. The first place to look is in the land of "firsts" and "bests." Being the first from your college to be recruited to your prestigious company. Going from the bottom to the top of your analyst class after a devastating but accurate mid-year review. Notice, I didn't say "ranking at the top of your class"—if you're a consistent achiever, then choosing that as your accomplishment would be showing off, not revealing a defining moment when you refused to surrender to an obstacle.

Breaking a mold or setting a standard are, objectively, real accomplishments by any measure.

Professional Accomplishments—
Beyond the Call of Duty

Some amazing candidates don't have "firsts" or "bests"—at least not in the professional arena, which is what this section is about. However, look closely at what you consider to be a "first" or "best." If you didn't have the opportunity to be in on the Hewlett-Packard/Compaq merger, if you're not the first person from Swaziland to be hired by IBM, or if you didn't write the code that allows cell phones to access the Internet, then you might start looking at where your work *contributed* to events like these. You weren't a primary player, but you were crucial.

Or better yet, you simply went above the call of duty and created some form of legacy.

That's Bradley's story. The "first" industry primer he created for his telecom group didn't rewrite the rules of banking or bring in billions of dollars. What it did do, however, was help future teammates hit the ground running. In one fell swoop, Bradley was not only a team player, but also a leader who was thinking in terms that were greater than himself.

The best part of the story, however, is that he digs down deep and honestly admits that his intentions were not initially altruistic. And that weighed heavily on the "why" of why his accomplishment was so significant. To some, including this insight in the essay might seem unnecessary or even risky; however, it is fundamental not merely to establishing the credibility of the accomplishment, but the level of his insight.

None of this, however, was clear to Bradley when he began working with Forster-Thomas.

On paper, there was nothing special about him. But the investment bank that hired him must have seen the same thing I saw: someone who goes above and beyond the call of duty, who thought about more than just himself.

When Bradley came to us, his GPA and stats were less than stellar, about a 3.0 and about a 620 on his GMAT. But if the GMAT was a test of spirit and tenacity, he would have scored a perfect 800. After all, he suffered from dyslexia. Academically speaking, this made everything a challenge. So when he joined a white-shoe firm as an investment banking analyst in the telecom sector during this industry's heyday, Bradley had to get up to speed pronto.

Within two months he had managed to master the lingo, the research, the players, the financial modeling and valuation . . . and he did so on his own time. Day and night, every weekend, he wrote everything down. Eventually he had compiled a 128-page primer on the subject. Although he wrote it for himself, he decided to share it with his colleagues. This required even more weekends cleaning up, organizing, and proofing his dyslexic first drafts (and I can vouch for that, having been the recipient of many an incoherent email). Thanks to his hard work and fearless attitude, his telecom primer ended up becoming the standard training tool adopted by the telecom group for all new hires once his vice president had seen what he had done. And the by-product? He was asked to lead new-hire trainings.

And that is the point in the tale where Bradley stopped.

"But Bradley," I asked, "what about the other part of the question? The part that asks 'why you view this as significant'?"

For a bit, I thought I had lost him. His face crinkled. But then, if GPAs were based on self-awareness, Bradley was a 4.0. I nudged and pushed him a little.

"Well, one thing I'm proud of is that I did something few investment bankers are willing to do: Put the group first by not hoarding information, which I quickly learned is the most coveted commodity on Wall Street."

"Are they still using your telecom primer today?" I mentioned a few other wheels that never had to be reinvented, like tax software and DVRs, and the light finally went off in his head that he had not only mastered an incredibly complex and difficult subject—definitely a worthy professional accomplishment—but had also made it so that no one else would ever have to start from scratch again.

And that is called "creating legacy." As I've said already, perhaps that is one of the single most important things a leader can do—leave something of value behind that is not dependent on your continued presence. Not only did Bradley gain a huge amount of respect from colleagues and superiors, but he also passed it on to others.

The Lesson

No one expects you to have an objectively significant professional accomplishment in your twenties. Not every industry is like Hollywood, where twelve-year-olds are in charge of studios. But who is to say what is significant? Well, the question generally makes that clear: You get to define what is significant. So, find the moment you went above and beyond your job description—something you're proud of in the context of what you've done, and what you believe is important (like lobbying for a new water cooler on your floor). Such achievements are there in everyone's professional career. They're often easy to overlook, and sometimes hard to spot, but when you do, don't minimize what you've discovered. Embrace it.

BRADLEY'S PROFESSIONAL ACCOMPLISHMENT ESSAY

My first day in Lehman's Telecom group, I was straight out of college with a liberal arts major and no industry knowledge. The first team meeting could have been in Sanskrit for all the sector jargon being bandied about. Every night for the next two months, I secretly compiled my own industry primer. I remember jargon better when I write it down and put it into my own words, and more than 100 pages of notes later, I was fluent at last.

After hearing a few teammates ask about terms in my primer, I wondered if I should reveal my primer. Information is power on Wall Street, and weakness is despised, so I was nervous to reveal my secret. But ignorance, in my opinion, is worse. So I asked my boss if he would mind if I shared my work with the team. He vetted it, then clapped me on the back: "This is the best primer I've ever seen. Let's make it required reading."

My primer is still in use today, and other groups have used it as a template for their own jargon manuals. Creating a standard that lives past me at Lehman, and sharing knowledge in an industry that hoardes it, is one of my most substantial accomplishments.

Service Accomplishments—Consultant, Heal Thyself

You're more likely to have objectively significant service/extracurricular accomplishments. Lucky for you, many MBA programs don't limit their accomplishment/achievement essay questions to the professional arena. Service accomplishments are excellent because they kill a number of birds with one stone: They highlight a part of your candidacy that may just get a brief mention in the Activities Description part of the application, they show that you transform communities as a leader rather than simply participate, and they prove there is more to you than eating, sleeping, and (of course) drinking.

As we've discussed, extracurricular achievements can range from helping a bunch of kids get into college to growing the recruiting efforts of Big Brothers/Big Sisters among young people in your industry. But both of those are pretty obvious. They have a metric: Did every kid you were working with get into college? Yes. Bravo. Did you meet or exceed your target number for recruiting? Excellent!

But let's say you don't have such an easy answer. You need to start examining that area that your driving instructor referred to as your "blind spot." In other words, look where you're not looking. You will find a treasure trove of possibilities. You may find that you achieved something that, because you don't have a metric, you tend to overlook.

A great place to find those achievements is in moments of failure or near failure. Creating a moderate success after almost-certain calamity is often more impressive than plucking low-hanging fruit off an overripe tree. After all, necessity is the mother of invention. For example, if you have a large, rich circle of friends, I'm not impressed that you raised $20,000 with a few phone calls. More impressive is when you barely manage to make your $2,000 quota on the night of an event—but would have made only $250 if you hadn't rallied the few troops who showed up, created an instant phone bank with their cell phones, and inspired them to call everyone they know to come to the fund-raiser *right now*. You've shown the committee a lot about how you operate: You don't back down, you don't take no for an answer, you rise to a challenge in the moment, you're committed to the result instead of the process, and you know how to inspire others in the moment as well.

One such invention occurred out of a necessity to change the way an entire program was approaching its mentees. Anya had no problem figuring out why her personal and professional accomplishments were so meaningful to her, but she had difficulty finding the "true" impact of her extracurriculars.

While she had many great moments in her extracurricular history, one that she downplayed was her membership in a team of volunteer small-business consultants whose objective was to help New York City entrepreneurs grow their businesses. Specifically, the mandate for her group of four was to help an entrepreneur immigrant develop a marketing plan to grow his business into a million-dollar enterprise.

When I said, "This sounds great! Why are you mumbling past this one?" she answered, "The truth is, we kind of failed." That always piques my curiosity. After pushing her, what she *thought* was just a dismissible failure, almost an embarrassment, began to reveal itself as an accomplishment of an entirely different nature. As I said, I've often seen people in her position miss such an achievement completely. That's the blind spot.

All she could see was that the "four young suits" on her team, herself included, couldn't seem to communicate with the immigrant. Simply put, they spoke "*Fortune 500*"; he spoke "self-made." As a result, they spent two months working with the guy, giving him marketing advice that was surely right on point, but which was so obscured by lingo that he didn't know how to apply it.

I wanted to understand what went wrong—I was already thinking ahead to how this might make for a great failure essay (as you'll read in

Chapter 13, some great failure essays come out of so-called accomplishments). "Did you come up with a marketing plan?"

"Yeah, we told him he needed to devise a direct-mail strategy whose cost didn't exceed $40 DC per MCM."

"Okay . . ." I said to her, fumbling with my *Marketing for Dummies* book and feeling like an idiot. "And that led to . . . ?"

"Well, naturally, we *something, something, something* [insert sound of Charlie Brown's teacher talking]—and as simple as all that is, he never followed through."

"Well, who can blame the guy? You need an MBA just to understand what the hell you were talking about."

She agreed, actually. "One of the reasons we failed was because we were speaking different languages to each other. I really regret failing our client. That's partly why I sat down with the heads of ServiceOrg and helped them create a training method to get young consultants to communicate more effectively."

That's when I slammed on the brakes. "You mean, you got the volunteers to actually speak English?"

"Yeah, something like that."

It was the "something like that" I seized upon. After all, everybody and his brother has volunteer-consulted a small-business owner. That's just the top-shelf version of mentoring an inner-city kid. Nice, but still *yawn*.

Working together on how she had transformed the way the organization helped young consultants be more effective, we both became very excited: It was as if we had just found a $20 bill on the sidewalk—no, better still, a pair of this season's Manolo sling backs at 50 percent off! There it was: She had transformed the way an entire nonprofit executed its mission by creating an action plan that reduced the level of bureaucracy, paperwork, and "consultese" to put the focus on operating within the small-business owner's comfort zone.

Thanks to Anya, the group began shifting to a much more "of the people, by the people, for the people" approach. True, Anya's particular team wasn't particularly successful with her particular entrepreneur, but she laid the groundwork for a much more lasting impact: one that revealed the values that truly made this one of her most substantial accomplishments to date. It had all the right moves: a challenge, an obstacle, changing people's minds, and a long-lasting impact.

The Lesson

You've got to look past the obvious result or the organization's stated objective, such as raising a specific dollar amount for a good cause or, better, raising more than expected as a result of your work. Metrics, while they're significant and should definitely be mentioned, should usually be secondary in your analysis. What has always made my candidates stand out is that while they mention the measurable results, they knock the rest of the competition off the court because they go further. In a sense, they downplay the metric and accentuate a more qualitative insight into the impact of their work.

It's the difference between the guy who says, "I raised a million dollars," and the guy who says, "I raised a million dollars, but more important, I created possibilities that were heretofore nonexistent." The ability to spot that is the mark of a true leader. Yes, Gandhi freed a billion people, but what he really did was change the way people valued themselves as deserving of their own country instead of accepting vassalage as an option. Make your admissions officer say, "Wow, the last guy didn't think about it that way!"

The lesson here is not to look for accomplishments in your failures; it's to look past the obvious. One way of defining "the obvious" is to look at what you were there to achieve. Anya wasn't a volunteer to rewrite the way ServiceOrg operated, she was there to help an entrepreneur. Her blind spot was all the work she did for ServiceOrg that didn't directly involve her entrepreneur. Once we expanded our field of vision to her entire experience with ServiceOrg, the blind spot disappeared, and it revealed an amazing accomplishment.

Last October, ServiceOrg asked me to form a team to help "Entrepreneur of the Year" Jordan Johnson with his marketing plan. The Guyanese immigrant wanted to grow his promotional products business into a million dollar company. In our business suits, spouting demands for customer databases, system integration, recurring business, cost structure, we just kept alienating Jordan. It was all Greek to him. After months of hard work, we failed to develop Jordan's marketing plan. Apparently, this was the norm at ServiceOrg. I went against the tide, not merely pointing out the problem but implementing the solution. I held countless meetings with the ServiceOrg Chairman and Founder, convincing him to adopt my execution strategy which included less paperwork and more personal interaction.

Through the transformation I created at ServiceOrg, I learned the significance of versatility and flexibility. Instead of trying to adjust our core competencies to help Jordan, we expected him to adapt to us: In hindsight, we were not helping others. Working on the multibillion-dollar Neiman Marcuses of the world, we had lost touch with the equally important needs of small-business people. With my action plan, ServiceOrg is poised to reestablish a connection with the small business community—the community it set out to impact.

Personal Accomplishments—Swimmer's Ear

Now that you've read about professional and service accomplishments, I've saved the hardest for last: the nonprofessional or personal accomplishment. On a basic level, I describe this as something you did on your own where you grew or matured emotionally, reinvented your worldview, did something extraordinary without help, or overcame an obstacle outside of the professional arena.

Significant personal accomplishments that my candidates have submitted have ranged from growth in a relationship you had with a family member to issues around weight loss to overcoming a brain aneurysm.

I'm not interested in the following: how great you are (that is, how big your dick is), your romantic relationships, or the simple fact that you, say, still hold the hundred-yard-dash record for your college (unless you can tell me what an underdog you were coming into the championship). And please don't tell me about how you put yourself through college or got your job, unless you can similarly tell me exactly what the obstacles were and how you overcame them (and they'd better be more significant than "my parents couldn't afford it and I had to do work-study"). While it's admirable, it's what you should have done.

And this brings me to the issue of "should."

We've already established that accomplishments go beyond the call of duty, outside of your comfort zone or natural talents. That's why I don't want to know that you still hold an athletic record if you've always been a jock. While some may not agree with me, my goal is to push you further, to make you Olympic in your choices and the way you define who you are and what is significant to you. While I'm not putting down your college record, all it takes is for one guy with one leg to also hold a record—*any* record. You just lost that game.

I had a client, Brook, who came to me with a very heart-wrenching story about her father's prostate cancer. She wanted to write about how she managed to stay on top of her game at work and still manage to be a supportive daughter, even often flying home to be at her father's side on the weekends. Her father was battling cancer while Brook and I were working together. And while I thought Brook's support of her father was admirable, as far as I was concerned, this was how she *should* have behaved. Brook couldn't see this, so I had to pull out my big gun: "Brook," I said, "all it takes is for someone to survive cancer *his- or herself* while working and applying to business school. And then for you, it's game over."

That said, the best personal accomplishments not only highlight an achievement, but better yet, highlight the personal values that drive you to succeed. For example, how do you behave when given an "out"? What personality traits do you draw on when challenged? How high do you set the bar?

All of these questions came into play when I worked with Susan, a Rolls-Royce candidate. She had a 760 GMAT, she was an associate at a bulge-bracket investment bank, and she was an Ivy League undergraduate with a personal story of triumph over a setback that, for the purposes of applying to school, we all wish we had.

But here's the kicker: When she came to us, she was a reapplicant. With all those great aspects to her candidacy, she had been denied by all top-three schools the prior year. After just one read of her original essays, Uncle David and I turned to each other in amazement and simultaneously said, "She told the wrong story!" ("Jinx!" I said first. Uncle David's not as quick on the draw as I am.)

She had managed to lower herself to the mediocrity of *writing what you think the admissions committee wants to hear*, you know, what your managing director would suggest: how much lingo you know, the biggest deal you've ever done, how you learned the nuances of a leveraged buyout. Or what your father would suggest: how you grew your savings account from your Bar Mitzvah money. Or what your mother would suggest: two hundred people read your blog, your YouTube video has been watched by everyone in the neighborhood, or you just sold an option on a Hollywood script.

Or, you can listen to your Auntie Evan: All of this is just playing it safe. Susan's killer mistake was thinking that she didn't want to blow her candidacy on the "soft stuff" like essays when her "hard stuff" like stats were so strong. So she had limited herself to the same old stories of taking over for VPs on vacation, working overtime to create a valuation model, and running a marathon.

Hello, people, if it's already in your résumé, tell us something in these essays we don't know. Susan just kept blowing out lines on her résumé into essays. Worse than that, she was telling us stories we could have anticipated for a woman of her caliber—in other words, she was still trying to prove that she did everything she "should" do. There was nothing that made her flesh and blood.

I shot Susan an email. "I knew all this stuff about you before you even signed up with us. Tell me something new!" She was on the phone in a flash, and that's when she finally let me comb through her life and hit below the belt (in MBA terms, that means covering the breadth and width of your life, telling me about things that you think don't matter, seem too corny, or are just too darn intimate).

When I started going there, however, I could imagine the bun on Susan's head tightening a little. In an industry run by men, letting her guard down was as likely as her going from active to glamour-length french tips. She resisted every attempt to discuss things like her favorite guilty pleasure. If I asked her about rebellion, this lover of classical music described going for Bartok over Beethoven. (It took my college roommate Tracy to say, "Evan, there *is* a difference.")

Then I thought I heard a giggle. And suddenly Susan lowered her voice, a sure sign of mayhem to come. I white-knuckled my desk chair, wondering what had she done (it's always the quiet ones). Had she transformed herself from the slut of band camp to Wall Street professional? Tape recorder on!

And she began to tell me a story. Apparently, she had been a very reserved, appropriate child. The one place she really cut loose was in the water—she loved splashing in the shallow end. Yet, when she was only seven years old, she wandered too far into the deep end and almost drowned. She developed a morbid fear of drowning that paralyzed her for years. This LA girl couldn't go to Zuma or pool parties, and she hated explaining why. She became even more shy. Then, at the end of eighth grade, a crisis erupted: Her school required all students to swim across a pool and back as part of their fitness test before they could graduate from middle school.

Susan's mother, a Bel Air helicopter parent if ever there was one, told her not to worry about it: "We'll get a waiver for the requirement; they'll understand your fear of water—you almost drowned!"

After a day's thought, Susan decided she had had enough of being the girl afraid of water. Over her mother's protestations, she went to the Y and learned how to swim a single lap across a pool. I could tell she had that look that one tween gives another when she admits she loves Mario Lopez in *Saved by the Bell*. "Of course I'd never write an essay about it," she confided, "this was the moment that made me realize there is no challenge I couldn't face."

"That's it!" I jumped up. "That's just the accomplishment I'm looking for. It reflects your values—you are a persistent thing, after all—it's unique, and it's something that we all understand. And most important, you are incredibly proud of it.

While she was incredibly proud of it, her misguided instincts that a "substantial" accomplishment required being at least twenty years old and generating several million dollars in transaction fees had steered her away from one of the best stories I'd heard in years. It had everything: a ticking clock (she had to master her fear by graduation), an obstacle, an easy out she refused to take . . . all of which tested her own mettle. For the rest of her life, it became the bar when faced with any challenge.

This time, Susan was accepted to HBS.

The Lesson

It's not about when you did it. An accomplishment is not tied to age unless the MBA program's essay question specifically limits you to recent achievements. (If in doubt about how far back you can go, it's not a state secret: Just pick up the phone and call the admissions office—what do you think my colleagues and I do?)

You don't have to have a fear of water to have a great personal accomplishment. However, you do have to have the guts to dig down deep like a visionary and a leader—the way Susan eventually did—and isolate the moments for you that really mattered. So, catch yourself off guard and let your mind wander. Do a tequila shot if you need to. Just loosen up and let your hair down. Again, they're looking for who you really are, not who you think you're supposed to be. Those things that pop into mind—even those things you've never told anyone about—might just be the perfect accomplishments to make a mark.

SUSAN'S PERSONAL ACCOMPLISHMENT ESSAY

When I was just eight years old, I almost drowned. For the next several years, I let that fear rule me. Near the end of eighth grade, however, I got horrible news: in order to graduate middle school, I had to swim one lap across the pool as part of my physical health assessment.

My mother immediately offered to talk to the principal and get the requirement waived. But I decided that I was done with fear. I wanted to join my friends at pool parties and put that awful memory of almost drowning behind me. I went to the YMCA and took a class—and almost quit when I realized I would be the only teenager in a class of five year olds. But the fear was even more humiliating.

Within two weeks, I had swum my lap. In objective terms, I don't consider this a noteworthy achievement. But I deeply value this as one of my most substantial accomplishments because it marked the moment in my life when I took charge. I'm now known among my friends as "the fearless one," and my work colleagues know I will step forward when we have bad news to report to our M.D. As long as I breathe, float, and balance, I can achieve anything I set my mind to.

CHAPTER 10

Leadership Essays

How to take all that great work you did on leadership and condense it into a great narrative example of how you take on challenges.

You've already learned about living life as a leader; now comes learning how to express leadership in your essays. The most important question is not what have you accomplished, but what is your leadership *style*? Rod Garcia, director of admissions at the Sloan School of Management at MIT, puts it this way: "It's important to us to find out, are you a visionary leader? Do you lead by socializing, or relating to others? Are you a big sense-maker? Or are you an inventor or innovator or creator? We want to find out what your capabilities are and whether you're developing those capabilities in action." What you look like in action, how you assess others' strengths and weaknesses to build a team, and how flexible you are in crisis are just a few of the possible details to include in the leadership essay.

Two specific examples will open your mind up to the possibilities.

Scenario 1: Queen for a Day

Remember Vinod, the Indian jazz cat who was a ring-tone engineer? Well, as far as leadership goes, he had the good fortune in his professional career that few junior analysts had: He actually was a project manager and already had a nest of potentially rich but inherently tedious and expected experiences, such as leading a rookie team at his telecom company that successfully reduced costs by over $15 million. While it was an amazing accomplishment that required substantial leadership—and could have made a very strong essay—that story wasn't so far out of the ballpark of expectations for an accomplished twenty-seven-year-old engineer who belonged at the top rung of the b-school ladder.

So, despite the potential gold mine, and the fact that he was able to successfully lead me in my long-standing quest to download Beyoncé's "Bootylicious" as my ring tone (which came up again during our conversation about Vinod's three greatest accomplishments), I decided the jazz cat had to go crazy, daddio, crazy, and dig deeper—something you should always try to do.

Just because you have a great leadership story doesn't mean a better, more unique one doesn't exist just below the surface of your consciousness. After listening to a snooze-and-booze-inducing list of leadership stories that included words like "javascript" and something about ones and zeros, I metaphorically reached into my backpack, pulled out my pompoms, and began my favorite cheer: "B-E different! B-E different!" When that started to scare him, he finally had a breakthrough (he was probably desperate to shut me up): "What about the Mumbai Statewide

Intercollegiate Music Competition?" he asked, as if he were referring to *American Idol*.

"Shoot," I said.

And the next thing I knew, Vinod had deeply engaged me in a story that had all the components of an outstanding and memorable leadership essay. What needs to be understood is that we all have a story lurking somewhere beneath the obvious. I'm writing about Vinod's experience not because he's one of a kind, but because there is a little Indian jazz cat finger clapping in all of us.

Vinod's story went something like this: With four weeks to go before the Mumbai Statewide Intercollegiate Music Competition, Vinod—like any good but unwitting leader—threw himself into the lion's den. His college was a winner in its traditional categories, including Hindu spiritual, but Vinod wanted to go out on a limb and enter his college into an area he loved but in which it had no experience: Western a capella.

And Vinod decided to start with a bang: Queen's "Bohemian Rhapsody," considered by many intellectuals, and frankly anyone who's heard it, to be one of the most vocally ambitious rock operas. *Mamma Mia!* To up the ante further, Vinod had only four weeks to lead five singers into this uncharted territory.

The cast of characters ranged from a newly minted Hindi Pop star to two Hindu spiritual singers and one computer geek who had a great voice in the shower. Early on, his best singer, Sudarshan—the budding Hindi Pop star—walked out. Vinod was incensed—how could Sudarshan not trust him, when he had won several instrumental-only categories in years past? Then, the rest of the team began to implode with fear. At this point, Vinod couldn't just make it about Sudarshan. He had to take note that if other people were having difficulties, perhaps the problem lay within him.

This became the first unusual detail in this essay that revealed Vinod's growth and confidence as a leader—his willingness to share the blame. This new attitude earned the trust of his remaining team to admit their specific sources of anxiety, such as stage fright. Armed with these insights, Vinod was able to tailor specific solutions for each source of anxiety.

That forms the second unusual detail in his essay: walking the reader through the specific steps he took as a leader to create a solution.

The challenge here was steering Vinod away from focusing on all the process-management issues and toward people-leadership details. You know, the egos and insecurities of his team, as well as an honest assessment of his own fears.

There is a big difference between managing a process and leading people. At Forster-Thomas, we call the former what "the essay-editing mills tell you to write about." Our clients take on the big stuff, and the big stuff always involves much more than meeting deadlines and pushing paper around (I call that facilitatorship, not leadership; Uncle David simply calls it "process management"). While leaders often facilitate, it's not what makes them great. England was a great weapons manufacturer in the 1940s, but its people thought of Hitler as a "Continental" problem. So Churchill didn't win what became World War II because he moved guns to the front line. He won because he influenced his country to send people there.

Although there were far fewer casualties in Vinod's war, in the end, like with England, his team won. But as Vinod said, that wasn't even the important part. What he highlighted was the following: When one guy was going to quit and another was focused on midterms, he learned to get rid of his own personal fears about looking like a loser. He realized that if he gave up, they would give up. Instead, he impassioned his team to get them to understand that what they were doing was creating pride in themselves, pride in their school, and pride in their community, and though it didn't seem so at the time, there would be greater value in doing their best, not just for themselves individually, but how great they could be together as a team.

While I was adamant that Vinod focus on a more left-brain leadership story in order to offset his relatively typical career/cultural back-ground and skill set, I believe you will find after reading his final draft, which follows, that what clinched this essay and pushed it well beyond the wonderfully offbeat topic and execution, was the bit in the last para-graph where he mentions the cost-saving initiative he led. That way, we were able to name-drop something professionally significant he had accomplished as a leader (with a metric as an extra added bonus). Fur-thermore, we were able to show that Vinod had that rare ability to learn from history and apply what he learned in an extracurricular life to his career.

What's the message to admissions officers? That he'll be able to take the knowledge he receives in his MBA program and likewise adapt it to his career. Thus, while the essay is about him, it's not all about him. He also was able to show what he learned and where he applied it. These are two significant details that should be in any leadership essay, whether the ques-tion requires it or not.

The Lesson

Look under a rock. You might find more than dirt and doodlebugs. Crawl through your attic. You might find more than your bronzed booties and your Bar Mitzvah photos. You might just find an old trophy that brings back an old leadership story like how you got your old underdog club soccer team to the finals. But just remember how you did it. And lastly, just because Auntie Evan isn't there to tease the story out of you, it doesn't mean that it isn't there. It just means you've got to think about the events of your past as a distant observer. And for God's sake, stop talking about how, as a leader, you made sure you had pencils and paper. No one's in-terested in how you ordered online from Staples. Leadership is first and foremost about influencing people, and the narrative in a leadership essay is about showing "what you look like" when you're leading. Do you cre-ate consensus, lead by example, encourage people to take ownership, bash heads, build your team from the bottom up? Or is it a mix of several styles? All these are valid, and the committee wants to know which one is *yours*.

The way we identify a good story is that it has some of the elements that really great leadership stories have: inexperienced team members, a ticking clock, an unfamiliar project, dissent in the ranks (which I'll get to shortly). When these elements are present, you're on to something really great. With respect to Vinod's original story, the $15 million cost-cutting venture, when weighing the scales, that story is as old as Methuselah. And while the significance of that story in someone's life is real—it says you're a great leader with something to bring to the table—it doesn't say, "I bring a fresh way of thinking to your MBA program."

Although it's great to have an irreverent and fun subject matter, don't get stuck in it. What you need to start looking at here are the unusual, out-of-the-box leadership skills you possess. You don't have to be a musician to make this happen. You'll see in the next chapter a very traditional banking story that tapped into nontraditional leadership skills because the candidate dug down deep and really was able to examine and reveal unique leadership qualities. What makes Vinod's essay work is not the topic (though as a vehicle it's entertaining and off-the-cuff), but the insightful way in which he describes his leadership style. Admissions officers are not fooled by pop and flash. "Flash" lasts for about a sentence; what the flash illuminates, however, will stick with the reader for a long time.

Finally, good leadership essays should focus on the process, not the accomplishment. As a rule of thumb, don't spend more than 25 percent of your word count setting up the story. Spend the middle 50 percent illustrating "what you look like" as you influence the people and situation. Reserve the final 25 percent for briefly describing the outcome and what you learned about what makes you an effective leader based on the preceding story.

VINOD'S LEADERSHIP ESSAY

Describe how you have engaged a community or organization.

—Harvard Business School

"We sound like chimpanzees!" said Ram, our usually diplomatic baritone. He was right.

I had convinced Ram and four other relatively inexperienced classmates to compete in the University of Mumbai's Youth Festival. We planned to sing Queen's "Bohemian Rhapsody," a difficult composition for singers trained in traditional Indian music. With one week to go, we met to discuss our progress.

Kamesh, the bass singer, frequently drifted off-key. Rashmi, the tenor, mumbled when she forgot lyrics. Both Ram and Kavita faltered in their counterpoint harmonies. Only Sudarshan, our ambitious lead singer, could deliver a solid performance. Then he lowered the boom:

"Vinod, we sound awful—and these judges are talent scouts! I'm out."

Despite my previous optimism, I knew this venture was doomed—unless I changed our group from the inside out. I started with myself, shelving my know-it-all child-prodigy attitude.

After a break, I called a brainstorming session. Consequently, each singer confessed his or her fears. Rashmi admitted to stage fright. I suggested she try the "picture the audience naked" trick. Ram and Kavita revealed they were scared of going off-key. Recalling their perfect singing of hymns during a Hindu festival, I suggested they pretend to sing a hymn instead of a rock opera. To my satisfaction, these strategies significantly changed the group's attitude.

Still, we needed a lead singer. I asked the disenchanted Sudarshan to tutor Kamesh, our remaining weakest link. This delegation of authority not only gave Sudarshan a stake in the team's success, it also showed him our progress. Reassured by that, he rejoined the group.

On performance day, the stage lights dimmed as we went on:

"Is this the real life, is this just fan-ta-sy?" sang Kavita and Rashmi.

"Caught in a landslide, no escape from re-a-li-ty," added Ram and Kamesh.

Sudarshan belted, "Open your eyes, look up to the skies, and s-e-e!" Soon, the thousand pairs of eyes watching in the audience were transfixed, and we received a standing ovation.

The most significant way in which I engaged this group was by encouraging each team member—including myself—to accept a kind of personal challenge previously unimaginable. Through this success, I learned that leadership requires the courage to guide people through uncharted waters during even the worst of times—a skill that helped me lead a team of novice developers at Sprint succeed in saving the company over $15 million in its billing processes. Keeping in mind that inside each and every team member is a scared little boy or girl, I can always make an impact.

Scenario 2: From Boys to Men

Good things come to those who take risks. Quantum transformation, change, or growth is a result of a quantum leap. Just when Zainab and I had exhausted all her extracurriculars, scoured through her college and post-college service leadership, we decided to take a little man-hating diversion as a ten-minute break. She apologized for not having a leadership story ready, but she was exhausted from refereeing the men she most hated at that moment, who happened to be the VP and MD on her current deal team. Let's call them Jack and Bobby.

Always up for man-bashing (they're such pigs!), I set aside our consulting session to get the details. After all, sometimes you need to take a break and let off some steam. Zainab agreed, and launched into a drama about being stuck on a seventeen-hour trans-Pacific flight to Hong Kong the prior week for a make-or-break deal meeting regarding an $8 billion merger and acquisition.

Letting off steam—talking about something that seemingly has nothing to do with one's brainstorm for an essay topic—is often a great way to clear your mind. After all, in the immortal words of En Vogue, "the rest will follow." Sometimes, just like with Vinod, a great story is waiting to come out, but you just keep shoving it back down. That's why I encourage "mind-clearing" sessions like the one with Zainab.

It seems that Jack and Bobby were fighting in their sandbox, and an epic battle of egos was in full tilt. Something about who was in charge of research had turned into a fly in the ointment and a referendum on their skill sets. This, in turn, had exposed some barely hidden personal animosities between them—their leadership styles were as different as Obama and Palin. The result? A cold war had gone radioactive, just a week before the trip to Hong Kong.

At the water cooler, it was all Zainab's deal teammates could speak about, but no one—from her fellow second-year analysts to the associate—had the nerve to approach the dueling duo and lead the boys to a resolution—even though their feud was putting the deal in jeopardy because of the miscommunications endemic to their animosity. When Jack or Bobby would walk into a room where the other already was, the deal-team members would disperse like roaches when you flip on the kitchen light for a midnight snack.

On the flight, the two were not speaking at all. For the first time, Zainab wished she was in coach; she couldn't even focus on the numbers she was crunching. She was so fed up that she got out of her seat and asked for a meeting between the three of them. "Can you imagine," she said, "two grown men and it took me, an analyst for God's sake, to make them kiss and make up?"

"How did you do that?" I asked gingerly.

"I was totally freaked out," she said. "I was afraid I was going to lose my job. Everyone else was snoring, and Jack and Bobby were on opposite sides of first class ignoring each other instead of hammering out the final presentation. So, somewhere after Hawaii, I scheduled a meeting in the center row. Thank God it was a practically empty red-eye."

To Zainab's way of thinking, she was being recklessly risky, and while her manner was professional, she had taken action because her emotions had gotten the best of her; she just couldn't take it anymore.

From my perspective, she had just brought two warring nations together—and hammered out a peace accord. She had done what Churchill, Napoleon, and Alexander had done: She unified opposing parties under her own banner and made them understand that they had two choices in this war of egos. One or the other could be "right," or together as a team, they could close one of the largest deals in the history of Goldman's private equity group.

To shift Zainab's perspective, I shared a little piece of advice: There are occasions when leaders *need* to let their emotions get the best of them. What Zainab looked down on as simply "emotions," I considered the "instinct of a leader." There's a difference between emotion and instinct—don't confuse that knot in your stomach as emotion; it might be instinct finding a way to express itself. When I was able to shift her perspective on her reaction, Zainab was able to see what I saw: a natural leader acting on her instincts, despite the risks, to create transformation in her environment.

So, finally, Zainab realized that she had just done what none of her peers had the nerve or leadership skills to do: Address the elephant in the room and broach the sensitive subject not just at the water cooler, but where it mattered: with the active parties themselves.

That is a hallmark of leadership. It didn't matter that she was the low person on the totem pole. It didn't matter that she had no title of leadership, no mandate to create change, and no authority by which to enforce it. She acted anyway. She created her own mandate and from that, authority was created in her.

By the time they landed in Hong Kong, the boys were acting like men.

The Lesson

Leadership is something you create, something you take hold of, something you're entitled to—not something you're granted. Without saying or even knowing it, Zainab was doing what leaders do: "taking one for the team" and demanding that the formal leaders start acting that way for the sake of the deal.

So when you're searching for leadership examples, don't forget to include instances of "up-management": when you got your boss to actually rise to the occasion for the sake of the team, and not just because having the "boss" title says he or she should. Don't let those stories pass you by just because you weren't elected or chosen, or just because you didn't get the result you wanted. In Zainab's case, she got the result she wanted, but had she not, she still acted like a leader, brought the men to the table, and took a risk on behalf of the team.

By the way, neither Jack nor Bobby would ever praise Zainab as the savior of the deal. Don't limit your search for successful leadership to times when others patted you on the back. Look into your heart for those times when you acted with courage and did what you knew to be right, even if you were worried it might get you into trouble. Leaders aren't worried about résumés. They're worried about results.

SAMPLE LEADERSHIP ESSAY

While Zainab's leadership essay can't be reprinted, the following essay includes all the same elements that make an outstanding piece: a quickly established setup, conflict between people that allows the writer to demonstrate interpersonal leadership skills, and analysis at the end that both shows the writer's awareness of how he or she succeeded, and an observation about what constitutes great leadership.

My IT supervisor dropped a bomb on me one day as I was about to go home: a prominent senator would arrive in town the next day to announce an important decision that would attract national media coverage. Someone had to lead a team of technicians to provision and install all communications for the senator's campaign and the press pool, in less than 24 hours. "Gonzalez, you have the ball. Don't fumble," he said sternly.

With only two years in the department, my selection to lead this massive effort was extraordinary. In the union culture of the phone company, leadership is usually correlated with seniority. I knew this breach of protocol could cause enormous tension, especially when Stan and Mauricio, veteran technicians, showed up with two rookies. Never had I been given such a formal and significant leadership position.

With 20 hours to go, I organized a pre-survey of the event location. The press-pool area did not even have a single phone jack. We would have to rewire the entire first level. I mobilized help from every department in the company to engineer the extra lines to this primarily residential area.

Fifteen hours to go. My team had resigned itself to failure. At the center of this negative cloud was Mauricio. I spoke to him privately and tried reason. But in his resentment at being passed over, he dug in his heels. Though I prefer persuasive leadership over brute coercion, I finally threatened to pull him off the job—sacrificing his overtime. He backed down. I separated him from the main group to run lines through the basement.

At eight hours to go, things were moving briskly along. I established a sleep rotation and implemented an organizational plan for charting our progress. More importantly, I started to change the way my team viewed the carrot: This project wasn't about overtime; it was about rising to the challenge. After each meeting, I started to understand their individual strengths and weaknesses and delegated accordingly. I even won over Stan, once Mauricio's sidekick.

We completed the job with 30 minutes to spare. I will never forget the exhilaration I felt as I coordinated every department to

*move in unison with graceful efficiency. This experience ignited a
quantum leap in my leadership and communications skills. I
learned how to manage expectations and conflict. Most
significantly, I realized that while leadership is about delegation,
political savvy, and results, it's also about transformation. If you
are not transforming your teammates' lives and abilities, you are
not a leader.*

CHAPTER 11

Impact/Opportunity Essays

A Beautiful Mind-Set

Not all leadership essays focus on the individuals you led. Here's how to shift your story when process counts as well.

In the last two chapters, we talked about leadership as it relates to working with and transforming others to make something happen. There's a whole subset of essays that focus more on the process of creating change rather than leading the people involved in the change. And while they certainly cross over and can be used as launching pads for one another, they are distinctly different in their intention.

Falling into this category are the "when did you create change" and "how did you impact an organization" essays often found in MIT Sloan, Stanford, Georgetown's McDonough, and Wharton applications.

In addition, slate in Columbia Business School's essay focusing on "the entrepreneurial mind-set."

All of my previous advice on leadership essays applies here, but impact/opportunity essays have an additional step that requires a slightly different kind of thinking: dissecting a process. While leadership essays are most compelling when they focus on people, "impact" essays often do best when focused on a process. "Entrepreneurial mind-set" essays are about seizing an opportunity, which can entail people or processes. Excellent sources of inspiration are your most hard-won challenges, like the example of Ziva, who seized an opportunity to bring together two stubborn people who couldn't see the benefit of working together.

My relationship with Ziva was a perfect example of what I call "creative high-speed competitive Ping-Pong." Both Ziva and I play to win, so when she chose to work with me, it wasn't so much about her inability to come up with ideas as it was to work with somebody who would push her already strong ideas to an Olympic level. If you want to flesh your ideas out and make sure you are playing your A-game, find another A-game player: someone who won't bullshit you, who will make fun of you, who will not tolerate mediocrity.

After all, that's the world Ziva lived in every day at a leading glossy food magazine. She had clawed her way up the ladder to become a food stylist, which included setting up and managing photo shoots of gorgeous victuals.

Ziva, a tall, confident Hebrew National, was unusually neurotic about applying to business school as a foodie. She assumed the admissions committees wouldn't take her seriously because she didn't come from a traditional business background. Yet, she had an extraordinarily entrepreneurial mind-set. She was a MacGyver of food photography, able to find an extension cord in the middle of the Guatemalan jungle during a shoot on Central American spices. However, every time I would ask her for ideas for various essay topics, she went straight to the one area of her amazing job description that was the least interesting: creating, proposing, and operating within budgets. (You know, $5,000 to shoot a plate of french fries.) She kept talking about how hard it was to keep people within budget, but it wasn't anything I hadn't already heard.

Remember: Don't confuse sexy players with sexy essays—Ziva is one of those rare people who wasn't name-dropping when she dropped a name like Rachel Ray or that silver fox from Savannah, Paula Dean. In fact, she consistently shied away from it. But too many times I've worked with candidates who spent five minutes in the same room with Meg Whitman and wanted to center their candidacy around it. Unless you're the one who got her to launch eBay or change her hairstyle, let it go.

The budgets and the Food Network stars weren't what was interesting about the photo shoots. It was the intense vision she had for bringing people together and making impossible visions a reality.

Although she had an entrepreneurial mind-set, we had a difficult time with her Columbia essay about the entrepreneurial mind-set. The heart of the essay was to describe how you had seized an opportunity and made something happen. After some sparring back and forth, one of the best shots that landed on my side of the table was about how she had forged an unlikely connection between two people who couldn't see how much they had to offer each other.

Martha and Reginald came from similar worlds—photography—but were polar opposites: Reginald was a veteran food photographer while Martha wanted to shoot portraits. Reginald was old school—dark rooms and chemicals—while Martha was 100 percent Photoshop. Ziva wanted to put the two of them together, but neither could see the benefit Ziva did. Yet, against the odds, she successfully forged an apprenticeship that turned into a powerful and productive professional relationship—one that eventually did not require Ziva's stewardship. But like so many people drenched by the familiarity of their knowledge and experience, the hard part was getting Ziva to actually describe what she had done to get them there.

"I don't know, I just did it," she kept saying.

"So, basically what you're saying is, your photo editor had no clue what she was doing when she asked you to take on that first photo shoot?"

"No, when she threw me into the fire, she said she had no one else to turn to. But that was crap. She was just testing me."

I glared right through her. "So she was manipulating you . . . hmmm . . . I wonder if that was an accident or if she knew exactly what to do to get a competent woman to finally have confidence? If I asked your editor how she got you to believe in yourself, do you think she would just whine, 'I don't know,' or she would tell me about her old trick of throwing her assistants into the fire?"

For all of you out there saying, "I don't know," please consider what you're saying about yourself: "I don't know how I succeed, I just do." If that's really true, that makes your success accidental instead of intentional. Which kind of success do you think business schools are drawn to?

If you're still struggling with how to pull out the details that create your success, here's an exercise to illustrate the problem: Describe how you get from your house to Target (because you know there's one near you and you know you love going). Go ahead, do it.

If your answer was, "I get in the car and drive," then you're like 95 percent of all candidates—and you just wrote a really boring essay and missed 50 percent of the question. You need to think along the lines of, "I decided to drive. I found my keys, opened the door, turned on the ignition, made a right out of the driveway, headed onto Route 7, took a left on Target Way, and parked illegally in a handicapped space."

That's the level of detail you need in a change/impact essay. I kept shooting down every one of Ziva's "I don't knows" until she finally got concrete about how she manipulated—like any good leader would—Martha and Reginald's initial introduction and relationship. Then she described how she nurtured their evolving dynamic until the two of them were off and running on their own.

Notice the level of detail in the fourth paragraph of Ziva's essay (page 154). That effortless second sentence—"I would call her at the last minute and beg for assistance saying none of my interns was available and could she come as a personal favor"—came only after hours of me refusing to accept "I don't know" as an answer to the question, "How did you get Martha into Reginald's studio in the first place if she insisted she had nothing to learn from him?"

The Lesson

In the end, the essay succeeds not because Ziva was able to come up with an example of her seizing an opportunity no one else saw, but rather because she was able to walk the reader through *how* she seized that opportunity. This level of self-awareness showed the admissions committee what Ziva's presence in their community would look like. They got to witness her leadership style in action, see her visionary thought style, and her leadership style when converting her vision into an action plan. The admissions committee, like Ziva's photo editor, knew exactly what they were getting in Ziva. That's why they accepted her.

ZIVA'S SEIZING AN OPPORTUNITY ESSAY

"We have established the mind-set that entrepreneurship is about everything you do." Please discuss a time in your own life when you have identified and captured an opportunity.

—Columbia Business School

During our shoot on indigenous spices in Guatemala, I spent an afternoon with Marco, a guide who knew all the secret spots where the plants we wanted to photograph grew, and the local village leaders who needed to be consulted before we set up our shoot on their land. Marco called his numerous connections and left messages in his optimistic Spanish accent: "Lee-sen, I'm here with the food pee-pul and they have a lot of opp-or-tunee-tees that we must discuss."

I laughed hysterically. I figured anyone hearing the message would expect to be featured on the cover of my magazine or given a sum comparable to winning the lottery, whereas in reality, we were offering $5 to use the picks and shovels hiding in their huts. But when our phone started ringing off the hook, I realized this crusty native and I have quite a lot in common: We both know opp-or-tunee-teess when we see them.

In fact, one of the other characters on the shoot was my close friend Martha, who I had recently introduced to a well-known photographer, Reginald. In each of them, I saw an opportunity to help the other that most people would consider crazy at worst, misguided at best. Martha had arrived in New York several months earlier, passionate about photography, journalism, and the digital age. She thirsted to photograph politicians in their statehouses, not steak frites on a platter, but I knew that Reginald could teach Martha how to set up the perfect picture, and in turn, Martha could show him how to deliver it in time. Yet, the two believed they came from mutually exclusive worlds; the trick would be persuading them to see how much they could offer each other.

I started my plan by finding opportunities for Martha to help me with styling on Reginald's shoots. I would call her at the last minute and beg for assistance saying none of my interns was available and could she come as a personal favor. Ignorant to my ulterior motives, Martha would happily oblige. Once on the shoots, however, she met Reginald and began to realize that food photography was not as banal and boring as she had previously imagined. She spent hours talking to Reginald about Hasselblads and Leicas, and she began teaching him about digital Cannons and the latest Photoshop software. Before I knew it, the studio was calling Martha to assist on shoots independently of me, and as soon as a full-time position became available, they immediately offered it to her. Today, Martha is Reginald's Art Director and responsible for all of the studio's digital retouching and printing—a field that did not exist before she arrived.

What was Marco's reward for calling up almost half the

villages of Guatemala in order to solicit favors for my magazine? Nothing, really. What did I get out of connecting Reginald and Martha? Nothing tangible. Yet, Marco and I both instinctively seek out and create opportunities not only for ourselves but for those around us—and, when necessary, help them to realize possibilities they could not see otherwise. Every day presents an endless series of choices, and being an entrepreneur is about seeing these possibilities and creating unexpected solutions that lead to even more opportunities.

CHAPTER 12

Ethical Dilemma Essays

Ethical dilemma essays are not about choosing right over wrong, but about how you extricate yourself from between a rock and a hard place.

One thing I'm famous for is hanging up on my candidates.

Occasionally, I do it in frustration, like the time Matthew called me to thank me for helping him come out of the closet—something he waited to do until *after* he sent in his applications. Admittedly, my gaydar should have gone off, since he had a tendency to go on for far too long about Hooters. *Me should have thought the lady doth protest too much* . . . But I didn't see it, and in fact I thought he was joking when he called me after Christmas to give me the news—and by then, he had been waitlisted at Stanford's Graduate School of Business.

That's when I hung up, in shock and disbelief. If he had actually written about how applying to Stanford had helped him face the truth about himself in the "What matters most to me and why" essay, he probably would have been a clear admit! *The long arm of homophobia had struck again.*

This circumstance did have all of the elements of a great ethical dilemma: (a) Do I congratulate Matthew and reveal the secret handshake, or (b) Do I scream at him for lowering my placement statistic for that year? Later, when he got into Berkeley's Haas School of Business, his number one choice, I graciously decided to forgive him. (Stanford had been his first choice, until he visited Haas and discovered that it had a more prominent MBA gay community. Matthew took great satisfaction removing his name from the Stanford waitlist.)

Usually when I hang up, however, it's to make a point that the candidate is not working hard enough—not digging down deep. Never does this seem to happen more often than during discussions about ethical dilemmas, be they personal or professional.

The question is pretty straightforward; it's usually something along the lines of "Describe an ethical dilemma and tell us how you resolved it." You wouldn't believe the crap that people insist are ethical dilemmas—they are really just bummers.

Or maybe you would. Take the test.

Ethical Dilemma or Bummer?

1. Your boss finds a material error in a spreadsheet—the night before the big presentation. He directs you to ignore the error; you'll correct the assumptions after you've closed the deal.

2. You find out in confidence that your work friend is going to be laid off next month. He then tells you he's planning an enormously expensive wedding.

3. Your roommate just got off an MBA waitlist, three weeks before he has to move. To sell his car quickly, he neglects to tell a buyer that he had it repaired after a major accident.

4. **You've been saving for a big ski trip in Zermatt. An acquaintance who is a single mother asks to borrow money to pay the rent that same month; your savings is all you have.**

The answer to each of these scenarios is the same: "Depends on how you look at it." And that is the whole reason the "ethical dilemma" question is so attractive to so many admissions committees: It forces you to describe not only how you make decisions, but also how you analyze problems before you. This is a great indicator of your leadership potential.

However, most candidates initially approach this question from an entirely different, misguided perspective: Did you behave in an ethical way? *That's not the question!*

Come on, people: Do you really think an admissions committee believes it's going to trip you up into admitting that you're the same kind of unethical bastard that flushed our economy down the toilet not so long ago? Give them the same credit they're giving you.

It's true that MBA programs are very sensitive to their role in shaping the ethics of tomorrow's business leaders—as they should be. But that's a different question entirely (one that HBS used to ask directly: "In your career, you will have to deal with many ethical issues. What are likely to be the most challenging and what is your plan for developing the competencies you will need to handle these issues effectively?"). This particular type of ethics-oriented essay disappeared long ago, however—it's very difficult to get candidates to address it in more than platitudes about how ethical they are.

If you're thinking about ethical dilemmas such as the one posed in the first scenario listed previously as "a choice between obeying your boss or blowing the whistle," then you're missing the sophisticated approach to analyzing this scenario. The way you're looking at it, this isn't an ethical dilemma, it is just a bummer: You either do what your boss says or get fired and/or removed from the deal. If you approach it this way, there's no real choice here. The more sophisticated approach is to position it as a choice between two values. The first value is obvious, and should be universal: your dedication to telling the truth and serving your client's needs before your boss's reputation. There are many values you can pit this against, and the one you choose will tell the committee something important about what you hold most dear. Just off the top of my head, I can come up with several potential opposing values:

- **You value experience. Your boss knows a lot more than you do about how to handle clients, and you've never known him to cheat a client. So perhaps there's something you're missing.**

- **You're ex-military or a team-sports player and you respect the chain of command. Period.**

- **You value loyalty. Questioning your boss would undermine his belief that you trust him and reveal you to be naive.**

- **You put the long term ahead of what's expedient. The error does not represent the nature of your relationship; therefore, it can be corrected later without damage to your client.**

To break it down, it's an ethical *di*-lemma. If you skipped one too many Latin classes, the prefix *di* refers to "two" (I haven't got the slightest idea about *lemma*, but this much is clear: You need two of them). You need to find a situation in which you are damned if you do, damned if you don't. You must find yourself in a situation in which you could have taken either road.

A question regarding an ethical dilemma, be it personal or professional, requires that everyone in the room is right. A bummer is when you're expected to do something wrong, or else. An ethical dilemma is when you have to choose between "right" and "right" (or occasionally "wrong" and "wrong"), and you don't know what to do. What makes a great ethical dilemma response is your analysis of how you come to a decision.

Think *Sophie's Choice:* Do you give up your son or your daughter? And if that's way too harsh for you to be able to apply to your own experiences, then let's take it down about twenty notches and look at the Julia

Roberts vehicle, *My Best Friend's Wedding.* In this movie, one of the 1990s critically overlooked masterpieces, Julia Roberts (actually her character, Julianne) has to choose between finally being true to herself and declaring her love for her best friend, Dermott Mulroney (Michael)—which would ruin his impending nuptials—or supporting her best friend's choice and respecting his love for Cameron Diaz (Kimberly). Dear Julia is right no matter which choice she makes. How she makes that choice, and what she learns about herself, is what the movie is all about—just as her essay would have been. Julia also has to choose between two competing ethics in *Erin Brockovich,* in which she has to choose between family—being there during milestone moments of her young children's lives—or dedicating her entire life to winning justice for the victims of nasty PG&E.

Bottom line: What makes a powerful ethical dilemma essay is not the topic or nature of the dilemma, but (1) how sophisticated an approach you take to analyzing the two ethics in competition with each other, and (2) how transparent you are in weighing your options and coming to a decision. Remember, sexy topics don't make sexy essays, but when you can come up with both—as in the story that follows—it's essay gold.

What Happens in Tokyo Stays in Tokyo

Oscar, a management consultant who had transferred to the Japan office from New York, was having so much trouble with the "ethical dilemma versus bummer" issue that his Forster-Thomas coach asked for an Auntie Evan intervention. Like so many other young professionals, Oscar went through his roster of shady superiors with even shadier requests.

Oscar kept telling me what I like to call "Dudley Do-Right stories"— black and white with no shades of gray. There were bad guys and good guys; like a game of cops and robbers, decisions were easy. To overbill or not to overbill? That always seemed to be the question.

That's when I stopped him and said, "Oscar, what I'm looking for is a circumstance when you had a difficult time *deciding* what to do."

Oscar gave me that long, slow exhale that lets me know there's a lightbulb going off over his head.

"Bring it on," I said.

And, finally, he did—he was struggling with something like that at this very moment. He was in Japan on a plum assignment with his vice president, Sandra, to help their Japanese client through an acquisition. As the two Americans on the job—the rest of the acquisition team was from Japan—Oscar and Sandra had bonded while antiquing in the countryside on the weekends (yes, they were good friends; no, Oscar was straight).

During one of their weekend jaunts, Oscar noticed that Sandra had seemed despondent and distant. When he pressed her, Sandra admitted that she was having difficulty working with her Japanese male counterparts. Ryuichiro, the owner of the company around whom the engagement centered, had been making inappropriate comments about Sandra's outfits and hair.

Sandra made it clear that she was taking Oscar into her confidence with the following revelation: While the same behavior in New York would have sent her straight to HR, she acknowledged that the culture was different in Japan and she didn't want to make waves.

Oscar's impulse as a friend was to suggest solutions and come to her aid, including offering to intervene on her behalf, man to man with the offender. Sandra was thankful but adamantly requested that Oscar keep his mouth shut. "I was only venting," she told him. He promised not to say a thing—"promise" being the operative word.

I knew from experience that it wasn't going to end here—and I knew Oscar had finally stumbled onto a real ethical dilemma story as soon as he told me that he had committed to the promise.

"So what happened to *you*?" I asked, though I knew the answer.

As the weeks in Japan wore on, Oscar said, he found that Sandra grew more and more withdrawn, and her usually exacting performance got sloppier. Oscar approached her again, demanding that if she wasn't going to do anything about the harassment, she should let him speak directly to Ryuichiro on her behalf—man to man. "Doing nothing was ethically wrong," he told me. "I was in a position to make a difference, but Sandra was tying my hands. I could not stand by while this ass treated her like a piece of meat."

Oscar wanted to be the white knight and come to the fair maiden's rescue—in essence, his thinking was just as sexist as that of Sandra's harasser. To Oscar, Sandra was a damsel in distress refusing to be saved.

When I pointed that out to Oscar, he just couldn't see it at all. Once again, he was trying to create a situation with right opposing wrong, casting himself as the hero. In his opinion, Sandra was becoming responsible for her own problem because she wouldn't let him save her.

It was time for me to sprinkle a little fairy dust on the situation and get Sir Lancelot to snap out of it. The ethical dilemma was right under his helmet. So I decided to reframe the issue for him.

"Oscar," I said, "do you consider yourself a man of your word?"

"Of course!" he responded in true white-knight fashion.

"So it isn't Sandra who is holding you back from acting, it is your own belief in keeping a promise. If you didn't value your word, you would have just confronted the harasser already and wiped this whole mess away. So, if an ethical dilemma is a choice between two equally valid but opposing ethics, what are the two ethics at play here for you?"

"Well . . ." he drawled, "I don't believe in sitting still while a colleague and friend is suffering, but I also believe in keeping my word."

And the trumpets sounded! Now Oscar had a real ethical dilemma with two competing ethics. Either choice Oscar made—staying silent as he promised or acting to make Sandra's situation easier—would be in line with his values. However, the actions he had to choose from were mutually exclusive. One negated the other, so unfortunately, he'd have to betray one of those—unless he found a third way.

That's where the "how did you resolve it" part of the essay question comes into play. And since Oscar hadn't resolved it yet, a little push and some strategic thinking from Auntie Evan helped put the strategic consultant on track.

"What exactly was your promise again?" I asked.

"That I wouldn't talk to Ryuichiro about the situation."

"One consultant to another," I said, "you didn't promise Sandra that you wouldn't tell anyone back in the New York office, did you?" This strategic thinker got my strategy immediately.

"No, I didn't," he said, "but I think that would be violating the spirit of my promise."

"I'm not suggesting you open your mouth, Oscar, so much as I am suggesting that you be on the lookout to make a judgment call. After all, if you're seeing a downturn in her performance, don't you think corporate will as well? If that's the case, your saying something isn't betraying Sandra about the harassment, it's having her back regarding her performance."

As I suspected, Oscar didn't have to wait long. During an update conversation with his boss back in New York, he was asked, "How are you and Sandra doing?" Oscar made his judgment call: "Perhaps you should ask Sandra how she's doing," he replied. To make a long story shorter, the colleague did, and that was the opening Sandra apparently was waiting for: The floodgates opened, and she explained everything that was going on with her. She even requested that he intervene directly with Ryuichiro.

So without betraying any confidences, and without having to be championed or acknowledged by Sandra for his support, Oscar created a situation that gave her an opportunity to make a decision about whether she would disclose or not. He resolved the situation creatively, reconciling two ethics that seemed mutually exclusive to someone without the keen eye of a problem solver.

The Lesson

Here's the secret to mastering the ethical dilemma question: Pose everything in terms of two competing ethics. At the beginning of the chapter, I posed a scenario where your boss directs you to overlook an error in a presentation scheduled to happen the following day. The first half of this ethical dilemma is clear: You believe in being honest with your client. There are any number of ways to frame the second half of the dilemma, however, and that's how we get to learn about you: Which do you choose as most important to you? (Remember, in a good ethical dilemma story, there is no "right" answer, just a decision-making process.)

When considering ethical dilemma stories, remember the difference between drama and melodrama. In melodrama, there's a really bad guy and he has a curly mustache and his first name is probably Snidely. If one of your alternatives is dressed in white and the other in black, you've got a melodrama—and the situation you are put in is called a "bummer" not a dilemma. Actual ethical dilemmas are the result of drama, and drama exists when every position or person's perspective is understandable, relatable, or possible and you are forced to make a decision between "right" and "right."

Oftentimes, the best way out of an ethical dilemma is by finding a third ethic that helps guide the choice you make, preventing an arbitrary decision. In Oscar's case, he relied on faith in his boss to handle the situation appropriately and sensitively just by suggesting he ask Sandra if she was okay. And remember, the reason an admissions committee asks this question is *not* to test your ethics, but to find out how you make decisions when stuck between a rock and a hard place.

Spend no more than a third of your word count on setting up the dilemma. Spend another 25 percent analyzing the pros and cons of taking one path, then an equal word count exploring the other path. Finish up with what broke the tie—often a third value coming into play—and what the result was. See Workbook 9 for more detail about how to structure this essay.

OSCAR'S ETHICAL DILEMMA ESSAY

Discuss an ethical dilemma that you experienced firsthand. How did you manage and resolve the situation?

—Harvard Business School

In Tokyo, I worked alongside a senior consultant named Sandra who shared my interest in Shinto temple architecture. Together, we scavenged the city in pursuit of perfectly preserved ruins. One day, as one such trip neared its end, Sandra shared with me a startling revelation: a co-worker was sexually harassing her.

Sandra told me I was the only colleague she had shared this secret with, for fear of professional estrangement. In Japan, she argued, successful businesswomen had to tolerate the indignities of this male-dominated culture straight out of Mad Men. *She had resolved to do the same. But I felt ethically compelled to convince her to take action, going so far as offering to volunteer to speak to her supervisor on her behalf. Despite my efforts, I could not persuade her.*

Each trip thereafter, our conversation circled back to this subject. Sandra would explain our co-worker's latest inappropriate act and question whether she had brought it upon herself. More often than not, she would start to cry midway through our conversation. Nonetheless, she remained steadfast in her decision against "ratting out" her harasser.

Sandra's tears made the severity of her situation undeniable. My conscience demanded that I advocate for her despite her objections. To manage my internal conflict, I weighed several issues. She understood the subtleties of Japan's corporate culture better than me, for example. On the other hand, what right had our co-worker to behave so hurtfully, without correction?

Then I brainstormed a strategy for having it both ways: opening up a dialogue on the topic without revealing her secret. The next time our supervisor called, he asked how our project was going. After giving him an update, I described that our cultural transition could sometimes be difficult. When he asked how Sandra and I were holding up, I answered for myself—and, after a pregnant pause, suggested he ask Sandra that same question directly.

Sandra wasted no time opening up to our supervisor. As she explained to me later that day, she felt weak bringing up the issue, but if asked, she had no problem describing how uncomfortable she felt in the given environment. Our supervisor was thankfully understanding, and asked if she wanted to transfer back. She asked him to speak to the Japanese staff himself.

During our next trip, the conversation again turned to the theme of sexual harassment. This time, Sandra explained how her harasser had been avoiding her. She felt like she was slowly returning to her former self. And at last, we finally found the perfect Shinto shrine.

CHAPTER 13

Failure Essays

The ultimate test of leadership is how you respond to—and write about—failure (yes, even *you* have failed).

Talk about the line going dead. During the creation of failure essays is when I really exercise my bicep: picking up the phone and hanging it up almost as quickly as the lame ideas for failure essays roll in. Everyone in my office is familiar with my shouting, "Call me when you're ready to get serious!" As difficult as failure essays are, I admit they are one of my favorite parts of the job. I get to ask future senators about their deepest darkest secrets. I'm sure my brother Neil—the therapist—would have a field day with this.

Considering how much pain the failure question causes, why do admissions committees love it so much? And they do love it. This question moves around from school to school, from year to year, like a cockroach. HBS has included its "What did you learn from a mistake?" question for several years, and Columbia Business School has similarly clung to its "team failure" permutation for a while as well. Wharton has long included this question, but sometimes lets you choose it among several others. Personally, I think the more courageous candidates embrace this option, and admission committees respect that. Note: If you're trying to prove you're in the top echelon of applicants, take the bigger risk. You'll set yourself apart.

If you're avoiding this essay for a bunch of reasons that all spell fear, chances are, you have a great story to tell, and that story will probably reveal your leadership potential. Remember, part of being a leader is having insight into those you're leading. How can you possibly have insight into those you're leading, and help them be *better* when they're running into their own demons, if you haven't faced yours?

If you're somebody who has screwed up, faced your demons, and is willing to talk about it, then you're likely to be better at leading your team than someone who lacks the confidence to laugh at himself when his pants fall down in public, or who can't admit to weaknesses. Who doesn't despise the boss who can't admit when he's wrong?

Here's another reason admission committees love this question: Admissions officers really value introspection. In fact, as Derrick Bolton of Stanford says, "introspection and self-awareness" characterize the successful Stanford applicant; these traits are near the top of just about every list of adjectives admissions officers I have spoken to. Yet, you have to *demonstrate* introspection to a committee. You can't just *say* that you have it. Failure essays offer an excellent opportunity to demonstrate this, because all too often we don't notice when we're screwing up. Worse, if we do, we shift into rationalization, which eventually leads to denial—and let's just say that denial is not one of the attributes common among truly introspective people.

Worse yet, when considering this essay question, most people seem to interpret "failure" to mean "came really close to failing but saved the day at the last minute." Congratulations: If you choose a story wherein you almost failed but didn't really, you've revealed yourself to be someone who fears failure rather than embraces it as part of your evolution as a leader. True leaders have truly failed, and those are the stories people like to start their "Man of the Year" speeches with.

Here are a few of my favorite ill-conceived failure topics. You'd be surprised how often these come up among candidates:

1. I didn't make the final cut of the varsity basketball team.

2. I didn't get the blue ribbon at the county fair (I only got the yellow ribbon).

3. I almost blew the client presentation by missing the FedEx deadline to send off the materials . . . but at the last minute I saved the day by chasing down the FedEx truck!

4. I didn't get into Princeton, but I'm really glad I ended up at Georgetown.

5. I got a D in art history.

Are these sounding remotely familiar? If not, you're either on the right track or you're in denial. Here's a quick analysis of why each of these don't work.

1. If you worked really hard and still didn't get on the team, then it's not a failure—there just happened to be somebody better than you. You may have felt like a failure . . . but you probably have your stage mother/father to blame for how you feel (if this is gnawing at you, call my brother and tell him you know Auntie Evan).

2. Getting a ribbon is pretty damn good. (If you don't get that the blue ribbon is a metaphor, then chances are you're up against our old client Heather, who really did win county fairs throughout the Northeast, including three wins in a row at the Guilford County Fair

in Vermont with her amazing Taffy's Lemon Blueberry Jubilee.) You didn't fail, you just didn't meet your own expectation. Reading essays that make this mistake is like watching an interview of Kate Moss complaining she's too thin. It just makes me want to throw up in my mouth a little bit.

3.   Okay, white knight, we got it—you're a stud. This is perhaps the most common "failure essay" error. It's really just a backdoor way to pat yourself on your back by how far you're willing to go to save the day. There is no mistake—unless you actually missed the FedEx truck.

4.   Princeton or bust? Here, your mistake is just your definition of success, which you revised after you went to Georgetown. There's two problems with this type of story: (1) You didn't actually let anyone down other than yourself, so it's a very safe choice; (2) You never embrace the failure as a learning experience because you find out you didn't make a mistake—the fates were looking out for you. How is it a failure when everything worked out for you? Do you want a list of how many candidates didn't get into HBS and still had the career of their dreams, due in large part to their experience at the MBA program they ended up attending?

5.   Academic failures simply make terrible essays. One reason is because they're not that uncommon, even among the kind of candidates that self-select into the top tier of business schools. What? You didn't study hard enough? You were so hungover that you missed the midterm? You weren't interested in the subject matter? That particular brand of mea culpa belongs in the "Optional" essay space (or Additional Information section—see Chapter 19).

In short, we're only as successful as our failures. I only ever know I'm closer to making the right choice when I am able to compare that decision to a time when I screwed up. And that means I didn't save the day, I didn't win any ribbon, I didn't make the team, and fate didn't teach me a lesson—only my failure itself did.

Since this question gives even my most evolved candidates a difficult time, with relish I present the stories of two of the most perfect people you could hope to meet. *Yeah, right.*

White Men Can't Fail

Enter Tommy, a Citibank associate who graduated at the top of his class at Boston College. To hear this former altar boy tell it, the only thing he'd failed at was not getting into Dartmouth, and he stopped admitting to that five minutes after getting the rejection letter. So, I was on my third attempt to get him to "open up" and get real. We had been through the *painful* leveraged buyout wherein his careless quantitative errors were causing the deal to head south and the time in college when his initial lack of VP savvy led to the near ruin of a campus organization he was involved with—both life-altering instances to be sure. Yet, in both, Tommy had managed to somehow come up smelling like a rose. An all-nighter got the right numbers into the model before the Incode Inc. meeting. (Tommy swore he'd always be more vigilant and managed to keep his job.) A six-month probation and a commitment to Boston's inner-city youth got his group off the hook. Needless to say, I had hung up on Tommy twice.

So, there I was, hanging out in my office making my crazy assistant Katie even crazier. Tommy had managed to steal an hour away from the daily rigors of buy/sell and stopped by. He was ready to admit to the error of his ways.

Tommy's story begins on a meaningful Monday morning in Merger and Acquisitions at Citibank. Apparently the deal was heading south and it was all Tommy's fault. So far, so good. And, just when I thought I could close up early, like a pimple that keeps swelling up in the same place on your nose, Tommy fell into the all-too-common trap I thought he was avoiding. There it was, the phrase that won't give up:

"But I managed to rectify the situation . . ."

Now, here is where I would have hung up if he hadn't been sitting in front of me. But Tommy was earnestly trying to talk turkey. It wasn't a case of outright arrogance, or even denial. It was simply years of what I like to call White Boy training.

White Boy training is what happens to people like Tommy who are raised to think they're the single greatest thing since sliced bread. (Oh, that's not you? You're African American or Indian, so you think you are exempt? Or you are a woman? Well, believe me, race and gender have nothing to do with White Boy syndrome. The disease just started in that highly pampered population. So, like Ebola, it takes the name of the place it originated.) Being a White Boy is a mind-set, a way of life. Not to be confused with "enlightenment," it's something called "entitlement."

If you've gotten this far, and all of this is sounding familiar to you, take a moment to test yourself for White Boy antibodies.

Answer honestly:

1. **Are you the firstborn?**

2. **Did someone else make your bed as a child?**

3. **Does a laundry service do your wash now?**

4. **Do you often think, "I could have done that better than he did"?**

5. **Do you pride yourself on knowing the difference between a Burgundy and a Montepulciano?**

6. **Have you climbed Mount Kilimanjaro, skied a glacier, or run a 5K for breast cancer?**

7. **Do you often save the day?**

8. **Are you proud of your multicultural friends?**

9. **Are your apologies often followed by "but . . ."?**

In and of themselves, these traits are not a problem, but if you have answered yes to four or more of these questions then *you* are a White Boy. If you answered yes only to the final question, you are still a White Boy.

Here's the point: TAKE OWNERSHIP. If you're a White Boy, be a White Boy. White Boys are in a position to turn the beat around. A little sense of entitlement, however, goes a long way. Claim more than your share of White Boyness, and you risk crossing the line from "person who has the strength, awareness, and resources to get things done" to "person who thinks all things should be done *his* way."

That leads us back to Tommy.

Tommy wanted to break those evil chains of White Boyness so badly. He is not arrogant and was doing his best to dig down deep and tell the truth. After all, he'd been schooled by the Jesuits of Boston College. There, in my office, a sudden wave of generosity came over me. I liked him. He was a good guy, but he was well-trained in seeing only the best in himself, especially the best intentions. What he could not see was when those good intentions were paving somebody else's road to hell. Enter his former best friend.

I had recalled a story he told me about an "ex"—in this case, an ex-best friend whom we will call Damian. They had spent four years together in college and had both gotten a job together at Citibank. They loved this because it meant they could continue their college tradition of hanging out every Thursday night—just the two of them. I reminded Tommy about Damian and immediately his face was awash with that all-too-familiar look of guilt. It was time to get personal.

One of Tommy's off-the-cuff comments had been about how bummed he was that, after several months at Citibank, his friendship with Damian had disintegrated. As much as he loved Damian, Tommy didn't invite him along when Tommy was asked by a few VPs and associates to join them at a lounge for their own Thursday night boys' club. And they were all white—really white, as in Caucasian—and Damian happened to be black. And rather than ask Damian to join in the reindeer games, he simply did what many White Boys do: Tommy took the better—or in this case easier—offer.

Interestingly, it was "around that time" that his friendship with Damian began to dissolve. "Um, Tommy, don't you see the connection?" I asked. "Those two things are totally connected." I watched his brain go to work.

"But I offered to go out with Damian on Wednesdays," he said.

I loved Tommy, but still I wanted to smack him across the head. "Tommy, you didn't invite him into the club! That was a failure on your part as a friend."

Silence. I reached across the desk and closed his jaw. His silence was all I needed to know that he knew I was right. He knew it, and as difficult as it was, he took ownership of it. And it was about Damian being black. After all, there were other recent hires who weren't "stand-out" who somehow made the cut. It could not be denied that all of them were white. While there was no intentional racism, the Thursday night boys' group was only reaching out to the guys they had most in common with. That goes to the heart of Tommy's failure: As someone with a lot in common with Damian, he needed to operate from a place of strength and share his good fortune with his best friend. Instead, he operated from a place of caution and kept his mouth shut.

"But I don't know if they were racist or not," Tommy told me as his last vestige of protest that this wasn't a failure.

"But you weren't willing to find out, Tommy. You weren't willing to find out."

And with that, we had a kickass essay. And Wharton agreed.

The Lesson

Take immediate ownership of your failure. The difficulty is in seeing the real failure in the first place. As a White Boy, Tommy felt he had earned his spot in the Thursday night club and didn't want to jeopardize and dilute all his hard work by inviting his friend Damian as well. To Tommy's way of looking at it, Damian needed to get his own invitation. To my way of looking at it, Tommy was the person to give it. And because his failure was not obviously related to racism, he refused to see how his actions failed to create transformation for his black friend. That truly is a significant failure, and one you can't whitewash at all.

TOMMY'S FAILURE ESSAY

While I am far from flawless, I must confess to struggling mightily with this essay topic. I wanted to answer this question honestly and openly, but choosing a personal disappointment that is neither superficial nor overly humiliating was challenging. So I asked my close friend Damian for help. After a few minutes of making sarcastic jokes about my flaws, Damian suddenly fell silent. What he had to say next—the story I am about to tell—revived disturbing memories of an incident long suppressed in my subconscious. I actually felt ill afterward.

Damian and I met years ago during a study abroad program in France. Although we come from dissimilar backgrounds, we have a lot in common and quickly became close. Damian grew up in poverty in rural Mississippi. His family pooled their money and sent him to Howard University ("a strong black school," his father said proudly). I grew up middle class, but in a poverty-stricken neighborhood in Maryland, and went to Boston College ("a strong Catholic school," my Italian grandmother said proudly).

We're both into sports and bonded trying to understand the British passion for soccer. In school we helped each other with international finance problem sets. We often went out together, debating such intellectual topics as the quality of local British ale and whether TUPAC or Notorious BIG was the best rapper of all time.

Coincidentally, we both started our careers at Citibank in two different groups. We looked forward to continuing our friendship there, but it wasn't long before my biggest personal disappointment occurred.

Thursday afternoons in New York, investment bankers like to go out for drinks before their weekend exodus to the suburbs. Because Citi can be cliquish, I was both surprised and thrilled when a few Vice Presidents asked me along. I seized the opportunity to be "part of the group" and raise my profile within the firm.

As I was exiting, I ran into Damian. Instead of inviting him along, I told him I was busy with "stuff" and would catch up with him later. The reason—which I now admit as a tremendous failure on my part—was because I was afraid of becoming known as "that guy with the black friend."

Compounding my disappointment in my actions is the likely fact that my insecurity and pathetic, nervous attempt to conform at all costs was unfounded. I had never heard a racist remark from my coworkers then, and in fact have never heard one since. I betrayed a friend, compromised my own values, and blinded myself to my actions simply to fit in with people I would have despised if I had seen real evidence they were racist.

Damian was not stupid; he knew what I was doing immediately, yet never confronted me about it until now. He currently has a great job with a hedge fund, and over some British ale, we talked a lot about the incident, about how he felt then, about how I feel now, and about the subtle racism that still pervades this country. Thankfully, Damian accepted my apologies with elegance and without hesitation. I am thankful we are still close, and I will always regret what I did. Never again will I let my insecurities compromise my values or my friendships inside or outside of the workplace.

What If Admissions Officers Hate Me?

Good failure essays come in two flavors. I've already discussed Tommy's. I call his "Ready and Willing," like chocolate—the flavor that's ready and willing to go anywhere: with nuts, cherries, whipped cream, and even coffee. That wasn't this former altar boy's problem; he desperately wanted to own the error of his ways. He simply had a hard time seeing where or what they might have been.

Once he realized the error of his ways with respect to his best friend and colleague Damian, and the fact that he had *not* gone to bat for Damian when he had the opportunity to bring him into a Wall Street "boys club," he was excited to take ownership of it and wrote the honest self-realized essay you just read.

However, as difficult as coming up with the topic for one's failure essay may be, equally difficult for so many is finding the strength to actually write it, let alone send it to Harvard.

Mahmoud was a textiles-mill heir from United Arab Emirates. With all due respect, he was raised like a prince and, for all I know, might actually have been of sheikh descent. He spoke beautifully, dressed impeccably, had a gorgeous British accent, and followed all the rules of the game—academically and professionally.

Again, I was forced to wade through a litany of acquisitions and LBOs nearly gone south. I also got the all-too-familiar "I failed Spanish in prep school."

I decided to put the "failure topic" aside for a moment—after all, he was so perfect, I even occasionally referred to him as the Prince of Abu Dhabi (to his face)—and moved on to accomplishments. I started asking him about his extracurricular efforts.

He began telling me the age-old "I tutor a kid in Harlem" story. Of course, it included how, via some amazing tutelage, Mahmoud had managed to raise Julio's high school math grade from a D to an A–. Over the course of several months in the New York State Governor's Tutoring Program, he and Julio had even started to become close. They met every week in the spring and in early fall at the park at the World Financial Center. The two would sit together on a bench looking out over the Hudson River gazing at New Jersey. This part of the story interested me more—I learned about Julio's desire to change his destiny, escape his abusive parents, put himself into the Marines, and eventually move across the Hudson River to the smelliest state in the country. Just as I was buying into the potential accomplishment, Mahmoud shut the whole story down: "Oh, this won't work. The kid ended up leaving the program."

"What do you mean? He just 'up and left'?" I asked. "He was doing so well and one day he just didn't show up?" Something smelled fishier than New Jersey. As I pressed for details, Mahmoud kept deflecting me and wanted to move on to a new accomplishment. But while many refer to me as Auntie Evan, there are others who call me Auntie Pit Bull. I can sense crap from a mile away, and once I sink my teeth in, I don't let go.

Mahmoud was so desperate to move on because unconsciously he knew what I suspected: Inside his accomplishment lay a failure. Many people have told Auntie Evan over the years, "Oh, it's nothing." To my ears, "Oh, it's nothing" is the same as "I'm guilty as sin." Their awareness of their guilt has no bearing on the equation.

Finally, realizing that I wasn't going to let go, Prince Mahmoud began answering my questions. Julio didn't just "not show up." As the story went, one of the rules of the Governor's Program expressly stated that "if your student mentions, in any way, shape, or form using or being around drugs or alcohol, you must report it immediately to the program office, and the student will be removed from the program."

That's exactly what had happened here. Mahmoud ratted out the kid for admitting to trying pot. "I didn't want to do it," Mahmoud insisted, "but the rules are the rules. And hey, what if anyone found out? I wasn't willing to take the fall for this kid by covering up for him."

"But did you, at least, first try to use this as an opportunity to make an impact?" I asked. "To actually *be a mentor* and use your hard-won influence and Julio's respect for you to get him to realize that he'd never make it to the Marines or New Jersey if he became a stoner?"

"Uh, I was tutoring him in math," Mahmoud said flatly.

"So how's Julio doing in school now?"

"I have no idea."

"How's his life at home? Are his parents still hitting him?"

"I have no idea."

"Is he still going to buy that house in Jersey and join the Marines?"

"I have no idea," Mahmoud answered again, getting perturbed, but obviously continuing this conversation in his own head.

After a silence you could dig a Holland Tunnel through, I had one last question for Mahmoud: "So, do you have a failure essay yet?"

He smiled weakly and nodded his head. "Yeah, I have a pretty good idea."

The Lesson

By the end of that conversation, Mahmoud viscerally understood his failure. Getting him to write it, however, required some arm bending. I finally convinced him to at least put it on paper and see what he felt then. The result was so powerful in its honesty—even including a line about how he had initially joined the Governor's Program to pad his résumé for an MBA application—that Mahmoud refused to go any further.

"What if the admissions officers hate me?" he asked.

Therein lies the lesson about failures: It's not what you did (or didn't do), it's how your failure changed you, what it taught you, and how you evolved as a person. And Mahmoud's lesson was one understood by all risk takers, world changers, and leaders: Sometimes, rules have to be broken. Adhering to a rule that hurts others, especially out of self-preservation, is the act of a coward—leaders don't follow such rules, they change them.

As I said, I don't do "essays by committee," where you show your work to everyone you know and let each one of them slowly grind any semblance of your personality out. But when I heard Mahmoud's mother had agreed with me, I enlisted her help to finally convince him to take the risk and submit the essay. Though in the effort, I almost lost him as a client. Like I said, I stop at nothing—that's what good friends and good consultants do. Let this be a mini-lesson: If you're not hiring a professional, don't ask any friends for help except the one who's willing to tell you that you look fat in that suit or "he's just not that into you."

Given all Mahmoud's resistance, you can imagine my surprise, when, a few months later, he sent me an instant message from Abu Dhabi: "You are the Dalai Lama. Harvard Business School not only accepted me, but specifically mentioned how much they loved my failure essay."

MAHMOUD'S FAILURE ESSAY

"I'm gonna get out of Washington Heights and move to New Jersey," Julio said as we sat in Battery Park, gazing across the Hudson. And by tutoring him, I was going to help him get there— until my dreams became more important than his.

I met the Dominican tenth grader through the Governor's Mentoring Program, an outreach program to tutor inner-city kids in New York. Quickly, we got to know each other well and, among many things that we shared, we talked about the importance of following rules, at school and in life. By late winter, his grades and our friendship were on the rise. Most important, Julio had set a new goal for his life: to become a Marine.

One day, however, Julio mentioned drinking and smoking pot. Somehow, his using them didn't shock me. Still, a feeling of dread came over me. All the tutors had been told to "report any sensitive information." But Julio had trusted me, and ratting him out would destroy the fragile bond we'd built—and the progress we'd made.

But hadn't I taught Julio that rules are there to assist, not hinder? And then, I asked myself, what if something happened to Julio and I had never said a word to anyone? Then I reminded myself that my own reputation was at stake. So I decided to tell the head of the mentoring program.

I never saw Julio again. He dropped out of the program and school. Like everyone else in his life, I had let him down—as a friend and as a mentor. I could have talked to him about what drugs do and how the Marines would never tolerate them. But I took the easy route and passed the buck.

Sometimes rules have to be bent, even broken. Sometimes risks have to be taken. Sometimes people have to be trusted, especially when they have earned it. Julio definitely had. He studied and completed his homework in the face of family violence, overcrowded classrooms, and low income. And he traveled all the way from one tip of the city to another to meet with me, on time, without fail. What had I done? Very little. When did I go out of my way? Not often. And certainly not when it could have mattered most.

CHAPTER 14

Background, or "What Makes You Unique?" Essays

It's the Little Things

You don't have to be a left-handed Lithuanian lesbian to bring diversity to your MBA community.

Who cares where you're from? Your future in-laws, for one. Not to mention many of the schools you'll be applying to. After all, it's all about "fit," people. You might think this process is about exclusivity—keeping people out—but it's actually about inclusivity: making sure the right people get in. It's all about a mix of individuals who are—each one—going to bring something unique to the table, be it cultural, social, or professional.

They're not looking for well-rounded people, they're looking for a well-rounded class. You don't need to be the whole puzzle, you just need to be the right puzzle piece.

This cuts to the heart of my message: Be precisely who you are. I've said this a million times, and nowhere is it more directly applicable than here in the unique and background essays: You are only in competition with yourself.

Too many candidates start off yearning to know what kind of person Kellogg wants, or Harvard wants, or Tuck wants. Well, the answer is that all of these schools want a whole variety of people. Just like a great DC dinner party—whose hostess makes sure to invite a banker, a scientist, a lawyer, an artist, a politico, a socialite, a community organizer, and a fashion model—you want all kinds present. You want the whole to be greater than the sum of its parts. And so we go through this with our candidates—making them dig down deep, scouring around in their lives via their workbooks (see the workbooks at the end of this book) to see who they are "in part." This is what defines their value, and their place in the whole.

When we met Garrett, an analyst at the securities research firm Omega Partners, he sheepishly asked, "How can I spruce myself up?" He actually thought he wasn't good enough. At first glance, Garrett was an average guy. He was a good man with a decent GPA from one of the second-tier University of California schools: nothing to write home about. Even his 670 GMAT was good but not great. At the time, he was very involved with the American Institute for the Andes. Put all that together, and you get a great potential candidate for Tuck, Darden, Haas, Yale, Kellogg, or any other school whose mission stresses commitment to community and social diversity.

But to hear Garrett tell it, he was basically humble pie. He was a white boy who suffered from anything but White Boy syndrome—in fact, he could have used a dose. His problem was that he couldn't see what made him unique or special, so, once again, it was time to root around and peel back the artichoke leaves.

At the center, it turned out, was quite an interesting story.

How do you peel back those layers? Simply go back to the basics: Where were you born, what did your parents do, what were the values they preached, where did you grow up? At first glance, Garrett seemed to shoot straight down the middle. He had grown up in central California during the 1980s in a middle-class family with what he described as middle-class values: a strong work ethic and a "love thy neighbor" attitude.

For this New Yorker, however, his earnestness brought something quite unique to the table right away. Had this been the 1950s, we could have stuck our hand in a pond and pulled out a million fish just like him. However, this is post-9/11, when reality TV and cynicism rule. At first, I was tempted to agree with Garrett. Did his home-spun demeanor have a place in a twenty-first-century business school?

But that question is a fool's game, and the easy way out. Deal with the deck you've got, not the deck you wish you had. Just embrace who you are, not who you think you should be. Somewhere in there you'll find a story that communicates the basket of values, skills, and unique traits that you bring to the table. It's not like Coca-Cola. There is no secret formula. And the more you try to prove you're just like everyone else at the school, the more faceless you end up becoming. It's better to be the Opie everyone remembers, rather than the hipster who dresses just like every other throwback poser.

Just as I ask all my candidates, I asked Garrett to think of a story that goes, as RuPaul would say, "back back back to your roots"—you know, that story that continues to be told at every Thanksgiving, funeral, or wedding since your childhood. That story that becomes part of your family mythology, like the way your grandmother Patty would gather all the leftovers from Thanksgiving dinner and make you take it to the homeless shelter in the next town over—and how now, even long after she's gone, you keep that tradition going. Somewhere in there are the values you grew up with, and no matter what they are, they say a lot about who you are.

So, let's just take it from the top with Garrett.

He was born in central California in what was a relatively small town in a place I'll call Paradise Valley, characterized by modest ranch homes; around the corner from Main Street, farmland as far as the eye could see. Somewhere in the near distance was the Pacific Ocean. His mother was a schoolteacher, his father a police officer. Garrett's story gelled for me when I asked him to relate some of the most significant moments he recalled from childhood. One immediately came to mind: the day the town almost burned down. California towns have a special knack for that. But what he remembered was not the flames or the choking smoke. His father organized the townspeople with the local volunteer fire brigade and managed to stop the fire from jumping from the mountain to the town. It was something right out of Jim Carrey's character in the film *The Majestic*.

This story didn't seem special to Garrett because it just showed what his father always did: It was people first. It was no surprise that, as a high school student, he worked at the local supermarket and became a volunteer fireman—being a volunteer wasn't unusual to him, wasn't out of the ordinary, and it didn't make him special. It wasn't something to be proud of, just what you were supposed to do. All he needed was a staple through his navel and he'd be the ultimate fireman's calendar pinup.

What he brought to the table was something that could not be ignored: integrity, commitment to community, love thy neighbor as thyself— the whole package. Then there was the biggest statement of all: This gift his father gave him—an attitude that there is more to life than a job. As a policeman, Dad easily could have bulldozed over people. And certainly, he didn't have to help put out other people's fires, so to speak, for free.

Being "of service" is finally what made Garrett unique. It was the element of his personal background that illustrated what he brought to the table. And it was integrated into his goals. Being a person who grew up loving the land and the people inhabiting it, his goals did not stray far: He wanted to create a venture capital concern that would invest in alternative energy sources and companies whose techniques improve how efficiently governments recycle. No shock, the guy wanted to have an impact on a clean environment.

What did he bring to the table? He was the guy who would come into a school with some very necessary intangibles. He had an absolute demonstrated commitment to community—no two ways about it. And it was no shock that his long-term professional goal, which he zeroed in on long before we discussed his background, gelled like a hand in a glove with his strong desire to make a difference in his community. This is what I made him see and stress. It's no wonder why Darden, Duke, and Tuck eventually saw his value as well. Thank God. Or rather, thanks to people like Garrett, there's a possibility that we might not have to rape the entire planet.

Don't get me wrong, you don't need to have Garrett's sense of social responsibility to be unique. Here's what made several people really unique: For Fabienne, it was her love and knowledge of diversity as ultimately revealed through her shoes. For Ian, it was the knowledge that he was *not* as progressive as he thought when a pro-employee stance he took made his colleagues suspect he might be gay, and how he ultimately decided he didn't care. For Shimon, it was his commitment to community as revealed via the method by which he made sure his college friends remained in touch with each other; Sunday brunch for alumni at Shimon's apartment became so well-known that out-of-town alumni passing through New York City would always ask if they could attend. And for Gerard, it wasn't that he was black and came from the hood—which would have been the obvious—but his commitment to raising his daughter on his own that taught him who he really is. Finally, for Edouard and Yeesan, it wasn't their upbringings in France or Malaysia, respectively, that they chose to highlight; it was that they thrived in an international team dynamic and learned to understand, accept, and value difference.

Those were the little things they all brought to the table.

The Lesson

We've all got a little "somethin'-somethin'" that makes us who we are. Don't shy away from it, don't avoid it—include it. The very thing you think makes you undesirable because to you it seems so common or was a problem in high school—like, say, you were too short or too tall, too thin or too fat—might be the very thing that informs your experience of the world, the thing that makes you a perfect addition to a particular MBA community. The key is your willingness to share it and be who you really are, not who you think they want you to be.

Remember, it's the little things. Note that each of the people mentioned previously took the story of what made them diverse at least one step farther than the obvious. One of the oldest educational consultant lines of all time is, "Schools are looking for a well-rounded class, not well-rounded people." The key is integration. To Garrett, being one of the youngest volunteer fire chiefs ever just didn't seem like a big deal. It's strange how others can help you see what makes you unique. You might want to look at Facebook and what your old friends value about you.

Be careful not to be "too busy being you" to see the difference that you bring to the table. Not everybody has the guts to sing a solo in front of a crowd, understand the unique importance of friendship (because you're an only child), be fearless in the face of new cultures because you were an Army brat, or have the courage to put out raging wildfires.

Stop worrying about who you're not, and embrace who you are. Every MBA program has got to have a really good guy, a gosh-darn-it Opie, a crazy ADD, a friend of Dorothy, an alternative guy, a dash of Euro-something, your requisite metrosexual, and somebody with a piercing. Yes, even business schools have somebody with a piercing.

Now, about writing the essay itself: Depending on the length, you want to pick three to five anecdotes about your life, spell them out in a little detail, and *loop the example into how this story illustrates the type of classmate you will be*. What makes the difference between an okay essay and a fantastic one is, as always, specificity: Don't just say you'll be an active member of the community; say you'll be an active member of the Have a Heart club and expand the club's service reach to the suburbs. Name speakers you'd invite to a panel discussion you'll volunteer to organize for a specific club. The more concrete and grounded your ideas are, the clearer it is that you can visualize yourself as a vibrant, active member of the community.

GARRETT'S BACKGROUND ESSAY

Tuck seeks candidates of various backgrounds who can bring new perspectives to our community. How will your unique personal history, values, and/or life experiences contribute to the culture at Tuck?

Paradise Valley in Central California was a rural suburb in the 1980s, when I was growing up. Open fields far outnumbered houses, and roads were paved around trees, not over them. Locks were considered a nuisance. Life moved fairly slowly, and everyone knew his or her neighbors. I certainly did, since my father was a police officer with the Sheriff's Department.

My father took his career and the impact he had on others' lives very seriously. I remember occasions in my youth when ex-convicts approached my father at the mall or grocery store. They would recall how well he treated them while they were in jail and wanted to thank him. My father believed in treating others as he would want to be treated, which is not necessarily common practice among police officers. This had a significant impact on my view of the world and treatment of others.

My commitment to community involvement was tested in 1990 when a forest fire nearly claimed our neighborhood. I remember my mother sniffing the air; it was the Saturday before Independence Day. "It smells like smoke!" she shouted. "Oh my God, the hill is on fire!" My mother, Gayle, is a very laid-back person who does not panic. She is an incredibly caring, selfless person who would do absolutely anything for her family. So, my father and I then knew the seriousness of the situation—and I was absolutely scared. Without a word, we knew we needed to take action. We ran to the door where my mother was standing, only to see the mountain we lived on fully engulfed in flames. With a great deal of teamwork, my father, mother, friends, neighbors, and I soaked the roofs, trees, and brush with water. We were able to save the houses. We were absolutely exhausted, but the rush of adrenaline kept us moving. The firefighters were concerned, but calm at the same time. Their mental strength and physical endurance really made an impression on me. After that, all I wanted was to become a firefighter.

When I turned sixteen, I joined the Paradise Fire Department, a small volunteer station ten minutes from my home, working my way up to Captain at age eighteen. Emergency calls were infrequent due to the small size of our community, but from the proverbial "cat in the tree" calls to collecting food for less fortunate families, I was very involved with the town and its people. This kind of dedication to community is what attracts me to Tuck, which shares my values. As a Tuck student, I would like to join the Social Impact and Have a Heart clubs, maintaining my long-term social commitment whether lending the strength of my back or the efforts of my mind. I would also like to join the Energy Management club. There, I would have opportunity to get involved with others who have a similar interest in the future of the energy industry. The opportunity to learn about other students' experiences and vision, share my own, and work toward objectives in this field would be invaluable.

My values are very important to me. My years as a firefighter taught me the importance of community and selflessness, my time at Safeway imparted me with a strong work ethic and the managerial skills, and my experience as an analyst at Alpha demonstrated to me the value of teamwork and communication skills. But it's the intangible qualities I possess that I want to bring to Tuck, such as my deeply felt understanding of the virtues of balance and perspective. There is more to life than work, and I want to share this outlook with the students in your program. I have always been involved in the community. Whether serving as a firefighter or volunteering now for the American Foundation for the Andes, raising money for orphanages, hospitals, and schools serving the Quechua people of South America, I work hard for the *causes I believe in. At Tuck, I would like to form an organization where student volunteers can offer consulting services to local Quechua business people and economic improvement organizations, thus helping them improve efficiency, add value to their products, and reap the reward potential of their efforts. In particular, I envision projects ranging from marketing strategies for craft producers, enabling Quechua women to earn a living, to promoting efficient ceramic coal stoves, greatly cutting resource depletion and pollution. I have committed myself to various communities throughout my life, and I feel this would be an amazing next step in my progression as well as help build relationships among interested Tuck students. I know this organization's members will reap as much of the rewards as I will, Tuck will expand its already impressive global focus and footprint, and the people we assist in the Andes will be able to break their cycle, share their experience with others, and potentially make a meaningful impact on the local economy. I cannot imagine anything more enriching to the Tuck community than creating a possibility like this.*

CHAPTER 15

The Whimsical Essays, or "If You Were a Tree, What Tree Would You Be?"

The "Whimsical Essay"—favorites of Haas, Kellogg, Darden, and Booth—is your single best chance to stand out, along with the "open" essay that lets you write about any topic you want. Here's how to finally take that big risk I've been going on about.

This chapter is dedicated to what I lovingly refer to as the Whimsical Essays. Some schools—in the past, the University of Chicago's Booth School of Business, as well as Emory Goizueta, Haas, Kenan-Flagler, Ross, and Darden, to name a few—have an institution-wide tradition of asking bizarre, one-of-a-kind questions of their applicants. Sometimes they mix the questions up radically from year to year. This chapter will ready you for anything.

Whimsical questions like to take you by surprise. They are anything but business-related. They want to bring out the real you—the "you" known only to those who know you best. The first part of this chapter is based on an essay question that has been asked by many schools and, based on our research, will likely be asked again. The second part is taken from Michigan's "passionate" essay, which is akin to so many other questions, like "What would the admissions committee be surprised to know about you?" And last, for the third part, I will dive into what we call the "open" question, which truly is whatever you want it to be—sounds easy, but perhaps is the most difficult of all.

Part 1: The Completely Random Topic

The University of Chicago's Booth School of Business has traditionally loved whimsical topics. Its PowerPoint presentation, which we will also discuss in Chapter 17, is so open-ended that you can do anything with it. The following anecdote relates to a 2001 Chicago question and one that Peter Johnson of Berkeley's Haas hinted that he'd love to bring back: "If you could invite any three people to dinner, whom would you choose and why?"

When I asked Shehzad who he would love to invite to dinner, he started his list by running through the usual suspects: Lee Iacocca, Madeline Albright, Bill Gates . . . you get the picture. But this question is not about being slick or cute, or God forbid, trendy (dare I say the number of people over the years who've said Madonna, and, if the question were asked now, I'm sure it would be Jay-Z or Kanye). The key is choosing people who reflect values you admire and skill sets you want to acquire.

That's when Shehzad shifted his list to Shaquille O'Neal and a bunch of other people whose fame has something to do with bouncing balls. Shehzad was a suburban California boy who worked for an oil company in the middle of nowhere. He was sharp as a tack, quick-witted, handsome (he had a body that rivaled The Rock), and a typical White Boy (despite his Indian Muslim heritage). You'd never know that behind that curtain he had a whole *Upstairs Downstairs* drama going on. When he was a young boy in Ahmedabad, Gujarat, his father died—shocking the family by leaving them massively in debt. His mother fled the country in search of a better life in the United States—only to become a veritable indentured servant in the southern home of his Cruella De Vil aunt. But his mother worked hard, saved her money, remarried a great guy, and always told Shehzad to keep his faith in God.

"And that's why I love Shaquille," Shehzad said. "He went from no one to someone!"

"So did Cinderella," I quipped. This is the first mistake people make: They go *really* obvious. The biggest message you're sending with a choice like Shaquille is that you have no imagination. Even if you do have no imagination, you could at least brighten up the admissions committee's day by researching other rags-to-riches stories and finding one that's a little more tailored to your own experience. As athletic as Shehzad was, he had nothing in common with a giant black man from the projects of Chicago.

I asked him to lose Shaquille for a minute and get to who *he* is. What you're really about is those values your mother taught: choosing a great partner (like your stepdad), never giving up, and giving back to the world. I told him to get back to me after he'd found three people who've done something with their lives that he'd like to emulate.

Three days later, Shehzad came back with the following triumvirate: George Soros, Mrs. Fields, and Jimmy Johnson.

George Soros, the financier, was a nod to the traditional great businessman but with a philanthropic twist. He got that one right straight out the box.

Mrs. Fields was just the opposite: Before he came up with her, I had to keep sending him back to the drawing board. As a Muslim who considered himself modern and progressive, it was important to him that one of his choices reflects those values. "Shehzad," I asked him, "what distinguishes you from your family and friends who are much more conservative in their thinking?" He laughed: "Well, I do know people who only seem to think of women as potential baby makers, and I couldn't disagree more. I want my wife to be a partner, not a baby maker."

Nothing said "modern man" better than choosing an inspiring woman role model. Note: His choice was a pure reflection of a relevant message he was sending about who he is, not a cynical strategy to curry favor with the admissions committee.

One of Shehzad's original ideas was—wait for it—Oprah Winfrey. Too obvious. I also dismissed Meg Whitman and the inevitable, as I said earlier, Madonna for the same reason. When Shehzad brought up Mother Theresa, I just sighed. At least the others were businesswomen; Mother Theresa didn't even practice the same religion as Shehzad. He sheepishly agreed he was just throwing out names at that point. Then Shehzad finally had the original thought I was pushing for: Mrs. Fields, the cookie magnate who embodied his values of putting a great team together to achieve one's goals. That's why Mrs. Fields worked so well—not just because she made you think, "Oh yeah!" but because everything about her said something about Shehzad's values: Mrs. Fields was an entrepreneur whose instincts and confidence were strong enough that she recognized her skill set was baking, not business, and who therefore surrounded herself with an amazing team who trusted her voice and whose business acumen she trusted.

Shehzad's final choice, football coach Jimmy Johnson, embodied the kind of strong, motivational personality Shehzad respected and was in the process of becoming. Jimmy Johnson turned underperforming sports teams into league champions—and was the first football coach whose teams won both an NCAA Division 1A National Championship

---

A Few Eye Rollers to Avoid When Addressing Whimsical Questions

DON'T BRING BACK THE DEAD. Dead people are great, but it's just an easy out
   to rely on any of those thousands of years of people whom history has
   already agreed on as inspiring.

and a Super Bowl. How did he do it? The power of persuasion—a skill, Shehzad felt, that would be the key to success.

The Lesson

As always, be who you say you are and start there. Shehzad's initial problem was his fixation on three people that made him look good. Problem is, his idea of what "looks good" was "what's appropriate, normal, expected." The committee wants to see the "inner you" through your choices, and that's what Shehzad accomplished after being pushed to be real. And that's ultimately the primary commonality among the Whimsical Essays: The goal is to get people on board with your choices—ones they had never considered that reveal the way you see the world and reveal an evolved insight into how you look at people and what they have to offer. Other than that, the Whimsical Essays have virtually nothing in common. How long they are, and the question styles, can vary dramatically from school to school and year to year. Here are some example questions:

- What great historical moment would you like to have been present for?

- You've been selected as the distinguished alumni commencement speaker for the class of 2032. Write your speech.

- What film, book, or play would you recommend to the admissions committee and why?

- What would you say to someone moving to your hometown?

THIS ISN'T A LITERATURE PAPER. Don't open essays with quotes! Cool quotes don't show us how well-read you are; rather, they reveal how insecure in your own voice you are. It was okay when you pulled that in high school. At sixteen, you didn't have a voice, but we're all expecting more from you now. And while I'm on a roll, don't use *Roget's Thesaurus*.

SHEHZAD'S "GUESS WHO'S COMING TO DINNER?" ESSAY

Each of the three people I would invite to a formal dinner represents a success story based on attributes I value. One is a successful philanthropic businessman, one a visionary entrepreneur, and one an innovative, motivational leader. Respectively, they are George Soros, the international financier; Debbi Fields, the founder of Mrs. Fields Cookies; and Jimmy Johnson, the former coach of the Dallas Cowboys.

Soros survived the Nazi regime in Budapest and supported himself with odd jobs until enrolling at London Business School. Although he lacked the best grades, he parlayed his tenacity into creating the lucrative Quantum Fund and netting himself billions. But Soros donated much of the money to his philanthropic foundation supporting liberal democracy. This man exemplifies self-made success through great risk-taking. At dinner, he would offer an intriguing perspective on achieving business success while helping humanity.

Fields believed that her cookies could be the basis of a profitable, nationwide business. Although she faced many

Leave *Roget* at home for your little brother's high school papers or your mother's crossword puzzles.

DON'T BE AFRAID TO FLY THE FREAK FLAG. A candidate recently answered a question about what book or play you would recommend with *Starlight Express*, the ultra-cheesy roller-musical about toy trains that come to life at night. While he could have run to Spark Notes and gone on and on about Don DeLillo's *White Noise* or Salman Rushdie's *The Satanic Verses*, he instead went with the embarrassing truth—something you'd never expect from this particular golf-loving former high school football player who listens to Dave Matthews.

naysayers, she raised the capital to pursue her dream. She achieved it by focusing unyieldingly on her ideals of high quality and customer satisfaction. Fields's strength was the cookies themselves; she was also smart enough to surround herself with other experts to grow her business. Fields is the ultimate model of entrepreneurship. She would bring to the table much knowledge about how to carry out a business plan by maximizing one's strengths and supplementing one's weaknesses.

Johnson became the Cowboys' football coach when the team was on a downturn. He had an unorthodox plan for success that many questioned: signing young, undersize players with speed and heart. The team had only one win his first season, but it won two Super Bowls within five years. He reached the pinnacle by infusing the team with confidence in his vision and methods. Johnson would have many insights on innovation, diligence, and group motivation.

These individuals possess particular characteristics that I hope to weave into my own life. I believe these attributes can carry me far in achieving my goals.

DON'T DRESS TO IMPRESS. For those of you who take any of these questions on from the angle of "I must 'dress to impress' by going super-highbrow," you may as well consider yourself heading backward on the Yellow Brick Road. These essays must come straight from the heart, not from the head. Which is not to say that there aren't those out there who love Bartok and string theory—if that's you, you should write about it. Just ask yourself one question when you choose to address the Whimsical Essays: Does the idea of inviting Lee Iacocca to dinner, being there at the Crossing of the Delaware, or actually recommending Fassbinder's *The Marriage of Maria Braun* (subtitled, not dubbed) really bring you to the brink of *le petit mort*? I hope for most of you that the honest answer is no.

Part 2: The Passion Essay

Dutch, a laid-off lawyer who had quit his legal career and was on his third (and finally successful) entrepreneurial venture, had a nasty little secret, one he was almost embarrassed to talk about (at least outside Boston): He was a diehard Red Sox fan.

Dutch was straight up about his passion: If you asked him about it, and you got him past what he thought the admissions committee wanted to hear—education, "my family," and world peace; you know, the quest for the Miss America title—he was quick to blurt out the "Boston Red Sox." But why? That's always the question. He certainly didn't answer that in his first draft. And that's the danger of writing about a passion: You focus on the facts of the passion and not yourself.

His first draft taught me all kinds of boring details that ran me through an entire emery board. The list included obscure dates, statistics on the number of fans, something about Fenway Park, blah, blah, blah. Even with all that information flying around, or perhaps because of it, his passion for this team came through, and it was quite clear we had the right topic. I sent him off to revise.

My mistake—it was too soon. I let his obvious commitment to the topic convince me he had an essay there. But the draft he sent me was just more of the same excited statistics he had babbled on about during our conversation. It didn't teach me anything about him.

Dutch had to connect the passion to his own life.

One simple line in the essay gave me the reason I needed to finally put the emery board down—it was when he mentioned that every spring this team of losers (my word, not his) kept coming back to the table and played as if they were going to win. They refused to let their repeat failures get them down.

"Dutch," I said after I crumpled up the paper and tossed it over my shoulder, "you graduated college, you had a great lawyer job . . . like these guys, the season looked good. Then boom—the economy went south and you lost. You lost your job, your ego was shaken, and certainly your nice Jewish mother was worried when you came home and said, 'I think I'll start a Laundromat.' In a bad neighborhood, no less! I think, Dutch, there's a ton of books at Barnes & Noble that talk about why small businesses fail. But that didn't stop you. Like the boys on the Red Sox, you picked yourself up, you dusted yourself off, and you started your life and career all over again. It's who you are."

He got it. "No wonder I love the Red Sox—I identify with them."

I finished my last nail (new emery board) and told him, "I might even go see a Red Sox game now, but not because of those facts and figures you listed here. I will sit through nine tedious innings and potential overtime in the summer heat, drenched in the smell of Pabst Blue Ribbon, because I am inspired by the parallel between your 'never say die' attitude and this nutball team that consistently gets close but never grabs the brass ring. In a world where most people are rolling their eyes, it's people like you who don't take no for an answer. Now get your ass back there and make this essay about *you*. The Red Sox are simply a metaphor. Period."

Dutch had a shit-eating grin when he handed in his new version, and he had every right to. He had dug down deep and told us who he was in the context of creating a successful Laundromat/coffee shop in the middle of South Boston with plans to open a whole chain (think, one win, 1918, and we're going for it again come hell or high water).

The Lesson

Don't be the runner-up in the Miss America Pageant. Ending world hunger says nothing about you unless you're a charter member of Farm Aid. Get real about what you love—become unreasonable about it. You know when you're on the right track when you're talking about something that you love—despite what anyone else thinks. It must be something that makes you get out of bed every single day.

But that's only half the battle. You have to figure out why you're so connected to this thing, the way Dutch did. The Boston Red Sox were a mirror of his life. And by the way, as history would finally tell, Dutch *and* the Red Sox won again.

Having worked with my clients and hearing some of the most bizarre "passion" stories, I want to thank many—in particular Gabrielle, for teaching me who Doug Flutie was and what the "Hail Mary Pass" is; to Reza, for teaching me names of fish in the Red Sea; to Susan, who corrected me when I thought she said "tassels" was her passion (what she actually said was "castles"), and I'm now versed in Neuschwanstein, the back garden of Versailles, and the Cloisters; and, finally, hats off to Ben, who taught me the secret formula of Mad Martha's Mint Chocolate Chip Milkshake, his favorite summer drink on Martha's Vineyard. They all had a secret passion; each passion mirrored their lives; most told an admissions committee something it was surprised to know about, and each one was accepted to Columbia Business School, Ross, Kellogg, and/or Emory.

DUTCH'S "WHAT ARE YOU PASSIONATE ABOUT?" ESSAY

What are you most passionate about in life?

—Columbia Business School

In 1918, the Boston Red Sox won the World Series. They haven't won since. Yet, I know the name of every player, I follow every game, and I can recite past line-ups like an old man tells war stories. Why am I so passionate about the Red Sox? They may lose games, but their attitude says "winner" all the way: pick yourself up, dust yourself off, and start all over when the season begins. That's a way of playing the game of baseball and life I admire— and I can certainly relate to it.

When my law firm downsized, I had no time to mope. I only looked ahead. Deciding to open my own business—a Laundromat in a poor neighborhood—posed a huge risk; failing at that could have created a worse situation than being laid off. It wasn't much different than being a Red Sox fan: After all, I am most excited

and fulfilled as a business owner when the odds seem impossible.
Likewise, every year, millions of Red Sox fans and I begin the
season with hopes of winning the World Series.

So a couple of seasons ago, I simply added the hopes of The
Big Spin Laundromat succeeding to my Red Sox World Series
dream. Now my business is thriving. The Red Sox are still losing.
Yet, I remain as passionate about my team as I am about my
Laundromat. Even if they keep on losing, I'll still be a fan. After
all, I wouldn't sell my business just because I had a bad quarter.

Part 3: The Open or "Wish" Essay

Essays that ask you to pick any topic that will help the admissions committee get to know you better are some of my favorites. They present such an amazing opportunity to really shine—to show the committee what separates you from the herd. However, from a candidate's standpoint, they are often terrifying for exactly the same reason.

It was one of the oddest situations. To date, I have never met Ms. Sadie in person, even though I've met many of the candidates she's referred to me, and we're in contact every several months. It's not unusual: I have many clients each year that I never meet in person. After all, it's kind of difficult to meet the ones who live as far as Paris or Hong Kong. In Sadie's case, she was in Atlanta during the time I took over her candidacy for one of my coaches, who had come to me asking for help with Sadie's "open" essay. All three of Sadie school's—Harvard, Wharton, and Stanford—had some version of the open essay that year. Wharton's question specifically asked, "Describe a personal characteristic or something in your background that will help the admissions committee get to know you better." For years, Harvard and Kellogg have asked this question on and off, asking what question does the candidate wish the admissions committee had asked.

Sadie was steadfast in her topic: She had a long history of fighting for the underdog, and that is the personal characteristic she wanted to talk about. By the end of a couple of conversations with Sadie, I knew she was incredibly accomplished, even more so than most twenty-five-year-old engineers; she had been in one of the most sought-after African American sororities; she had a GPA that matched her wit and a charm that could be deliciously barbed. But I was shocked by the way this powerhouse wrote about her commitment to fight for the underdog. Her essay was a sentimentality-filled screed about her compassion for the marginalized that was filled with such lines as "growing up black made me realize how important it was for me to help and be there for others who are disenfranchised and suffer the slings and arrows of outrageous misfortune."

Ouch.

And she began to describe how, when she was a kid, she used to be called Sasquatch by some of the kids, which would send her running out of the room in tears. The way she told this story was much more powerful than anything she had said about being marginalized as a black woman. I had a thought.

"Sadie, just how tall are you?"

"Let's put it this way," she admitted, "I have to have my shoes specially made."

Then I asked if most of the kids in her school were black. They were.

"So honey, you being black had nothing to do with those kids making fun of you."

As we continued talking, I confirmed that the origin or Sadie's feelings of disenfranchisement and defending the underdog had nothing to do with her being black. It had to do with her size. As she finally put it, "I could have been the love child of Serena Williams and Shaquille O'Neal."

Now that we were finally being honest, we were able to tell the story from a different point of view. I told her, "*Open* with the Sasquatch story. Embrace it! Champion it!" And then I promptly reminded her that it was time to find her inner Sasquatch. Specifically, that part of her that took her junior high basketball team to state champions for the first time. Needless to say, she had stolen the spotlight—and she had dominated every other game thereafter in her life: She was the largest woman ever to be invited into her sorority, and she kicked butt as an engineering consultant, managing to succeed in a world where men come first.

She was so exalted by the end of this conversation that she crowned herself "Sadie the Sasquatch." She stopped using namby-pamby words like "big-boned" and took ownership of who she is and used it as a source of power.

It's no wonder Wharton made room for her.

The Lesson

When you're considering your life, don't just tell sweet and lovely tales about how meaningful life is to you. Think about what you mean to life, and how you have been a role model to others. This essay is the ultimate "show not tell." In Sadie's honesty and openness, she didn't just tell us she was a leader, she demonstrated the qualities of leadership. Hence, the spirit of all the things she was trying to communicate in her original version was there: Sadie is someone who is fearless and dependable. The essay, like Sadie, was fearless. What she learned about herself was that something she was ashamed of was actually the locus of her power.

SADIE'S OPEN ESSAY

What is a personal characteristic or something in your background that will help the committee get to know you better?

I sprouted up faster than every kid in my Birmingham, Alabama, elementary school—and I just kept growing in junior high. "Sadie is a Sasquatch!" one kid shouted one day, and the phrase blossomed into a chorus after that. While no one dared pick on me physically, I would start crying the moment I stepped off the bus each day. At home, my mother would soothe me with platitudes about how one day, I'd make those kids regret their words. I never believed her for a second.

While I excelled academically, I wanted to be beautiful. I tried out for junior high cheerleader but awkwardly crashed mid-cartwheel. I tried out for the square-dance troupe because I loved the gingham dresses girls wore, but my teacher, Mrs. Randall, couldn't find a single boy my height; she told me I looked ridiculous dancing with a partner and asked me to find some other activity.

Then, in eighth grade, Coach Whitacre grabbed me by the back of my T-shirt one day in gym class and told me I was henceforth on the basketball team. I was horrified—I had always avoided athletics; growing so fast had made me clumsy all my life. But during practice, I found my footing. I scored 24 points in my first cross-town game.

On the court, I was lightning. Graceful, fast, powerful. Soon, my school's girls basketball team became as popular as the boys team, and whenever I scored, the crowd went wild. I may never have gotten to wear a cute little cheerleader skirt, but I found my place in school and soared. Only a few years later, in college, I did don that skirt as the tallest girl on the Ole Miss cheerleading squad.

Now I wear a business suit, and I know I look good—even if I do top six feet tall in heels. I may not be a size 4, but I own my court and can command a business meeting with confidence and style. Sadie the Sasquatch is here to stay.

CHAPTER 16

What Matters Most

Never Settle for the B-Plan

Stanford's "what matters most" essay is the most feared application essay on the planet. I unlock its secrets.

In just seven words—"What matters most to you, and why?"—Stanford GSB strikes fear into the heart of even the most accomplished candidate. With good reason: This is perhaps the most difficult essay question of all. Answering it requires a level of digging down deep that doesn't come easy for most. It separates the men from the boys—and I'm not talking about just the candidates. Educational consultants who aren't just a little afraid of this essay clearly don't understand the question. In fact, I see this question as the line in the sand that separates educational consultants who are in the business of inspiration and transformation, and "admissions con-sultants" who try to game the system through "branding techniques." Save that for your company, not your candidacy. It's like the difference between a journalist and publicist: A journalist reports the truth, while a publicist spins it.

I'm going to break this essay down first by what NOT to do.

PITFALL 1. Overconnecting your long-term professional goal to what matters most to you. One common version of this is that you're commit-ted to a long-term goal wherein you want to go into private equity so that you can grow Goldman Sachs's new media group. Because you are pas-sionate about this goal, it's only reflexive that it matters *a lot* to you. On the surface, it probably even matters more to you than anything else at this particular moment, especially if you've only recently realized how passionate you are about transforming Goldman. The key word here is "surface." Derrick Bolton, director of admissions at Stanford GSB, wants you to dig a lot deeper than that; he has even suggested that you use the essay as an opportunity to learn about yourself, and invited you to be transparent about that in the actual writing of the essay.

PITFALL 2. When "what matters most" makes your goal look like a strategy or gimmick as opposed to a value you deeply care about. Those who have found a long-term goal that is about transforming the planet in that *Free Willy* way—you know, ending world hunger, irrigating the Ir-rawaddy River through venture capital—are particularly susceptible to such overkill. In their case, the mistake is also particularly tragic: Having a persuasive, convincing *Free Willy* goal is a powerful thing, but it can easily be dismissed as an eye-roll-inducing gimmick when beaten into the ground in a what matters most essay.

Linking this essay with your long-term goal essay does seem like a nifty idea, but don't think you are the first person to come up with it. It's been done thousands of times, but in perhaps only ten of those times was it done well. As someone who probably has strong quantitative skills, what do you think the odds are that you'll be one of those ten?

Connect the Themes in Your Life

While a great goals essay should encompass what matters most to you professionally, what Stanford GSB is looking for in this essay is what matters most to you as a whole person. As Derrick Bolton, Stanford's director of admissions, wrote in one of his online letters from the director, "This probably sounds strange, since these are essays for business school, but we don't expect to hear about your business experience in this essay . . . Tell a story that only you can tell. If you concentrate your efforts on telling us who you are, differentiation will occur naturally; if your goal is to appear unique, you actually may achieve the opposite effect." Again, something a good leader should be able to do—again and again and again. Often, this essay goes hand in hand with open-ended questions like "What are you most passionate about?" and "Tell us something to help the committee get to know you better." Similar soul-searching applies. And along the essay trail, you may have lightbulbs go off about who you are and what makes you tick in ways you have never before realized. For example, after thinking through his leadership, accomplishments, and failure while writing other essays, Edward realized a common theme had popped up throughout his life: Many of his decisions were based on being different than his father. What he learned while writing this essay is that what really mattered to him was not being different than his father, but rather making the impact (or difference) his father never seemed to make. "Making a difference" by itself would have been a big yawn (everyone tries to get that one past us). But "making the difference my father never made" is a highly personal spin that teaches the reader a very intimate story about how one man's values and self-understanding evolved over a lifetime of experience.

Sabrina's lifetime of experiences led her to understand that what mattered most was "being true to myself." Any corniness this theme may have dissolves instantly when you hear the backstory. Sabrina spent her childhood training to be a world-class athlete—and succeeded—yet, on the eve of an Olympic-level event, was forced to choose between attending college or pursuing a medal. That's when Sabrina realized she'd never wanted to be an athlete, and had lived her life to please her father. After she walked off the field, she vowed to remain true to herself from then on—and embarked on a lifetime of accomplishments she truly cared about.

Because of the level of sophistication this essay calls for, what matters most (or any open-ended question) is often best answered after all other essays for all other schools have been tackled. Just because a school with an open-ended question like Stanford's what matters most may be your first choice—and you want to finish that application first—is no reason to jump forward and answer this question early on in your essay-writing process. In answering all the other essay questions, you'll be exploring many aspects of your life. All the introspection that's required for those essays needs to percolate in the brain for some period of time. This percolation most authentically leads you to what really matters most to you. After the other questions have been answered, if there's something important still left unsaid, still nagging at you because it seemed just too personal, that subject may be a great starting point here.

I'd been working with Gene for several months. He was, by all accounts, as pure as the driven snow on the White Boy scale. He knew a mere Cuban from a hand-rolled Cohiban, graduated from a select university, and knew his Chardonnay from Shiraz. But there was a twist: The Marines had paid for his degree—a degree that began with two years at a community college. That thrilled me to death—what a way to distinguish oneself—and Gene did not disappoint. His stories of rising to E-4 pay grade in only six months, leadership among his peers, and parlaying discipline and perseverance onto a Wall Street fast track, helped me make Gene's job as easy (and as all-American) as apple pie.

As I got to know him, his life story revealed parents who were local public school teachers, and two older siblings who had graduated top of their high school classes as well but had opted to play it safe in harmless, secure, barely white-collar jobs in West Texas. They had one other thing in common: big dreams that had been crushed under the thumb of a mother who, while she had their "best interests" at heart, was filled with a fear that made her a dream killer. You know, someone who always reminds you that "seventy-five percent of all businesses fail in the first year" or "don't give up your day job."

As a result, the most that everyone in Gene's nuclear family attempted was talking about what they were "going to do." For example, his brother wanted to start a company that managed professional athletes' money. His father always wanted to be an expert Mini Cooper restoration mechanic. In passing, however, Gene mentioned that to this day, on the front lawn of Gene's home, sit three rotting Mini Coopers. It's no surprise that his sister and brother talked and talked about how they were "going to conquer the world" yet played it safe, never leaving their own neighborhood.

Not having the good fortune to have a fortune, and determined to actually live out his dreams despite his mother, Gene decided to join the Marines. He wanted to see the world. He wanted a world-class education. He wanted to chart his own course. In discussing his goals, Gene hit upon an idea that had long been percolating but (being his mother's son) he had never really taken seriously: launching a sake industry here in the United States, the same way it had happened for wine in the 1980s in Napa (who knew there were more than twenty different types of sake?). Once I gave him permission to follow his real dream, Gene tackled that goal with the same gusto that had gotten him out of the suburbs and into Merrill Lynch.

Despite his go-for-it life and visionary goal, however, Gene just couldn't get past the usual "what matters most to me are my family and friends."

Have you all figured out what mattered most to Gene yet? If you haven't, first consider what Derrick Bolton says: "Your task in this first essay is to connect the people, situations, and events in your life with the values you adhere to and the choices you have made. This essay gives you a terrific opportunity to learn about yourself!" In doing so, just like with Edward and Sabrina, a theme will begin to pop up over and over again.

Let's look at some Gene themes: His brother could have gone to a top school, but stayed nearby; Gene got himself into a top university. His family talked about conquering the planet but never got as far as the corner of their street; Gene traveled the world. Dad didn't go for his Mini Coop dream job, but instead became a local high school teacher; Gene followed a path that led him to a bulge-bracket investment bank.

Gene's theme was staring me right in the face, but Gene was just too close to it. So I looked at Gene and said, "Let's see if I can't help you out here. When you told your mother you wanted to go travel the world, what was her response?"

"She said, 'What's wrong with West Texas?'"

"When you told your mother you were going to leave community college to get a finance degree from Rice, what did she say?"

"'What's wrong with the school you're in?'"

"And when you recently told her you wanted to leave investment banking to live your dream of opening up a winery, what did she say?"

He laughed and said, "She knows me by now."

Let's just say she didn't bake a cake.

"So, Gene," I told him, "despite every time someone told you 'be careful,' 'life is good enough,' 'what if someone beats you?' or 'you are better safe than sorry . . .'"

And I saw the light sparkle behind his eyes. "I just ignored them, and did what I wanted to do anyway."

Ding, ding, ding. Despite the risk, despite the naysayers, and in the face of no, Gene refused to follow anything other than his A-plan. What mattered most to Gene was never settling for the B-plan.

Once we had a theme, I made Gene read between the lines of his life.

You need to do the same thing. Put the puzzle together. Everyone who's still got this book open is a Gene. Make lists: What are the patterns that have popped up in your life?

Peeling Back the Onion

LEVEL-ONE THINKING. The trick is to think big and, even more important, to be sophisticated in your thinking. For example, one way in which Gene interpreted his own life early on was to say, "All I've ever done is gone after a better salary." That validated his very existence when he finally got to Wall Street. But that's level-one thinking. He wasn't digging past that. In level-one thinking, what mattered most to him could have been phrased as "making lots of money." But that didn't feel right to him, and not just because it would make him look like an ass (though that can be a good barometer).

LEVEL-TWO THINKING. Connect your level-one thinking to the bigger picture. Many of Gene's decisions, for example, came out of reactions against the way his mother thought. Therefore, he could have arrived at, "What matters most to me is making more money than my parents" or "What matters most is proving my mother wrong." Again, these negative spins didn't feel right to Gene. So he tried rephrasing the same idea in a positive light: "What matters most is proving myself able." That's not bad. It's certainly in the ballpark, but it's still the minor leagues, and Stanford doesn't do minor league. Where's the sophistication, the introspection . . . frankly, where's the Dalai Lama in "proving myself able"? That's just all about you.

LEVEL-THREE THINKING. Closer examination of his life and finding the pattern made Gene realize two important things: (1) He is someone who says "yes I can" in the face of no—otherwise known as Mom, the dream killer. That's level-three thinking, when you pull all the pieces of your life together and you have a moment when you realize that you just can't live without that value or state of being that matters most. When you'd rather die than live any other way. Settling for the safe path, the "B-plan," would have crushed Gene's spirit, and the definition of what matters most to him. That's why "family and friends" just doesn't work, at least for this essay: You can lose your friends and make new ones; you can build a family of choice (it's what people hopefully do every time they move to a new city alone). Losing his "family and friends" would have devastated Gene, perhaps even for years, but it wouldn't have crushed his soul the way that accepting life on his mother's terms would have.

Case in point: Barack Obama's grandmother—the person who arguably mattered most in his entire life—died the day before he won the 2008 presidential election. Yet that single person wasn't what mattered most to him—bringing change to America is what mattered most. So losing that person did not stop him, and, like him or not, the world knew him to be a true leader when he was able to get through the most amazing day of his life on the day after the most devastating day of his life.

When you read Gene's essay, notice that he made certain to share his realization that he did not blame his mother, father, or anyone in his family for being who they are. In fact, he makes a point of saying how important they are for him and how much he loves them for so many reasons, not the least of which is their work ethic. They weren't slackers, they just valued safety above all. There's nothing wrong with having a safe life, it just isn't commensurate with people who get chosen for top business schools. The very least expectation they have is that you have the mind-set to change the world, when they give you the schools to do so.

Also note that Gene is transparent about discovering what matters most to him in the course of writing this essay. As Derrick Bolton wrote in his director's letter, that's gold. But I'm not saying copy that idea: When it's natural, it's natural . . . it's not part of a formula. Formulas are for admissions consultants; realizations are for educational consultants.

And if you're still having trouble or looking for a formula, you might consider having a talk with God, your therapist, or your significant other. If none of those work for you, perhaps try looking in the bottom of a bottle of tequila. It worked for Hemingway.

Final note: Gene was accepted to Stanford—fittingly, his A-plan for business school.

GENE'S "WHAT MATTERS MOST TO YOU, AND WHY?" ESSAY

All summer, I had been preparing for the day when I could start practice with my high school football team and put on a set of pads for the first time. I was still a young kid out of junior high school, five foot six and barely 125 pounds. I was an easy target, and on the first day of full-contact practice, I got killed. I could barely breathe after getting the wind knocked out of me twice that day, but I was happy. So what if I could hardly walk? At least I had followed through with my decision to play and be part of the team.

My parents wouldn't let my older brother play football, but knowing my personality and resolve, they were resigned to let me learn the hard way that I was too small and weak to last very long. One day, however, Mom caught me limping. Horrified, she tried to make me quit right there. I shrugged her off.

Throughout my childhood and into high school, my parents always tried to steer me to the safest, most conservative, and risk-free decisions in life. I often heard the naysaying about things I did being too dangerous or too risky; looking back, that's probably why everyone in my family considered me "the adopted one." Both my parents were teachers and lived a life as far from risk as they could. That's the world I grew up in—play it safe and avoid uncertainty—and the rest of my family followed in lockstep. My older sister gave up her dream of becoming a child psychologist when she fell in love and got pregnant. My brother graduated valedictorian from his high school class, but rather than chase his dream of an architect, illustrator, or draftsman, he chose a safer path—majoring in accounting. He went no further than the local university and majored in accounting.

Long before my siblings gave up on their dreams, my dad had given up on his. Working on cars was his passion. He dreamed of a career repairing and restoring old cars. But my mom thought Dad should use his college degree to build a teaching career. So he did.

I never put the whole situation with my dad together until I started analyzing my past and thinking about what really matters most to me. Their world did not make sense, and I knew I was different because of it. To me, it only makes sense to go after your dream, no matter what, and that's how I have lived my life. So far, I've won some and lost some, but "going for it" is what matters most to me.

Throughout my childhood, I always had a love and knack for business. At six years old, I made Christmas ornaments in art class and sold them around the neighborhood. At seven and eight years old, my friend and I ran a lemonade stand so we would have some pocket change. Based on my entrepreneurial appetite, I decided I wanted to pursue a career in business. But even more, while my older brother and sister had stayed at home for college, I wanted to go far away and attend a major university like UCLA—one that had things like great sports teams and a challenging education and like-minded individuals going for their dreams.

To pay for college, I joined the Marines. When I made my decision to join, my parents neither stopped me, nor supported me. The only people who raised an eyebrow were my high school teachers, who were stunned as to why a scholar-athlete was not heading to a top university. While it was lonely and scary the day I had my physical and signed four years of my life over to the Marines, I knew I was going after my dream.

I made the most of my enlisted career. As a result of leadership community volunteerism and graduating number one from technical school, I was given a promotion opportunity to advance from E-1, the Marines's lowest rank, to E-4, a supervisory rank, in exchange for extending my enlistment one year. I did not want to delay going to college by another year, but I also wanted *the increased responsibility and experience that came with a higher rank. So I went for it. I had to learn how to be a boss as well as a friend. In doing so, I had to motivate others to get the job done, while at the same time, build a mutual respect for one another.*

I enrolled in community college after the Marines and had always wanted to be a leader on campus and make a difference in the community. After two years, I attended Rice University and became president of the Business Club, and landed a summer internship at Bank of America. I took the full-time offer after graduating.

Although I noticed ways to improve efficiency and presentation analysis, I was afraid to suggest anything or change established systems. For the first time, I was hesitant to "go for it." Was I maybe not "the adopted son" after all? I quickly realized, however, that going for your dreams is not the same as recklessness or fearlessness. My managing director, after all, had strictly prohibited using some of the very techniques I knew would improve our efficiency, and I did have respect for chain of command. Still, it just didn't make sense to duplicate things and ignore resources that would benefit us. In the end, the additional effort on my part to convince my managing director to adopt some of my suggestions paid off and has saved fellow analysts and me several hours of unnecessary work each week.

As a child, I could not understand why my family had dreams about working on cars, producing great art and architecture, or helping children as a child psychologist, but do little or nothing to go after them. It was frustrating to witness it because it just didn't make sense to me. I suppose that to some people, "dreams" is another word for "fairy tales." To me, however, going after my dreams and making them the guiding principal in my life is what I strive for. I will continue to shoot for the stars, building a U.S. sake empire. What if I never grow past one small brewery run by my wife Kayoko and me? That would surely be both a surprise and a disappointment. But I also know that what matters most is not how successful my business is, but knowing I'll always be able to say, "I went for it."

CHAPTER 17

Creative/Slideshow Essays

Finding Your "Wow"

NYU Stern's creative essay and Chicago's slideshow essay are like the open essay on steroids. Here's how to up your own game to keep up.

For years, NYU Stern has asked one of the questions that keeps educational consultants in business: "Please describe yourself to your MBA classmates. You may use almost any method to convey your message (e.g., words, illustrations). Feel free to be creative." Stern sets the bar high with a candidate-terrorizing podcast (search online for "NYU Stern School Marketplace from American Public Media" to find it; or click on http://marketplace.publicradio.org/shows/2005/12/27/PM200512276 .html), which describes some of the most memorable approaches to this essay.

I write "*approaches* to this essay" because Stern's creative essay and

Booth's PowerPoint slideshow invite you to burst outside the box of a standard five-hundred-word essay and instead submit, in Stern's case, a pop-up book of your life, a paper doll with different outfits that symbolize your various interests, a description of the plants in your garden and how each one reflects an element of your personality, or the much-used-and-abused "personal recipe" including all the ingredients that make up you. Please put that one on the back burner, because that dish went stale a long time ago.

So how do you stay fresh? It's about finding your "wow"—that thing that makes people sit up and listen at a cocktail party, that thing that closes the deal, gets someone to call you back, want a second date, want to be in your life in both a personal and professional capacity.

Approach this essay question in two parts. The first part is the "wow" factor: Ask yourself, "Why do people like hanging out with me? What role do I play in a group of friends—the charmer, the organizer, the party animal, the pot-stirrer, the peacemaker? What surprises people the most to learn about me?" The second part is figuring out the vehicle that most readily and broadly reveals the wow (e.g., the pop-up book or paper doll).

This essay is not a trick question. Like the Stanford what matters most question, the best answer is usually the simplest. All too often, however, people don't give this question its due and they try to come up with "groovy," "cute," or "clever" ideas. Just stop. There is a huge difference between *clever* and *creative*. As Edward Hopper said, "Clever is next to nothing." The question is designed to get you to reveal the "who you are" while exploring your creative mettle. But remember, revealing who you are is always paramount. Rose Martinelli of Booth told us, for example, that the PowerPoint slideshow is meant to be an open-ended showcase for you to express yourself in any way you choose—it is *not* a test of your PowerPoint skills. Simple words on the slides, if they teach the admissions committee what makes you unique, will win out over a vapid but brilliantly designed slideshow any day.

In other words, you get two pages, double-spaced, and you get to do anything you want in that space. Very tight parameters are put around your flexibility to communicate who you are and get people on board with it. That's what leaders face all the time. NYU has created a great test. Nothing says "leader" like being able to communicate an idea using eight crayons when it takes sixty-four crayons for others to do the same thing. You have to think like a fifteen-second commercial: You have limited time to get a complicated message across. The story that follows illustrates the creative process in action.

Dancing Desi

"Frankly, my dear, I don't give a damn" is what I told Ankita when she began to list the things she wanted her classmates to know about her: "I love my friends, my family, my job, blah, blah, blah." My forehead smacked against my desk as I chimed in with, "And you love long walks on the beach, sunsets, and puppies."

And to tell the truth, dear reader, so do I. How do you think I ended up with my black pit bull–Lab mix, Mz. Keesha, and Uncle David's two cats, whatever their names are. Right there, I'm already more interesting than she is! She had started off with the same litany of personal and work-related aspects of her life that all of my more initially guarded candidates do: What is it about the academics, family, career, and good works that everyone defaults to instead of cutting to the heart of who they are?

Ankita had a fair to middling candidacy, truth be known. She would tell you the same; in fact, she seemed to be best at telling me what she wasn't great at. She had a decent GPA and a barely passable GMAT score; yet, like so many in her position, she seemed unaware that her innate creativity, inner beauty, and humor could go a long way toward vamping up her candidacy.

The bottom line is, while many of the "common" things about Ankita were interesting—her parents were immigrants from India who had successfully ridden the IT wave; she had worked hard, including on a few interesting mergers and acquisitions—the point is that she wasn't "working it." And this was a girl who had "it." The gods had shined their lights on her. She was funny. She made great conversation. And the real bottom line is, she was hot. I was like, "Girl, if I was going to creatively describe you, the first thing I'd mention would not be your ability to split atoms or balance a spreadsheet. Nor would I be getting into conversations about your love for your mother and father." That's not exactly what I would call the "OMG! Keep talking!" conversation. The one that makes you want to ignore call-waiting.

So what do we know about Ankita? What was she up to or into in her life that could help to reveal the most interesting and important 360 degrees of who she is? That's the way you have to approach this. I already knew all about her family, friends, and good works. But what was the icing on and around her particular cake? What is the thing within which all of her important, revealing stories could be cradled? The ones that reveal her as a self-reflective, insightful, evolved, yet fun gal to be with? The girl you want to call up late at night because she'll be ready to either work on that team project into the wee hours or be there for you at a moment's notice when you're in the pokey.

I have a tried-and-true way of getting there: Explore every aspect of your life, make a list, and leave no stone unturned—the things that are most important about you will always rise to the top and they will have stories to exemplify them. And one of them will rise to the tip-top. And that is where the *creative* as opposed to the *clever* of your essay lies. So we went through a number of aspects.

Eventually I found it. Among all the things that she had to offer, in addition to her beautiful face, her perfect body had been honed to precision through years of practicing an ancient Indian dance form known as Manipuri. Manipuri's most salient feature is its precise, controlled hand gestures. Think sign language put to music. No surprise then that for years at the local Hindu temple, she had been passing this dance form down to younger girls. She was the Manipuri Madonna of Miami. Another important part of Manipuri is a sense of modesty. But modesty is not something Auntie Evan has time for. All she needed was a runway to work, and that's exactly what the creative essay is.

I did a little research of my own and found out that each Manipuri gesture represents a concept, character, or aspect of human emotion. That's when I figured out how to set her free. Manipuri hand gestures, I explained, would serve the same purpose that baseball cards had for Andrew: a springboard to talk about the things you want people to know about you. Andrew had picked baseball players that represented different values that were important to him (for example, Jackie Robinson represented his pioneering spirit and gave him a platform to discuss something he had pioneered).

And with that, Ankita's path to enlightenment became clear to her. Excited, she erupted with ideas: The result was a beautifully handcrafted scrapbook of Ankita in Manipuri poses whose size and word count, in the end, approximated the two-page double-space requirement. Each photo was accompanied by a paragraph explaining the meaning of each Manipuri gesture, such as "passion," and its relevance to her life. Her Manipuri manual had all the components that she originally wanted to include, from work to good works, from family to friends, but in a way that kept bringing out the "wow" of her: a divergent thinker with an ability to express universal concepts and unique aspects of her persona—the very hallmarks of great leaders and certainly a great asset to the Stern community.

The Lesson

It's no holds barred. Nothing is sacred and nothing is off-limits (except, it should be noted, perishable items and a few other things specifically proscribed by the admissions committee). Some of our greatest slideshows and creative essays have been:

- The summer-camp king who wrote a letter home to Mom

- The computer consultant who sent his essay in on a Chinese scroll

- The Societe Generale analyst whose photo montage was a walk through his life

- The Dallas banker who created a paper doll of himself, along with different outfits appropriate for the various activities he enjoyed

- The ice skater whose halftime choreography for an NHL team revealed her as an unconventional thinker

Please note: Some of these required Elmer's; others required Photoshop or PowerPoint; and some simply needed a bending of the brain and the good old-fashioned written word. But none of them were "cute" or, dare I say, "clever." First and foremost, they were straight from the heart. They showed real people with real emotions revealing who they are through things they love.

CHAPTER 18

Culture Shock Is a State of Mind

Whatever you wanted to write about "culture shock" or cross-cultural differences is already boring the admissions committee, and you haven't even written it yet. Here's how to have a fresh take on a very stale topic.

INSEAD has long enjoyed tormenting applicants on both sides of the pond, not to mention Asia, with its question, "Have you ever experienced culture shock? What did it mean to you?" INSEAD lets you choose between that essay and another, "What would you say to a foreigner moving to your home country?" Both options are asking you to explore the same concepts: How deeply do you understand cross-cultural issues and vast and various ways mankind expresses identity? How adaptable are you to difference? How experienced are you at seeing the line between understanding, tolerance, and acceptance? You can understand without accepting, for example, and tolerate without understanding. You can even accept without tolerating, as our friend in Japan learned during his ethical dilemma described in Chapter 14.

Just as all politics are local, all business is increasingly global. Masterful leaders must learn how to navigate cross-cultural differences to some degree if they want to make an impact on a scale larger than what they can see with the naked eye from a hilltop. And that leads us to the heart of acing the culture-shock question: Exotic locales, disgusting foods, and unfamiliar rituals aren't necessary. An Arizonan in Boston may experience as much culture shock as a New Yorker in Paris, perhaps even more so because the Arizonan may not have expected culture shock in the first place. You can experience culture shock without leaving your own hometown, when you have to work with a team that's moved into your headquarters from the Shanghai office.

So, you don't have to have lived or studied abroad to write a compelling culture-shock essay, but if you do have significant experience abroad, you should write about that. But, as I've written for every other essay question in this book, you want to push your thinking to the next level. Level-one thinking is culture shock related to food (this isn't an episode of *Survivor*), issues around time ("I finally accepted that everyone arrives fifteen minutes late in Trinidad"), or language. Level-two thinking pushes past those issues to more unexpected, deeper-seated issues. This is how you set yourself apart.

Because level-two thinking is subtle, let's look at how Vijay and I tackled this issue to learn how to think through the nuances and distinguish yourself in this question.

Vijay had moved to the United States from India. But when we started to talk about this question, the list he gave was not very different than if he had moved from California to Colorado. The food was different, the people spoke differently, they wore different clothing, they had a different skin color . . .

What I was looking for was deeper insight. So I asked him, "Tell me what surprised you," and it needed to be grounded in specific personal stories versus a treatise on his observations about how life is different in America. While this is not a travelogue, like all great essays, it should tell a single story that prompts some sort of transformation in your adaptability and facility for relating something specific to you that can be translated universally into all new situations.

I asked him what most challenged his value system, what embarrassed him? "Were you ever dumbfounded? Let's cut to the chase, Vijay—did you ever feel like an idiot? Did anything you were raised to believe ever get called into question?"

He sat there silently and then recalled a simple story wherein he had been in the United States for X months—enough time to meet some locals while a student in Utah—when he dropped by a good friend's house at 10:00 p.m. His new American friend, Michael, obviously distressed, immediately asked, "What's wrong?" Vijay was completely confused—until Michael explained that people just don't drop by your house that late unannounced unless something was wrong.

We had struck gold with a very simple tale about two friends and their very different ideas about personal space—about, as Vijay put it, "how one man's heaven can be another man's hell." At first Vijay decided that his friend's way was bad, until he realized that decision was based on his own very personal experience of the world. After the experience, their relationship had not changed: They still shared their love of computers and Xbox. Except that in Michael's world, there was a beauty to having your own private time. And while Michael might have found it overly crowded in Vijay's part of the world, another way of looking at it was to see Vijay's point of view: That same crowd was a warm blanket.

Experiencing and adapting to culture shock is, ultimately, about understanding that you give meaning to the world, the world doesn't give meaning to you. The fact that the Chinese do not stock their public bathrooms with toilet paper is neither positive nor negative—until you assign one of those values based on your expectations. The "shock" in culture shock comes from believing that your view of the world is based in fact, which is why it's "more" shocking that four-star Chinese restaurants don't stock toilet paper either. You've been hit by double culture shock because you believe that high-end establishments should not neglect any of its patrons' needs.

Want to get rid of culture shock? Then stop giving meaning to our differences. That takes you from transformational leader to international leader.

The Lesson

Look for those realizations when you had to bend your beliefs or change your way of looking at something so that you could fit in to a new circumstance. This could potentially happen by transferring from the track team to the soccer team. After all, you still have to run around, you still have to exercise, but in soccer it's not all about you.

A great culture-shock essay is not about how you came to accept cultural differences, it's how you came to understand those differences. If you were to open your own high-end Chinese restaurant, you may not even consider for one second that patrons should supply their own toilet paper. *Accepting* means no longer making the Chinese wrong, and learning to carry your own supply. *Understanding* comes when you realize that most Chinese people find the idea of applying someone else's toilet paper (you don't know where it's been) to such an intimate area to be as distasteful as picking gum up off the sidewalk and plopping it in your mouth. Could it be?

Cultures do not have to take place in an actual foreign country. In this day and age, geographic travel is easy and cheap enough that just about anyone who wants to, can do it. So the natural default is to discuss an experience abroad. While the question is designed by schools with diverse communities like INSEAD, it is designed only in part to find out if you've left your own backyard.

If you've never traveled abroad, you can still have a great culture-shock essay. If you come from Tupelo, Mississippi, where gay people are expected to maintain their own separate underground culture, and then move to San Francisco to join a private equity firm, you might be shocked at how "the gays" walk openly hand in hand in the streets. But if you wrote your essay about your shock and how you came to accept that people operate differently in the Bay Area, you're only scratching the surface.

A more profound form of culture shock is when your stodgy managing director decides to open a gay-business investment arm. At first you raise an eyebrow: What is it about your managing director that is *really* driving such an unorthodox move? Why would he be willing to risk his and the firm's reputation by endorsing such a community? Does he have a secret his wife should know about? Then your new drinking buddy in the cubicle next to you explains that gay-themed merchandise has one of the highest profit margins in consumer goods, and the gay community has more disposable income than most. You either have to start raising the eyebrow at *everyone*—could your new wingman also be on the down low?—or you graduate into *understanding* the firm's decision, not just accepting it: A business is not defined by its clientele, and guilt by association has no place on the West Coast. And that doesn't require joining PFLAG (Parents Families and Friends of Lesbians and Gays).

Stepping into foreign territory, figuratively or literally, may drive culture shock, but no matter what, culture-shock essays are always about how you opened up to the world's differences *and/or* its similarities. So remember, "shock," in this case, does not always equal "this is so different." It can also mean, "This is just like it was in my own backyard." It can be about many things (not the least of which is a belief system), things you held so dearly to that you couldn't see yourself aligning your beliefs and values with your new surroundings or circumstances, be they physical, cultural, spiritual, or related to state of mind: Think, if you're a true-blue Democrat who just got a job at the Red State corporate office of Wal-Mart; if you're an inner-city survivor now working in the hallowed halls of Greenwich, Connecticut; or if you are the only male working in corporate finance at Lane Bryant, you probably have a culture-shock story to tell that doesn't begin with you getting on an airplane. Each of those stories revolves around learning how to understand and operate in the cultures of others different from you.

In the immortal words of Frank Zappa, "High school isn't a time or place; it's a state of mind."

VIJAY'S CULTURE-SHOCK ESSAY

Have you ever experienced culture shock? What did it mean to you?
—INSEAD

One crisp autumn night, when I dropped by my new American friend Michael's house at 10:00 pm, he immediately asked, "Is everything alright?" He was relieved, but clearly surprised, that I had come over just to shoot the breeze. I learned then that in America, unscheduled after-dinner chats—which I took for granted back in my native India—bordered on outright invasion of privacy.

His reaction was my first culture shock in the U.S. The American dream is about owning one's own land and stretching out into the suburbs. In contrast, we Indians live on top of each other like a warm blanket. Yet, I do not feel smothered; I feel swaddled instead.

Now I see how one man's heaven can be another's hell. India and the United States share much in common: both are democratic nations, former British colonies, a collection of unique states, and extremely diverse ethnically. Yet, their cultures, lifestyles, customs, and attitudes are drastically different. I would never trade my experiences during my first few months in Utah, when I was both enthralled and distressed. From adopting new bland foods to learning to live without chauffeurs and stay-at-home maids, I was constantly adjusting. As I expand my niche in the world, I realize that I will face change continually. I am no longer shocked by the unexpected or unfamiliar; I embrace it. I am part of a growing global melting pot—and can take on new flavors without losing those basic ingredients that make me "me."

CHAPTER 19

The Optional Essay

The Dog Did Not Eat Your Homework

For those with a problem in their application, the optional essay is almost as important as the goals essay. In this chapter, I teach you how to get the admissions committee to fall in love with you despite your flaws.

Warning: Do not read this chapter if you still think your mother was right when she forced your fifth-grade math teacher to let you retake the final exam. Everyone but you and Mom know the truth—the "evil" teacher was not out to get *you*, you just didn't study as much as you should have (and deep down, you know it). This chapter is dedicated to those of you who have never had a friend good enough to say to you, "Mr. Preston hated me more, and I still got an A."

Most schools have optional essays that read something like this: "Is there any additional information that you wish to provide to the Committee?" Some schools, like Harvard and Kellogg, don't have an optional essay per se, but they do provide space for "additional information" that is intended for the exact same purpose: *to provide an explanation of any areas of concern in your academic record or your personal history.*

The reason I started this chapter with a warning is because if you do *not* fall on your own sword, but instead make excuses about why the problem was really somebody else's fault, then the mistake will take on double the significance. Admission committees like nothing less than someone who points fingers, and they worry when that finger is going to point *their* way.

There is really only one effective way to use an optional essay: to fall on your own sword, take responsibility for whatever you did that precludes you from ignoring this essay, and give solid, hard evidence that you are no longer the person who made the mistake. If you do this, the committee may decide to overlook your black mark and assume the best of you going forward.

So, the optional essay is a place to put any "red flags" in your candidacy into context. Here are acceptable reasons to write an optional:

GPA below 3.1

GMAT of 650 or below

Disciplinary probation

Felony arrest or prosecution

Dishonorable discharge from military

Never, never, never, never, never (have I said it enough?) write an optional essay or fill in the Additional Information section with extra accomplishment stories, achievements, or other great moments in your history that you couldn't find a place for in the other essays or parts of your application. It is, in Auntie Evan's opinion, the kiss of death.

Many schools don't limit the number of words you can write. In the absence of a word limit, your optional essay should never be more than the paragraphs I outline later in the chapter. Try to keep it to three hun-

Other Triggers for an Optional Essay

No current direct supervisor rec

Rec from father or family member

Missing or misleading data ("My bonus is smaller this year because they changed the bonus date from January to July, so I only have half what I normally would this time; the prorated amount would be *X*.")

Explanation of data (I included my study abroad in my GPA against the directions of the application because my school actually administered the program . . .)

dred words, and certainly don't exceed the word count the school dictates for its other essays. If you have a learning difference or disability, you may have other information (such as a letter from you psychoeducational evaluator) to include as well. See Chapter 7 for specifics.

Jim's story will help you understand how to determine whether you should write an optional essay and how to achieve the mind-set you need to draft a successful essay.

According to Jim . . .

Jim thought that everyone at Bowdoin had it out for him. All his GPA problems could be traced back to a single element: getting cut from the lacrosse team. To hear Jim tell the story, his lacrosse coach's decision to cut him was unwarranted, petty, and vindictive. He was just as good as everyone else; it's just that his knee sometimes acted up. Oh, Jim.

The whole lacrosse conversation arose when I was combing through his transcripts: not pretty. There seemed to be a consistent downward spiral starting the spring term of his sophomore year. When I asked Jim about it, he told me about being cut from the team. He spent that whole spring semester in an angry funk, so "of course that affected my grades."

"So what happened your junior year?" I asked him skeptically. "Were you cut from another team?"

He hopped back on the excuse train. "The truth is, I had always been an athlete, and when I got cut from the team, it took me a while to figure who I was and where I belonged. I wasn't really focusing on academics."

The violins must have been playing at a very high frequency—like a dog, only I could hear them, it seemed. So I had to ask this now-successful private equity professional, "How long are you going to hold on to this story?"

Jim was stunned. He looked as if I had just asked him when he was going to get over the death of a child. I was going to have to reframe this conversation in terms he could understand.

"In your firm's current investment portfolio, how many consistently underperforming companies get to stay on the list? Is it petty and vindictive when you sell them off, or is it just, how do I say, 'good business'?"

He took the bait and told me that his firm would warn companies that they needed to turn around profits within a certain time frame.

"You mean, the same kind of warnings you got from professors all the time when your grades began to spiral?"

"Well, yeah. But I told you, I wasn't in a place where I could do anything about it. It was a really fucked-up time for me."

"I'm sure it's no walk in the park for those underperforming companies. Do their CEOs get to tell you about how difficult emotionally this is for them?"

"Yeah, right. These are professionals. You can see how it's not the same thing."

"After all, you tried your hardest, right?"

"Yeah!" he agreed eagerly.

Click! The trap was sprung. "But you already told me you were too

Don't Play the "I Can Top That" Game

Somebody's always got it worse off than you do. If your mother had cancer and that affected your grades, and you think the committee should cut you some slack for that, consider the girl who *herself* had cancer and managed to pull a 3.8. After doing this for so many years, I guarantee I can win the "I can top that" game—with someone facing worse hardships who performed twice as well.

If you think you've got a good "the rules shouldn't apply to me" story, you can't top what happened to Doug.

Remember the holiday season of 2005, when a devastating tsunami killed more than three hundred thousand people in Southeast Asia? A few days after Christmas—not even two weeks before the HBS second-round deadline—I received a frantic call from an Indian guy I'll call Doug.

"I was in Thailand during the tsunami," he started to explain with earnest urgency. "Thank God I wasn't in my hotel room because the whole thing was washed out to sea—including the Mac I'd been using for my application. It's all gone. Now I don't know what to do, because— can you believe this—I called Harvard to ask for an extension *and they wouldn't give it to me!*"

I took a breath deep enough for both of us. "Let me guess: They told you to apply third round."

distracted by figuring out who you were to do well. That means you weren't trying your hardest."

"But I was trying my hardest given the circumstances!"

This Ping-Pong game could have gone on forever if I didn't stop pussyfooting around.

"Come on, Jim, I'm a more experienced player than you. I've heard and come up with every excuse in the book. You can't convince me to let you off the hook, and do you really want to? Your post-college life has

Doug just couldn't understand why Harvard was being such an asshole. "I was in a *tsunami*!"

Doug was desperate for my help—third round may as well be called the kamikaze round—but I almost didn't accept him as a client. I'd seen what I feared was his type a thousand times before: "the adults for whom excuses still matter."

Doug got over it. After a little conversation, we were able to transform his perspective of "the tsunami story" into an interesting life experience, not a crutch or excuse. We created a very compelling candidacy—the candidacy of a man for whom the tsunami was an experience, not an excuse—and he was indeed admitted to HBS third round.

Are you playing Doug's game? You just might be if two or more of the following has come out of your mouth since graduating from college:

"But I tried my hardest."

"There was a family crisis."

"I've been going through a difficult time."

"So-and-so had it in for me."

"I refused to play my boss's game."

"Nobody told me . . ."

"Nobody ever called me back."

"I didn't think it counted."

"It's not the same thing."

been phenomenal! You're now a varsity player in private equity. You work your ass off. You wouldn't let others make excuses, so why make them for yourself?" And then the coup de grace: "When one of your analysts comes in late wearing the same outfit he had on the night before, what do you hear when he insists that the F train wasn't working?"

Jim cracked a smile. "'The dog ate my homework.' You just make yourself look stupid."

And that was the danger Jim faced. He needed to address his GPA issue in an optional essay, but his answer sounded like "the dog ate my homework." You can see how it all sounds like a line.

Whether your coach hated you or the F train was late or whatever, I'm not here to debate. But if you see a pattern (see page 234) of being the victim, please be careful about writing that. This pattern will follow you in all things you do if you don't nip it in the bud. But at least for now, for purposes of your application, you'd better pretend that you are enlightened enough to "take 100 percent responsibility" for your circumstances. Blame nobody but yourself, because that is what will get admissions officers on your side. You don't get some credit for winning if you're not willing to take credit for losing.

Jim didn't just follow my advice, he embraced it. He came to realize after close examination of his experience at school that he had spent two years whining and had used it as an excuse. And post-college, he had turned it around professionally to become a "varsity player" in finance and could not accept excuses like "the world's out to get me" or "but I work so hard" or "I tried" or any of the "dog ate my homework" excuses that functionaries give. Why would he even begin to run this routine in an essay that gives you the opportunity to do two things: (1) give perspective to a weakness or problem in your candidacy, and (2) reveal whether you're still the person who made that mistake or you've grown and matured past it emotionally, professionally, and academically. And as a result, his whole perspective changed. And so did his approach to the optional essay.

Steps for Building an Optional Essay

MEA CULPA. First, you need a "mea culpa"—you need to own the truth. Start the essay by acknowledging that there is a weakness and summarizing what it is. Don't dance around it, don't offer excuses or reasons (at least not yet), and be straightforward. If you don't start out this way, you'll be raising eyebrows before you've even gotten started. In Jim's case, he had bad grades, and that's the truth. Lay out the land using actual metrics: Don't just say that you want to add context to your *low GPA*, but to your *GPA of 2.8*.

TURN THE BEAT AROUND. Second, define the circumstances, don't dwell on them, don't make excuses for them, and describe what you learned from this experience—how you've grown to reinterpret your circumstance in a more sophisticated way. (For example, you turn "the coach was out to get me" to "I let myself wallow in self-pity, a mistake I now can spot a mile away and will never make again.")

This also goes for someone who truly was the victim of someone else's circumstances, like the daughter of a sick mother. Someone else's cancer is not your free pass. What needs to be revealed in the essay is that you learned over a period of time that to truly be there for somebody else, whether helping them through sickness or mourning them after their passing, requires you to keep your own life together despite the fact that walls are falling down around you. This kind of synthesis is what makes an essay compelling: Your failing was not in vain, but actually makes you a more valuable member of the MBA community having learned this lesson. The dog will never eat your homework again!

PROVE THE NEW YOU. Everything in the essay until now is just promises and talk. You need to show them that you have been walking the walk. And to do that, you need PROOF—data to substantiate the "new you." After acknowledging your weaknesses—be they grades, standardized test score, or an employment gap—find the ultimate strength of your candidacy and put it here. Jim's was threefold: a stellar career marked by promotions, the intellectual rigor and discipline to get through the CFA, and an excellent GMAT score. All pointed to his personal transformation. They are the proof Jim needed to back up the story of his transformation—and the reason for which the admissions committee honored his request to evaluate him not as the immature underperforming boy he was, but as the successful, intelligent, and disciplined man he had become.

The Lesson

Even if all of Bowdoin had truly been out to get Jim, no admissions officer would believe it, and they certainly don't want to hear it. In short, grow up and take ownership for your weaknesses—be they partying too hard, somebody died, you were ill (with or without a doctor's note), separation anxiety your freshman year, senioritis, or, one of my favorites, "The professor had it out for athletes who missed class for away games."

Excuse making is a dangerous game, because there's always somebody in your same predicament who figured it out, rose to the challenge, and did well anyway. And heaven forbid, one of those people is one of your admissions officers. In short, get on bended knee and chant, "Mea culpa, mea culpa." It's what a leader would do.

Remember, if you decide to include an optional essay, *you are asking your admissions officer to do extra work*. It had better be worth their extra time. If you couldn't figure out how to get everything you needed into the space the application provides, then it's arguable you're not savvy enough to market yourself in an impactful, pithy manner. It says, "I can't color within the lines. I'm long-winded."

And as a final note, do not write about something only *you* think is a problem. This may be the most common mistake you can make in this space. If you got a 690 GMAT, do not try to explain this away as a "failure" because you think you should have gotten above a 700. It's like the thin girl who keeps whining that she's fat: It's an eye roller and makes her look, frankly, kind of pathetic.

JIM'S OPTIONAL ESSAY

I would like to address the glaring contrast between my less-than-stellar undergraduate GPA of 2.9 and my GMAT score of 740 (95% Verbal/90% Quantitative).

Regrettably, my past academic performance cannot be undone. To be sure, the contrast between the GPA and GMAT score suggests a disparity between effort and ability. When I think of the young man I was in college, I must agree. However, when my candidacy is examined through a different lens—solid intellectual capacity as measured by the GMAT in combination with sustained strong professional performance—the picture arguably shifts. After college, I hit the ground running in the face of rigorous demands from my first day at Prudential to my current position and status as a Level III CFA candidate. I am no longer the undergraduate who struggled to find himself, but an adult who knows what he wants and achieves his goals.

I am embarrassed to admit that while I was at Bowdoin, I actually justified my poor performance through a litany of excuses led by my having been cut from Bowdoin's lacrosse team—a distinction by which I defined myself in those years. Today, the conversation is quite different: I take sole responsibility for every failure and every success in my life. This transformation of attitude is the key factor of my present success.

Again, I can't change the past, but my life experiences, my transformed view of myself, and the resulting career success is proof that, if given the opportunity, my performance as a student in your community will bear no resemblance to my undergraduate record.

To that end, please consider my candidacy in aggregate, taking into account the simple concept of "growing up." In that context, I trust the committee will see past the boy who attended Bowdoin to the hardworking, dedicated, and value-added adult I will be at Columbia—in whom there no longer exists a disparity between effort and ability.

Now That You've Hit "Submit"

Once you submit your application, the waiting game begins. The hardest part may be over, but the emotional roller coaster has just begun.

This section covers the next steps in the process: sitting for the MBA interview, as well as what to do should you be waitlisted and/or rejected. You haven't come this far to go down without a fight. And hey—the waitlist and reapplication processes are just two more opportunities to get your message across to an admissions committee.

Real leaders, after all, make sure they're heard, even if they have to change strategies.

CHAPTER 20

Interview Skills

Up Close and Personal

Congratulations: You've scored your first MBA interview. Whether you set it up or got there by invitation, the same thing is true: It's all about being who you are, not who you think they want you to be.

Sitting for your interview is the culmination of everything you've learned so far. Now you have to convert it from "on paper" to "in person."

Being interviewed is just scary. There's nothing theoretical about it: It's completely visceral. You are there. You can't backspace, hit the delete button, or send it to a friend for review first. You can't run and hide. You're very much exposed.

Face it, they *are* going to get up close and personal, and make a judgment on who you are. In this chapter, we'll help you stop resisting the inevitable and embrace it. You're going to have to accept that you are short (or you're tall). Yes, you do have blond hair (or you don't). You do have an accent (or you don't). You're heavy (or you're thin or you're somewhere in the middle). You're everything or nothing. You are who you are. All of these things are out of your control. At some point as you walk through the door, give it up. Nothing is worse than walking through the door fear first.

Interviews Come in Different Flavors

There are two types of interviews. The types can change from year to year for each program, but one thing is consistent: Understanding the different interview types (and subtypes) gives you a big leg up in preparing.

1. INVITE ONLY. The first and most common among top programs is the "invite only" (Harvard, Stanford, Columbia, and Wharton all prefer this method). You must be invited to interview. The good news is that getting an invitation almost certainly means that the admissions committee has deemed you *worthy* of the school. Score! But the game's not over yet. Understanding that you're already considered worthy is the key to success in an invite-only interview. Don't go in with something to prove, or you'll look desperate or, worse, like you lack confidence. Instead, be yourself. They like you, they really do. The interview is about judging if you're a good fit for their MBA community.

In short, the interviewer is less interested in *what* your answers are than *how* you go about answering. Your interviewer is judging if you're articulate, how you respond to questions, whether you are someone he or she would like to get a beer with. Are you self-aware—can you answer difficult questions off-the-cuff because you know yourself, or do you stumble with answers because you haven't figured out the "right answer" yet? How do you behave when challenged? (Some interviewers deliberately ask questions they hope will make you uncomfortable, so they can see how you cope under pressure.)

Rarely, a committee may be so intrigued by your candidacy that, despite reservations, they want to take a good look at you up close and personal to see what you're all about. In this case, your interview is likely to be more focused on your goals, your background, and even your qualifications. It's even possible that you'll be asked about a "red flag" in your candidacy, such as a low GMAT or a disciplinary suspension in college. If you have a red flag in your candidacy—something you likely wrote about in an optional essay or had to describe if you answered yes to questions about whether you've been convicted of a crime or put on academic or disciplinary probation in school—make sure to practice your answers so you're comfortable. You don't want to break into a nervous sweat when such a question comes your way.

2. OPEN. The "open" interview is less common (favored currently by Kellogg, Tuck, Darden, and Duke). Anyone who asks can schedule an interview, though you may first have to jump through some kind of hoop, such as coming to campus or submitting part of your application (usually just the data forms, not the essays or recommendations). Open interviews are more likely to focus on the types of questions you'd expect, such as "What are your goals?" as opposed to the more probing and personal questions often found in invite-only interviews. They can happen before or after you submit your application; make sure you closely follow a school's procedure for signing up, and *act early*! Some schools have limited slots and they "sell out" quickly.

Open interviews are fantastic for candidates whose primary strengths are their interpersonal skills (for example, the kind of guy who would never get chosen for a blind date on the sole basis of his photo, but always seems to get the number of a girl he meets face-to-face at a party because he can dazzle her with his wit, confidence, or personal story). If you're worried that what you most bring to the table—such as raw personal leadership charisma—will not translate through the essays and/or recommendations, then your chances at an open-interview school might be better than an invite-only institution. The committee will have already gotten a glowing report about how fantastic you are from the interviewer before they even see your application, so they might be more favorably inclined to read "fabulous" into your entire candidacy.

This type of interview is also great for people with a black mark on their candidacy (that could be anything from a low GPA to bouncing around multiple jobs). You get to address the weakness head-on and exploit an opportunity to cut the knees out from under it before the committee has read your application—which could mean the difference between trashing it during the first round of cuts and deciding that there are other elements of your candidacy that inspire them to put aside the black mark.

Interview Styles

Now it gets even more complicated. Within these two types are three subtypes, each with its own caveats.

1. BLIND. "Blind" interviews are by far the most common subtype, among both "invite-only" and "open" types. The "blind" interviewer has only your résumé when the interview begins: He or she has not seen your application. If it's an invite-only interview, the interviewer knows you're well-qualified, but is also interested in your answers to questions such as "What are your goals?" because he or she doesn't already know them.

2. FULL MONTY. Extremely rare is what I call the "Full Monty" interview—wherein your interviewer has read your entire application and will ask you questions designed specifically for you, even following up on essays you've written. HBS loves this type. All my advice for the first two interview types applies to the Full Monty—the emphasis is on how you answer the follow-up questions, but you also get to address specific weaknesses or other issues knowing that the interviewer is already aware of your situation. While that sounds like the optimal situation, it can be the most grueling of all, because you truly have to worry about style *and* content.

3. BEHAVIORAL. Rarer still—in fact, MIT Sloan is the only top school that rigorously practices this, as well as Stanford to a lesser degree—is the "Behavior Event-Based Interview" (or BEI for short . . . leave it to MIT to create an acronym). Sloan's website describes in explicit detail what a

BEI is, what to expect, and how to prepare (they created another acronym for that—STAR, which stands for Situation Task Action Result). In short, Sloan is interested in how you articulate your behavior when faced with specific situations in the past. Sound familiar? That's because it's exactly the Auntie Evan way! This entire book should have prepared you to blow a BEI out of the water: Most significant, B-E specific! Don't say I didn't warn you.

What They're Likely to Ask

Now that the gruesome interview landscape has been laid, I'd be remiss to leave you without a sample of specific questions many schools ask (all of these were actually asked during interviews). The first batch of questions in particular is likely to crop up no matter what the interview type and subtype are.

Sample questions whose answers are inherently relevant:

- **What are your short-term and long-term career goals?**
- **How can an MBA help you to achieve your goals?**
- **How can our specific program help you to achieve your goals?**
- **Name a CEO you admire.**
- **What would a coworker say is another weakness of yours?**
- **What character trait is most responsible for your professional advancement?**
- **What will be your biggest challenge in business school?**
- **What project are you working on?**
- **What would you do if an MBA was not an option for you?**
- **Tell me about a conflict you recently experienced.**
- **Tell me about a leadership experience.**

Sample questions designed to ferret out how you think and articulate:

- Who are your best friends and how did you meet them?

- If I called your friends and asked them to tell me about one of your leadership weaknesses, what would they say?

- How do you make friends?

- Tell me a time when you helped someone to succeed?

- What three movies and books do you like?

- What would an organization you propose look like?

- How would you secure funding?

- What do you do for fun?

Just about every interviewer will ask you the first three questions in this list. Practice your answers only to whittle them down to a lean, sharp, tight two-minute max. If your interviewer wants more detail, let the interviewer follow up. Babbling on aimlessly about your professional goals, for example, is about the worst thing you can do. If you're truly passionate about your professional direction, you should be past babbling about it. One would assume you're comfortable (and practiced) enough talking about it that you've got your "elevator pitch" down. Don't memorize a prepared text, however—elevator pitches are just horrible when they're overly rehearsed. And when they ask you about "projects" or "conflicts" or other situations without requiring a specific context or environment, feel free to draw from personal, professional, or extracurricular arenas as you see fit.

If you've read this book from beginning to end and have taken the advice to heart, you're already prepared to answer these questions. The goals chapter taught you how to answer questions about why you want an MBA (answer in terms of the impact you want to have, not a job title or set of responsibilities) and why that certain school is a fit with you (your answers will be specific about courses, professors, and the type of learning community the school fosters). Questions about specific traits that help you lead is a topic I covered in the leadership essay (remember, talk about your leadership style, not the bottom line: It's details about "how you motivate people," not "what did you accomplish as a leader," that they want to hear from you).

Regarding the more intimidating questions, such as "How do you make friends?" and "Name three books you enjoyed," remember to be honest. Telling the truth, rather than packaging an answer to make you sound good, is much more compelling. Your face will light up if you talk about three books you really love, rather than struggling through canned answers about why Salman Rushdie is so brilliant. Show all sides of your personality in your answer: For the friends question, include a friend you made while young, a friend you made through an extracurricular, and a friend you made at work. Let them see how you operate in all these different settings. For questions about books and movies, leaders you admire, or other more topical issues, again give answers that show your range: from lowbrow to highbrow. Everyone loves hearing about a guilty pleasure, but they also want to see what kind of intellectual challenge engages you.

"Be yourself" is good advice for any school, no matter what its personality. Just as you should wear a suit to an interview at buttoned-up Tuck or laid-back Berkeley, you should let your own real personality shine through. Remember, schools are looking to build a diverse class; they want a rainbow of personalities, styles, and attitudes. As long as you show leadership, teamwork, community spirit, intellectual curiosity, clear goals, and confidence, you can't go wrong.

Baxter: From Nervous Nelly to Powerful Pro

I wasn't as shocked as Baxter was when he received word from HBS, Wharton, and Haas that he had been invited for interviews—it just goes to show you that it's not all about GMAT and GPA; I always thought Baxter was refreshingly wonderful—honest and forthcoming with all of his faults. It's perhaps why Uncle David and I got behind his candidacy despite the fact that he was gripped by a fear that, one year earlier, had caused him to miss his deadlines. There was something about the way he owned who he was—the good, the bad, and the ugly. He was the only one who couldn't see it.

Baxter, an entrepreneur in his mid-twenties who had once fancied himself a lawyer (so did the law school of the big state university he went to), a film producer, and an inventor of technology for seniors, could not break a 620 on his GMAT, and his GPA—a 3.1—was anything but remarkable. What he had going for him was a variety of successes, albeit not exactly in one particular industry. It had taken our dear Baxter some extra time to get it together with respect to his career. It's not the most unusual of circumstances—let's face it, it's not like Auntie Evan grew up thinking, "Hey, when I grow up I'm going to be an educational consultant!"

But Baxter had a little voice in his head with one constant concern about what people were thinking about him from the time we had met two years earlier: "You're unfocused, you're unfocused, you're unfocused," it screamed. So when he got word of the interviews, rather than being excited, he went into a panic. "Maybe before the interview, I could have my CFO send in a letter of support. He's Chinese." I swear that's what he said, followed by, "I know, I know! I can highlight the work I did on the budget for the design of the senior-targeted tech! No, I know, I know . . ." Halfway through his diatribe about his excellent organizational skills, I stopped him. Baxter's ADHD is only slightly more frenetic than my own. It takes one to know one, and I knew Baxter was in full-blown interview panic.

Note: Interview panic is a completely common occurrence. Don't freak out! You might be asking yourself, "Why am I freaking out? I don't have a background like Baxter's." The truth is everyone has a skeleton in his closet, including your admissions office interviewer. Just tell the truth. Don't be afraid to get all Oprah and reveal your inner demons.

The more Baxter tried to cover up his weaknesses, the worse it got. Smart people tell the truth, and the truth was that neither the startup company he worked at nor the University of Colorado had said yes to Baxter because of his mathematical aptitude. They hired/accepted him precisely because he was not another math genius. Baxter had other qualities—insight and creativity—and these were the strengths he needed to play up during the interview. There's only one way to do that.

When faced with obvious blemishes, the only thing to do is what I call "getting Oprah with it," and that is precisely what I told Baxter to do. He looked at me as if I had been drinking and asked, "You want me to go through my erratic career?" To which I said, "Yes, if asked, give them the fits, the starts, the everything."

His interview panic was so intense that, rather than jump for joy that he got an interview in one of the bloodiest admit years on record, where 770 GMAT Wall Street studs were being rejected left and right, all he could see himself as was a "screw-up." All he could focus on was every mistake in or blemish on his career. Nevermind that he had launched the first-ever safety cell phone for seniors, that he had produced two movies, that he had been accepted to top law schools, that he was over six feet tall and devastatingly handsome, or any of his other personal and professional achievements, Baxter was certain that the interview would be his downfall. Somehow, the interviewers at Harvard/Wharton/Wherever would unmask his deep dark secret: "Baxter is a phony!"

Sound familiar?

I got Baxter to think about every time he hired people to work on any movie or at a company that he had launched. I got him to remember how he had sat there all day long, one interviewee after the other, hoping against hope that everyone he ushered into his office would be "the one"—that individual who would be the answer to his prayers—the perfect fit, the one to get the job done, and of course, the one that would allow him to go home for the day.

The same is true for admissions officers. Imagine how many nos they have to wade through before they get a yes. Just like you when you were holding tryouts for the soccer team, football team, debate team, or cheer squad, or you were interviewing prospective interns for the bank, the concept is not that you are hoping that your three o' clock will be another letdown. Instead, each time somebody walks through the door, it is your hope that they're going to be an *answer* and no longer a *question*.

There were several unavoidable truths when it came to Baxter's candidacy. Yes, he had a 620 on the GMAT. True, his GPA was nothing to write home about. And it's true; his fifty-sixth percentile quantitative section was not a big selling point. But there was another truth. Despite the fact that he had gone from one career to another, in each one he was a star. In each one he was innovative, thought outside the box, and, in a sense, had scored the highest of marks. This was his selling point. And sell himself on this point is exactly what I coached him to do. However, in order to sell yourself on your strong suits, you must be willing to be *out loud and proud* about your weaknesses. They're going to find their way out of the closet at some point. They always do.

Baxter came out of his daze. It seemed to be making sense to him. Under his breath, he began to chant, "Be the answer not the question, be the answer not the question, be the answer not the question." Admittedly, I was a little worried.

Give them who you are. Do not try to sell someone on who you are not. If you suck at math, then you *suck* at math. Trying to hide it or work your way around it simply screams, "I suck at math . . . and at lying."

Baxter had his interview with HBS, and he realized (thank God not *too* late) that what got him to the interview in the first place was the same candidness with which he approached his essays. He had no lack of either courage or honesty, and his interviewer apparently found his willing honesty to be as refreshing as I did: Baxter interviews, he said, seemed "oddly long." It didn't seem odd to me—I wasn't even surprised when he got his acceptance letter to his school of choice.

You Are What You Wear

What you can most control is how you look. Yes, even you. It's not about whether you're a ten by the standards of *Allure* or *GQ*, it's about how

YOU present yourself. And we're talking about any contact you have with an admissions office. The equation is simple: you = a million bucks.

As Randall Sawyer, Cornell's director of admissions, said, "If you're not dressed as well as I am, you've blown it."

So let's get you dressed.

I know people have laughed at consultants who tell you what to wear. And I've talked to people who say khakis and a crisp-clean Ralph Lauren polo shirt is "fine." But as my mother used to say when my step-father told her she looked "fine" before they headed out to the club, "'Fine' is what other people do." Then she'd head back into her dressing room.

Why not look like a million bucks when you can? Unless you're wearing Brooks Brothers to the office—and not many twentysomethings do anymore—don't dress for an interview like you do for work. The point is not to show them how you look now, but to give a glimpse of how you'll look as a captain of industry.

It's not just the boys who slack on this one: I've known some women who think that Betsey Johnson is really hip and groovy, or who think vintage wear has some sort of romantic appeal. I don't care if Haas is on the Berkeley campus, you're not going to a protest march. I can only imagine the look on Peter Johnson's face when you roll up in your hemp wear.

In short, while expressing your own style, women should wear a smart, conservative suit with heels and light jewelry. If you are comfortable in a skirt, wear one. Men should wear a dark suit, no pinstripes, and a bold tie. Men should *not* wear the khakis/oxford uniform that is so acceptable at most offices today. I would also avoid sports jackets with khakis, even to Duke.

Don't say I didn't warn you.

CHAPTER 21

You've Been Waitlisted, or "We Love You, But . . ."

Getting waitlisted is a far cry from being accepted, but it's even farther from being rejected. Here's how to seal the deal for good.

You spent the last six months, not to mention the last six years, preparing to go to business school. Now it's December, you log on to check your application status, and staring you back in the face is the most perplexing of three possibilities: You were neither accepted nor rejected, but WAIT-LISTED! You just entered admissions limbo—the place where all great candidacies go to sit and wait for further judgment. Psychologically, it's almost worse than rejection: You don't know whether to pack your bags and plan your pre-MBA summer in Ibiza or play the waiting game. (Never play the waiting game, no matter what the waitlist letter says. Even when the waitlist notification letter says, "Don't call us, we'll call you.")

At least when you're rejected, it's like dealing with death: It is what it is, and you eventually come to some sense of acceptance about it. You get to heal, you get to dust yourself off, and you move on, in this case to the next school.

So what does being waitlisted signify? I see waitlisted candidates create all kinds of meanings for their waitlisted status. The most common—and most incorrect—is that they weren't good enough. And even if they were to get accepted from the waitlist, they think they're a second choice, an also-ran.

Here's the deal about waitlists: Being waitlisted means you were qualified and worthy. But there was one element that was lacking or in question. What that element is directly relates to how you get yourself off the waitlist. There's no one-size-fits-all recipe.

Actions You Can Take to Get Off the Waitlist

Waitlisted candidates can choose from a variety of actions designed to add some fire to their candidacy. Not all of these actions are appropriate for everybody. See the three profiles in the following sections to determine which of the following actions are right for you.

1. **UNDERSTAND YOUR WAITLIST STATUS. There are two kinds of waitlists. The opt-out waitlist means that a school automatically puts you on its waitlist unless you tell them to remove you. The opt-in waitlist requires that you accept a position on the list, usually within a certain time frame. Always accept a waitlist offer, even if you're not sure what you want to do. You can always withdraw later.**

2. **IMMEDIATELY ASK FOR AN APPLICATION REVIEW. Some MBA programs, like Cornell's Johnson School, will give you feedback as to why you were waitlisted. They may even make specific suggestions for how you can improve your chances of getting off the waitlist and into the incoming class. (I have known Columbia to ask people to raise their GMAT thirty points, for example, for automatic entry.) If your**

school offers reviews, the waitlist letter will say so. If it specifically tells you not to contact them, don't ask. If the school is unclear, or if you get an obviously personalized waitlist notification from a specific individual, feel free to ask for feedback.

3. WRITE AN UPDATE LETTER (see Anatomy of an Update Letter). You only write a single update letter—they don't need to be notified every time your boss says "good job." Submit your letter via email three

Anatomy of an Update Letter

On the most basic level, an update letter, not surprisingly, updates the committee on improvements to your candidacy since you submitted your original application. A more significant effect, however, is that it establishes a connection between you and the admissions committee. Here is a template for writing a powerful and effective letter.

PARAGRAPH 1. Thank them for putting you on their waitlist, and let them know you're excited that they are continuing to keep you in consideration for the matriculating MBA class.

PARAGRAPH 2. *Optional.* Let them know you will accept if given a spot in the class—even on the last day (I'll never forget Rabia, who was accepted to Columbia a day before classes began, or Jorja, from DC, who was in the car in her driveway about to head south toward UNC's Kenan-Flagler when she received the call that she was accepted to University of Chicago's Booth School of Business). Nothing feels better than knowing you're number one. If, and only if, it is your number one choice, let that specific MBA program know. Don't be shy! Few in admissions will admit to the following, but yield is everything. What is yield? That is the ratio of those who are accepted to those who say yes and actually go—and everyone in admissions may hate me for saying this, but yield is one of the top factors in a *U.S. News & World Report* school ranking, be it college or grad school.

PARAGRAPH 3. Update. This is all about the new and improved you: new to four weeks after getting waitlisted. If you were waitlisted as a first-round applicant, send your update letter in about four weeks before the second-round decision-announcement date, as many waitlisted first-round candidates are actively considered as second-round candidates as well.

4. GET A NEW RECOMMENDATION. Unless the school specifically asks that you do not send in a new recommendation, you'll want to take

skills gained, new lessons learned, new insights, and recent accomplishments. Give the schools an update on what you've learned, what you've accomplished, and what you now bring to the table since you applied. For example, if you implemented or helped close a recent IPO, let them know, and let them know the impact your newfound skills and experiences will have on specific courses or clubs at their school.

PARAGRAPH 4. New stats. Write about courses you've taken or are taking, and about the high grades you're receiving. Of course, if you've retaken the GMAT, break it down and tell them about your improved quantitative and/or verbal scores.

PARAGRAPH 5. Initiate a dialogue. Ask what you can do to bolster your candidacy. Seek their advice, and re-enroll them in your long-term goal and mission. Make them part of it, and find out what more you can do to make yourself a fit for their school.

PARAGRAPH 6. Put a face to the name. Let them know you're on your way. Find a reason to visit their school again, and ask to meet with them.

PARAGRAPH 7 OR NOTE. These final two paragraphs are what initiate a dialogue between you and the waitlist manager/admissions office, and let them know you will continue to be in contact—that you will follow up, and when. As in standard business correspondence, invite them to contact you if they have further questions, and provide all contact information right here (even if it's in your letterhead). And remember, this letter gets sent via email *and* snail mail.

this step. If you applied to a school that requires three recs, like Harvard and Stanford, you've already got a third rec "in the can" you could use for any school that originally required only two recs.

5.   GET LETTERS OF SUPPORT (see page 64). Now is when letters of support are most effective—an additional voice to weigh in now that the school has already judged you worthy.

6.   TAKE CLASSES. If your GPA is low, that probably factored heavily into why you weren't a clear admit. Immediately sign up for a couple of community college classes at night—and get As—to prove you've got the intellectual ability as well as the discipline to do well in a rigorous quantitative curriculum. The four best classes to choose from are any kind of accounting, microeconomics, calculus, or statistics.

7.   RETAKE THE GMAT. Let them know your plans in your update letter—including the date you intend to take the test—and send them the result in a "ping" email (described later). If you've already got a 700-plus GMAT, or at least an 80 percentile quant score, raising your score further won't likely help. If you were waitlisted with less than a 680 GMAT, raising it to at least 680 may dramatically increase your chances of getting off the waitlist. If you were waitlisted at a very competitive school with less than a 680 GMAT, chances are the school *really* liked you—they simply have concerns about your score. Raising that score removes the most likely reason you were waitlisted rather than accepted outright.

8.   VISIT THE CAMPUS AND VISIT AGAIN. No matter why you've been waitlisted, you should get yourself to campus ASAP. Ask to see an admissions officer; include this request in your update letter. Many schools will be happy to accommodate you; for the ones that won't, camp out in the admissions office and ambush someone. Seriously—that has worked for many of our candidates in the past! Tell them you were in town on business and you simply wanted to put a face to the name. Don't spend more than five minutes with an admission officer unless they invite you to stay longer.

9. **PING THE COMMITTEE.** Your first contact will be your update letter, and you'll continue to ping the committee after that with a brief note. Send a brief note to your waitlist manager (if you were assigned one) or to the director of admissions expressing your continued interest in the school, willingness to provide further information, or anything else you feel is appropriate. "Ping" emails should go out about once every three weeks. When decision time comes, it is your name they will remember.

Profile 1: We Think You're Worthy, but We Can't Remember Your Name

Jason had a 730 GMAT, had worked at McKinsey for two and a half years, and earned an economics degree cum laude from one of the Southern Ivies. He even hired an admissions coach to help him with his essays. He was stunned when a good friend was accepted to Tuck, while he was only waitlisted.

"Parker only had a 710 GMAT!" Jason wailed. "I don't get it. He went to the same school and had the same grades as me, and I beat him hands down in the GMAT department. What happened?"

While I was telling Jason the following for the first time, I hope you already know the answer: "It's not just your stats. Stats are one measure of your candidacy: how academically capable you are. In other words, can you do the work? Both of you could do the work, Jason. The decision didn't come down to your statistics."

I asked about Jason's extracurricular profile. And once again, Jason couldn't stop talking about Parker, the guy in the other lane. "I had just as many extracurriculars, if not more. We both volunteered for the same big-name nonprofit, and we both were fraternity leaders in college," he whined. "And we were both at top strategic consulting firms (but mine was even better)," he couldn't resist adding.

The way Jason kept talking about his friend clued me in to the most likely reason Jason got waitlisted—and I hadn't even read his essays yet.

Jason had made the classic swimmers' mistake I talked about at the beginning of this book: He was so busy keeping track of the guys in the lanes next to him that he lost focus on his own race. He was perpetually playing "catch up," wondering what everyone else was up to.

When I read Jason's essays, my suspicions were confirmed: He had played it safe. He focused on what he had done, instead of what specific action he took and character traits he drew on while doing it. He forgot—or never knew—that the essays are not where you prove your worth, but where you stand out from the crowd.

Jason's strong stats proved he could handle the rigorous Tuck curriculum, and his history of service, leadership, and achievement proved he was ready for a world-class MBA education. His résumé and stats had already proved his worthiness before an admissions officer read a single essay.

But by focusing on *what* he had done—which could be found elsewhere in the application—instead of *how he did it* (that is, his personal style and characteristics while in action), he gave the admissions committee nothing to remember him by. They had nothing to judge what he would look like as a member of the Tuck community. *How* does he achieve his objectives? *How* does he interact with others?

Jason's prescription for getting off the waitlist starts with an update letter. First and foremost, Jason needed to let the committee know that he's excited about Tuck and wants to attend. Next, he needed to explain how he's a perfect fit for the Tuck community. In doing so, he's letting the *school* know that *he* knows what makes their community unique: Tuck, for example, highly values collaboration, community service, active participation in the MBA community, and what one Tuck application reader once described to me as "soul."

If you're the Jason-type profile, your prescription for getting off the waitlist is all about doing what you didn't do the first time around: In the update letter, give them a strong sense of what you're like as a person, what you have to offer, and why you're a fit (see detailed description of what goes in an update letter mentioned previously). Most important, your update letter must be an injection of your personality, points of view, and sensibility. You have nothing to lose and everything to gain. By the way, Jason graduated with his best friend from Tuck.

Profile 2: We Love You So Much, but We're Not Sure If You'll Even Come

Another dirty little secret in the MBA admissions game is using the waitlist to increase yield. If a school wonders if you're actually going to come if accepted—heaven forbid Columbia, for example, thinks you're God's gift but fears they'll lose you to Harvard or Wharton—they may waitlist you to test your commitment to coming. For the admissions committee, it's a win-win situation. If you reject a position on the waitlist or withdraw from the waitlist, it doesn't count as a rejection. Conversely, if you lobby hard to get off the waitlist, especially if you write a compelling update letter that expresses a strong statement that you will come if accepted, including persuasive details about why you are a fit for the school, then you stand a great chance of converting the admissions committee's fear about your commitment level into the belief that their program is indeed your number one choice.

You're most likely in this category if your GPA and GMAT are above the school's averages, and no other part of your candidacy is noticeably weak. If you're asking yourself, "How did my friend get in when I didn't—I was the stronger candidate," then you might have scared the school off.

Profile 3: We're Madly in Love with You, but Your Stats Are Weak

This profile describes candidates whose GPA and/or GMAT are below average (sometimes far below average). Some schools, like Columbia and

Wharton, are known to offer a lucky few such candidates "conditional acceptance," meaning they accept you on the condition that you meet a certain metric, such as raising your GMAT thirty points or taking a community college calculus class and getting an A. Most applicants in this category, however, will be waitlisted. It's up to you to decide if you're going to improve your candidacy. If you know you've got a higher GMAT in you, start there. That may be all it takes. If you're like Drew, however, and you know you can't raise that score, you must take a more aggressive approach.

Close, but no cigar: Drew got waitlisted. He was like a really good lover with a really small . . . GMAT score. He had taken the test five times, and his best GMAT was so low I won't even print it (in the 500s). It doesn't matter why; there are many reasons why people don't score well on the GMAT. You may have a learning disability or learning difference (see Chapter 6), or perhaps you just plain don't do well on standardized tests due to nerves, whatever. In Drew's case, schools like Johnson at Cornell understood perfectly well that he was never going to *do well* on the GMAT. They needed some other indicator that he could excel in its rigorous mathematical curriculum: He had only taken a couple of quantitative courses in college and made Bs in both. What they told him outright was, "We really want someone like you in our community"— someone who has a clear, strong sense of who he is, an entrepreneurial mind-set, and a demonstrated ability to lead a team, as exemplified by his stellar essays, recommendations, and résumé. This is why he was not rejected but was instead waitlisted.

Drew's prescription for getting off the waitlist required proving he could do the work. Uncle David had him immediately sign up for two classes at Westport Community College. Drew, a history major, had already taken calculus and microeconomics, two of the four unofficial MBA prerequisites. The other two are statistics and accounting, so Drew signed up for Statistics and Probability and Financial Accounting.

By signing up for those two classes, Drew was going over and above what Randall Sawyer, Johnson's director of admissions, had asked Drew to do when he called to share the news that he had been placed on the waitlist. The only specific request Sawyer had was that Drew sign up for the online pre-MBA math course at MBAmath.com. But it was going over and above expectations, not just all these classes, that was truly the hallmark of our strategy for helping Drew get off the waitlist. One skill we helped Drew develop was "pressing the flesh." Drew wasn't exactly Mr. July, but any girl with half a brain would have snapped this boy up in a heartbeat. He had the kind of charisma, confidence, and character that got people's attention (in fact, he had infused all of these characteristics so well into his essays, that this was why he was waitlisted instead of rejected in the first place).

So Drew had the basic skills to show up at the admission committee's door and remind them of why they were in love with him in the first place. Drew was just nervous about being aggressive. He needed an Auntie Evan intervention, one in which I reminded him of how he had negotiated a groundbreaking trade agreement in his industry. Also-rans don't do that. Once we finally convinced him that being waitlisted wasn't just a stroke of luck but a true indicator of his business mastery and acumen (or as they say in investment banking, a BSD—big-swinging dick), he had the confidence to travel up to Cornell to keep them mindful of what they'd lose if they turned Drew down. Between his repeated campus visits, his update letters, and the perfect scores he got in his classes, Cornell finally offered what we saw as inevitable: a place in their community.

DON'T take no for an answer. Don't let laziness or pride stop you from doing whatever it takes to prove you've got the stuff successful MBA students are made of. And remember to play to your strengths: the elements of your candidacy that vaulted you into the waitlist to begin with. Remember, it could have been so much easier for the committee to reject you outright. The death of any candidate with Drew's profile is believing you weren't good enough. As Patricia Dowden of HBS once told me, "Somebody has to be in the bottom ten percent, and those people are sometimes the most likely to do the most amazing things with the rest of their careers." After all, if you can get into a top school despite having stats that are below average, you must be doing something right.

CHAPTER 22

Reapplications

Guacamole, Meet Lemon

There's an old saying that no is just the last word you hear right before yes. That's how we see it when even the best candidates receive a rejection letter from the school of their choice.

So, the answer was no. When the dust of despair settles, what follows may put your rejection letter into perspective:

I've been told no countless times. No, you cannot raise money for a nonprofit like CIS during an economic recession; no, you'll never get that inner-city kid's parents to agree to let him go away to college; no, you'll never get 40 twentysomethings to show up on summer Saturday mornings to mentor teens; no, you'll never sustain a business based on graduate educational consulting. It may have taken me a while, but I eventually got my yeses. So can you when it comes to a little thing like HBS or Booth MBA programs.

Everything Uncle David and I do operates through the lens of what we call the Forster-Thomas triangle—but it's nothing new, so like every other piece of advice in this book, please steal it, take it, call it—nay—make it your own. The sides of the triangle are simple but immutable: "It works for me. It works for you. It works for a community."

When any of these is not in the picture—the agreement, outcome, result, transformation, possibility, or whatever transcendental phrase you want to use—your desired goal will result in a big bust. In your case we're talking about getting into the b-school of your choice.

So, the first thing to do is pick yourself up, dust yourself off, and start reviewing what happened—which side of the triangle did you leave out, and what can you do to get the admissions committee to take a second look?

For practical guidance on how to achieve that, please consider the following profiles. Which is most like you? Once you determine that, follow the advice.

Profile 1: You Did Not Demonstrate Quantitative Proficiency

While you in no way have to be Fibonacci, it doesn't work for the school to have a member of the student body who cannot do the basic quantitative work. It doesn't work for the community. So if you had a low GMAT, low GPA, no quantitative coursework in college, and/or performed poorly in quantitative coursework, you need to prove you can do the work in the eight months or so that you have before reapplying.

No matter how many test-prep courses Lewis took, how many times he saw his private tutor, or how hard he studied, Lewis, a Morgan Stanley associate, simply could not get his GMAT over the 640 hump. By itself, this might not have been so bad. After all, we've helped plenty of 640s get accepted to top schools. That's why he came to us after he was rejected on his first go-around.

His GMAT was not the issue, nor was it his great 3.8 GPA as a literature major. Upon closer inspection during his initial candidacy assessment, the festering pimple was sitting right on the tip of his Cyrano-like nose: Lewis had placed out of the only quantitative course he was required to take, and without a strong GMAT score, there was simply no evidence that Lewis had the ability to take on the quantitative aspects of a rigorous MBA program.

So what did we have our boy do? Enroll in three tough quantitative classes: Statistics, Micro Economics, and Calculus for Accounting. The result? He worked his ass off and got two As and a B+, respectively. The proof was now in the pudding, as they say. Wharton, one of his two first-choice schools, recognized his dedication, saw that he was a value-add (it worked for them), was excited to get his reapp, and in 2009, sent Lewis his acceptance letter.

Profile 2: You Have Weak Leadership and a Lack of Substantial Extracurriculars

Winnie, a private equity analyst, had all the right stats—a 770 GMAT score, a 3.6 GPA in computer science from MIT, and recs from the top of the Apollo Management heap. So when Kellogg et al. said no, Winnie and her entire private equity superiors were stunned. I was not. A quick glance at her application and résumé revealed the glaring problem: no evidence of leadership.

Okay, so some of you are thinking, "At our analyst level, there's little or no opportunity (let alone time) to get a lead role on a deal or engagement." That's probably true, but as I have said about a billion times in this book, leadership is a state of mind—not something you have to be voted into or chosen for. While Winnie was an awesome number two, and could always be counted on to complete her work with precision, accuracy, and dedication, she simply did not do anything more than just that—her assigned work. And not because she was selfish or single minded, but because she waited to be led. She thought in terms of being of service to others, not in service to a cause. She also couldn't see that a cause could be right there in the workplace. For example, she could have done recruiting from her alma mater. A great functionary sees something that needs to get done—like the toilet paper is almost empty—but because it's not in her assigned role, she wonders when the attendant will refill it, rather than going to the supply room to get more.

So, when Winnie came to us wondering where her application was deficient—"One of my colleagues got in with a 700 GMAT!" she complained—I probed a little more about what her colleague was "known for" around the office. "While he does his job fine, he's always getting into other people's business."

"What does that mean?" I asked.

"He's always got a scheme for getting friends who are graduating college a job at the company. He annoys people to get better coffee in the break room."

"Was he successful with the coffee scheme?" I asked.

"Yes. He got a Krupps machine that made Starbucks one cup at a time and saved us a few cents."

"So basically you're saying he's someone—annoying or not—who creates change, gets involved, leads, and creates his own extracurricular activities?"

She got defensive. "I worked at a soup kitchen last Thanksgiving and volunteer every other weekend at New York Cares doing all kinds of projects. I even painted a classroom."

Winnie wasn't getting it. She was looking at extracurriculars as a box to check off. Her "annoying" coworker focused on creating change.

I set out to transform Winnie's idea of leadership and service. After working with her like I worked with Ned and Carl in chapters 1 and 2, we created an Extracurricular Action Plan wherein she became the volunteer lead for a new small-business consulting program. She ended up becoming one of the most annoying people her friends knew—demanding that everyone be on time for their meetings with mentees. While at first she focused on the organizational part of her role, with a little coaching she soon grew comfortable inspiring and motivating her mentors as well. And her essay about how she made an impact on an organization made MIT Sloan take a second look—and finally extend an invitation to attend.

Profile 3: You Told the Wrong Story

Lily was an associate from a bulge-bracket investment bank. She was also a dwarf. Despite her short stature, she had very high stats—in fact, they were some of the best I've ever seen. This economics major had not only a perfect 800 GMAT but also a 3.85 GPA from an Ivy League school to go with it. Still, she was denied acceptance to HBS. She wasn't even asked to interview. Her dwarfism even added an element of diversity. When she walked into my office, all she could say was, "How could they have missed me?"

In addition to her great stats, she had launched a women's networking group in her office, and she made sure to write all about it . . . again and again. So what was the problem?

After close examination of her essays, what she had never written about was that one small item: her size. At the risk of mixing metaphors, it was the elephant in the room. Here was someone who had overcome not only stereotyping but also a range of physical challenges—like being able to reach Z at the back of the file cabinet.

The point is that her dwarfism was a major factor in her development as a leader. She learned at a very young age how to get people to judge her based on her actions, not her appearance. Lily didn't like to talk about her dwarfism because she didn't want her identity to revolve around it—and that led to a major mistake in her candidacy: ignoring it altogether. To the admissions board, she was just another overachiever who didn't understand how she achieved. Her candidacy got lost amid all the other overachievers who think their accomplishments alone—rather than the high level of self-awareness that tends to create leaders of consequence—qualify them for admission to HBS.

By ignoring her dwarfism, she also had to ignore how dwarfism was the fuel to her fire. The depth of her denial shocked me. When I asked how her size contributed to her development as a leader, she said that if anything, it held her back. "I have had to work twice as hard to be taken seriously because I'm a dwarf," she said with more than a bit of bitterness.

I had to connect the dots for her. "So if you weren't a dwarf, you might not have worked twice as hard?" She didn't want to cop to that, but she had basically already admitted as much.

I know it's difficult to turn your perspective around when you've hewn tight to a particular point of view your whole life, but MBA essays are an excellent opportunity for you to see your life in a clear, fresh way. Once I caught Lily in her catch-22—I have to work harder because I'm a dwarf, but being a dwarf has nothing to do with why I work so hard—she finally accepted that the two were connected. And voilá, her whole life snapped into an entirely different focus.

We were able to help her craft a leadership essay that included details on the lessons her dwarfism had taught her about how to read people, how to inspire skeptics to trust her, and how to overcome challenges. It was a powerful essay that showed Lily as an evolved leader who turns weaknesses into strengths and knows how to change perceptions and expectations to succeed in any mission.

She got into HBS the second time around.

By the way, just because you don't have an elephant in the room doesn't mean you told the right story. I've had countless reapplicants come to me, and those who got what I was saying were successful: It's not enough to just regurgitate your good deeds, your great grades, and your successful professional achievements. We need to see what makes you *you*. What defined you growing up? What drives you? What are you trying to prove or disprove? What have you learned about yourself? How do you see the world?

It's not just what you've done, it's how you took it on. It's how you got yourself to the point of being successful in the face of a challenge. Not to mention, your ability to see it.

Profile 4: You Chose the Wrong Recommenders

If your stats are above average, the first place I look for a candidacy to have gone off the rails is through a bad choice of recommender: someone who doesn't know the applicant that well but who has a high title, an important name, or a close connection to a particular MBA program. Read Chapter 6 on choosing recommenders to see whether you might have made one of these classic mistakes. The chapter will also help you manage your new recommendation(s) for the reapplication. Many schools allow you to use the same recommenders as the previous application, but you should *always* ask your recommenders to update the rec.

Profile 5: You Didn't Differentiate Yourself (You Played It Safe)

Ms. Wang was flawless. When she entered my office in her jungle red Tahari suit, I sat up. Ms. Wang was the epitome of perfection. However, the suit exploded into my office in a way that her dejected demeanor did not—despite her top GPA, prestigious Wall Street investment banking position, and her 760 GMAT. "How did my friend Liz get accepted with a 700 when I did not?" she groaned.

It was like two ends of a color spectrum. On the one end, jungle red just entered the office in a well-tailored Tahari suit, but the attitude was all Filene's muted earth tones off the rack. She sat there, quietly, with Asian demure as I perused her essays. They were grammatically impeccable, clearly a result of a stint at Miss Porter's School for Girls with a side order of Vanderbilt. Her essays were like Christie Brinkley's flawless beauty when they should have been Lauren Bacall's gap-tooth smile: While the former may be perfect, the latter was distinctive and unforgettable. I had heard some version of her leadership story a thousand times. She had stepped up at the last minute and brought a deal to a successful close, when both her VP and her managing director were preoccupied with saving their jobs during the 2008 implosion of Wall Street. Yada, yada, yada. And her failure essay? During another transaction, she stood by silently while members of her team committed error after error. Her failure was saying nothing, trusting their experience, and ignoring her own instincts to pipe up and set everything right. Blah, blah, blah.

Those are two of the oldest stories in the book. If I wanted to create the Stepford candidate, those would be the stories I'd tell. She had the common yet mistaken idea that the most attractive candidate is the one whose paradigm meets all expectations: Like a math equation, one part "step up where I save the day," plus one part "inspire team members," equals one successful deal. Yawn. Instead of creating the ideal candidate, she had sewn together a Franken-candidate. It was no surprise that she hadn't been accepted. Even though her qualifications were superior to many accepted candidates, in the bigger picture her candidacy was like disappearing ink: completely invisible until you rub lemon on it. But she had forgotten the lemon. "Lemon juice" is that element of your candidacy that's memorable. Avocado may be nice and smooth, but without a squeeze of lemon and a dash of salt, it just doesn't have that Oliver twist—"Please, sir, I want some more!"

Unlike Sarah, who admitted fully in her leadership essay that the way she got the predominantly male team on board with her project included a sprinkle of flaunt and flirt, or Mohammed, who, in an essay about a defining leadership moment in his life, told the story about a time in high school when he had to either do what was right—stand up for his socially ostracized best friend—or take the easy way out. In the first draft of the essay, Mohammed left out the detail that he actually considered betraying his friend. He wanted to jump straight to doing the right thing and navigating the rest of the school out of this crisis. It was only when he admitted that he was tempted by the easy way out that he became remarkable for doing the right thing. Guacamole, meet lemon.

The Lesson

This time around—in your reapplication—don't use your essays to tell the admissions committee what you think they want to hear. I've said this over and over again, but nowhere is it more important than in the reapplication of a well-qualified candidate who still didn't get in—take risks, face your fears, and write what you're really thinking and what you really went through. As my friend and colleague Ms. Blanton, a former Dartmouth admissions staffer, says about getting in: "It's all in the strengths and the edges. The worst thing you can get written on your application is the letters LMO: like many others." After all, you've already lost once doing it *your* way. Now, you have *nothing* to lose and everything to gain.

Epilogue
The Joke's on You

There's another story I've told many times about a different guy (not Harry from the Prologue) who also wanted to get into private equity. Only in this case, it was a little more noble than "$40 million by forty." His goal was investing in medical devices as an alternative to drug therapy, and he simply wasn't going to take no for an answer. Like Harry, Julian thought he had to get into a top-ten business school to make that happen. Unfortunately, all of the top-ten business schools said no to his membership in their elite club. We did everything to make certain that Julian looked at more than just a list of top tens, but also applied to schools that would be a good fit personally, professionally, and with his goals. After all that's really the Triple Crown.

Cut to several years later, upon completion of the final chapter of this book. It's April 2009, and after a year of plunging markets and the demise of countless hedge funds and the unceremonious farewell to Lehman Brothers, the phone rang in our offices in Manhattan. I could hear Katie, our office manager/client flirt machine, jibber-jabbing on the phone, repeating, "That's great news." We were well into our next season. Which one of our handsome young candidates (male or female) was it this time?

She yawned and handed me the portable phone. "It's just one of your old candidates, and you need to talk fast." She yawned even bigger. "He's in the middle of saving the planet."

I took the caller off hold. It was Julian, now a principal at a prestigious medical-device private equity company. We hadn't chatted since his graduation from b-school. It was great to hear from him. He wasn't necessarily saving the planet yet, but he was clearly on his way. He began to tell me about his life since graduating from business school.

Back in the day, when Julian began talking about medical devices, few people had imagined them as more than simple tools such as blood sugar meters and stents to hold open vessels during surgery. But Julian had a grander vision, which helped drive his application to business school. Since we had last spoken, he had managed to make his way into the medical-device company of his dreams and was poised to deliver devices with actual therapeutic and curative abilities. Clearly, he had not given up. And clearly, he did not need a top-ten business school to help him get there. In fact, Georgetown's McDonough School of Business had served him well.

To be sure, Julian wasn't happy about being rejected by his number one top-ten choice (Columbia), and to be fair to Columbia and its admits that year, his GMAT didn't quite stack up. He came close—very close—but was on the waitlist till the very last minute and didn't get in. What did stack up was his drive. But I'll get to that later. Uncle David and I cheered as he sent his deposit in to Georgetown. We knew something he, like so many of you, couldn't conceive of—that a good business school is only a good business school. Neither Harvard nor Columbia nor Kellogg can ensure that there's going to be a bridge waiting for you when you get to the Red Sea. You have to make the Red Sea part on your own. Your future ultimately depends on you, not which school you go to.

In the summer after Julian's first year at McDonough, the strangest thing happened, although it didn't seem strange to us. He landed an internship at the medical-device private equity firm he wanted—he was the first-draft recruit. Couldn't have done better if he'd gone to HBS.

Go ahead people, roll your eyes. But there are plenty of HBS graduates who are still sitting in mid-level jobs, dragging themselves from one glad-handing event to another, and they're not getting any younger or closer to their goals. As one HBS admissions officer told me off the record, "It's great to go to Harvard, but you still have to *bring it*."

So for those of you who have now read this book and still think you have to go to Harvard, Stanford, or Kellogg and *that's* how you'll change the planet—the joke is on you. On that April day when Julian called to catch up, his voice was more alive than ever. "I couldn't have done it without you," he said.

That's where he was wrong. Julian couldn't have done it without *Julian*. He didn't need me. He clearly didn't need Harvard or Columbia, he also didn't *really* need Georgetown. He just needed Julian, and the singular belief in himself—that he will reach his goals no matter what. And if you don't, you will surely end up like "$40 million by forty" Harry. Maybe not now, but at some point in your life.

The moral of the story: There are many great MBA programs that are invisible to those of you for whom always making top ten in every aspect of your life is what defines who you are. *What truly defines who you are* is the way you live your life in every minute of the day. And in the case of business school admissions, *actually going* to business school, and then your career, it had better be as a leader hell-bent on making a difference. Not so that you can get into HBS but so that you can create a tectonic plate shift somewhere on the planet, be it in your country, your industry, or even in your family. Because the goal of this book never was, never has been, and never will be to ensure your place at a top ten. The goal, I would like to hope, is assuredly the goal of many who have gone unnamed in the pursuit of making this whole thing a better place for all of us. I'm pretty sure the top MBA programs in the world want the same thing.

Oops, sorry if I tricked you.

Be bold. Take risks. Be willing to fall down in public.

I love you,
Auntie Evan

Workbook 1:
Taking Your Inventory

PERSONAL INVENTORY

Name
_____

Age
_____

Nationality
_____

Residence
_____

Geographic limitations (if any)
_____

Schools of choice (as of now)
_____

PROFESSIONAL INVENTORY

Years in workforce
_____

Years at current job
_____

Title
_____

Promotions
_____

Other jobs
_____

NOTABLE PROJECT/TRANSACTION LIST

Leadership roles (formal)
_____

Leadership roles (informal)
_____

ACADEMIC INVENTORY

University
_____

Degree
_____

Major
_____

(Category: business, economics, sciences, social sciences/humanities, engineering)

_____

Certifications _____

Honors and awards _____

Scholarships _____

Do you have a diagnosed learning difference? If so, describe:

_____

_____

EXTRACURRICULARS IN COLLEGE

(Note leadership roles, and if tapped or elected)

_____

_____

YOUR STATS

GMAT _____

GMAT % _____

Quant % _____

Verbal % _____

AWA _____

GPA _____

IN MAJOR

Quant GPA _____

Verbal GPA _____

List any F's, W's, or I's on your transcript

_____

_____

_____

BRIEFLY DESCRIBE YOUR EXTRACURRICULARS SINCE COLLEGE
(Note leadership roles, duration)

_____

_____

_____

Nontraditional Extracurriculars (Note leadership roles, duration)

_____

_____

_____

Extracurriculars in Past Year

_____

_____

_____

Workplace Extracurriculars

_____

_____

SPORTS (If not listed already)

_____

_____

HOBBIES

_____

_____

Workbook 2:
Your Family Inventory

FAMILY BACKGROUND

(For each family member, list living/deceased, profession, age, academic status, etc.)

Father _____

_____

Mother _____

_____

Siblings _____

_____

_____

For each family member, please describe in one sentence what you find most valuable about your relationship. What story comes to mind that you would tell about them? _____

_____

_____

_____

_____

Where did you grow up? _____

What were your favorite activities/interests _____

    As a child? _____

    As a teen? _____

    As an adult? _____

What three adjectives would your family use to describe you?

_____

_____

_____

What three adjectives would your friends use to describe you?

_____

_____

_____

Consider your answers to the above two questions. How different are they? If very, what factors influence why your friends and family perceive you so differently?

_____

_____

_____

_____

What's the best thing your parents would say about you?

_____

_____

What's the most embarrassing thing?

_____

_____

Your turn: What are the best/worst things you could say about them?

_____

_____

Workbook 3:
The Hard Questions

List three professional strengths.

_____

_____

_____

List three professional weaknesses.

_____

_____

_____

List three personal strengths.

_____

_____

_____

List three personal weaknesses.

_____

_____

_____

List three professional/academic development needs.

_____

_____

_____

What three adjectives would others use to describe you?

_____

_____

_____

Defining moments in your history (personal), and what did you learn?

_____

_____

_____

Defining moments in your history (professional), and what did you learn?

_____

_____

_____

Defining moments in your history (social), and what did you learn?

_____

_____

_____

What are you most passionate about? (e.g., Boston Red Sox, world peace, Kurt Cobain)

_____

_____

What are your three guiltiest pleasures? (e.g., watching _Charmed_, drinking wine coolers . . . Something fun, innocent, yet embarrassing)

_____

_____

_____

Describe your spirituality. How much of this is inherited from your family?

_____

_____

_____

If you have a favorite quote/saying, what is it?

_____

_____

What are your three favorite movies?

_____

_____

_____

What are your three favorite books?

_____

_____

_____

Which crowd did you hang out with in high school?

_____

What responsibilities and/or aspects do you love most about your current job?

_____

What responsibilities and/or aspects do you like least about your current job?

_____

What code do you live by (think morals, values, ethics)?

_____

Please list where you have created/plan to create change or transformation at work, in your community, in an organization, in your personal life, or anywhere: _____

_____

_____

    In the past: _____

    Currently: _____

    In the future: _____

What's the most embarrassing moment you're willing to talk about in public? _____

_____

_____

_____

What has been the most difficult time in your life and what did you learn from it? _____

_____

_____

_____

_____

What are you worried about most with respect to your candidacy? (Besides getting in) _____

_____

_____

_____

_____

If you could do whatever you want with your life professionally, what would it be? (e.g., running a sleepaway camp, fashion design, being MLB commissioner, produce movies)

_____

_____

_____

_____

_____

_____

Ever notice that people tend to help you when you level with them? Like that time when you, say, actually admitted to your hard-nosed supervisor that you were nervous about presenting before the board of directors, and she unexpectedly sat down with you after hours to help you polish your presentation? Or that time you admitted to that beautiful French girl on the streets of Lyon that you had no idea how to get back to your hotel—and suddenly you received a full-on tour of the entire city?

News flash! Admissions officers are people too. The truth is universal, and when you reveal it, people tend to get on board with whatever you are doing—your goals, your needs, even your desire to get an MBA. What is at the core of your truth is also at the core of an admissions officer's truth. In you, they see themselves. And they want to help.

Tell them the truth, get them on board with your personal mission, and they will want to help you get into their school. Is it that simple? No, but the truth will not only set you free, it will give you an edge. Shore up all the edges and eventually you'll secure your place on the inside of a top MBA program.

Do you really know what you want to be doing with your life ten years from now? Very few people can talk precisely and passionately about their long-term hopes and dreams—and even fewer dare to dream with real conviction or clarity.

The same can't be said for most ten-year-olds: They're going to be a fireman, an astronaut, president of the United States, the guy who invents the transporter beam!

When approaching the goals essay, get in touch with your inner ten-year-old. Admissions officers are asking this question more to gauge your "belief in self" and "capacity for vision" than to sit in judgment of your aspirations.

In other words, what you write about isn't a contract you're signing with a school: It's okay if you don't know exactly what you want to do.

What is important is that you think in terms of how you will make an impact somehow, not what job title you want. Also, to write compellingly, your professional goals should seem connected to your personal interests.

So before you start your goals essay, consider the following:

- **Spend quite a bit of time just thinking about your life with friends and family. Kick back with a pen, a pad, and a cocktail and go through your history from day one to the present.**

- **Connect the dots: What defining moments led you to your first after-school job, your choice of college and college major, your first post-graduation career move?**

- **When looked at together, how do your experiences start to form a narrative you can extend to your future aspirations?**

We will talk about how to integrate these ideas into an actual essay, but the origin of all goals concepts can be broken into two broad categories:

- **THE LEMONADE STAND: "Since my first lemonade stand, I've always . . ."**

- **THE EPIPHANY: "Last month, on this deal, I had the wildest realization . . ."**

GOAL IDEA 1: "The Obvious"
Moving to the next level in your current professional track

The backstory

_____

_____

_____

_____

_____

The long-term professional goal

_____

_____

_____

_____

GOAL IDEA 2: "Career Transformation"

You were in finance; now you want to be a retail magnate.

The backstory

_____

_____

_____

_____

The long-term professional goal

_____

_____

_____

_____

GOAL IDEA 3: "Dream Job"

What do you daydream about, yet don't give yourself permission to do?

The backstory

_____

_____

_____

_____

The long-term professional goal

_____

_____

_____

_____

Workbook 5:
The Impact/Leadership Essay

Leadership is the "it" concept of business school today. B-schools are most specifically looking for candidates with demonstrated leadership potential, however: They understand that most applicants are too young to have had opportunities to truly test and refine their leadership abilities.

For the purposes of this essay, let's draw a sharp contrast between "management" and "leadership": the former is a low-level skill that involves stewarding processes (doing things like calling meetings, writing memos, creating spreadsheets); the latter is people-oriented (up-managing supervisors, enrolling peers in your vision, communicating ideas and changing attitudes). When it comes to writing, if you're focusing on what you did, you're emphasizing management; if you're focusing on how you interacted with people to create change, you're emphasizing leadership. General rules when brainstorming ideas:

- **Draw from job, extracurricular, and even personal experiences.**
- **You don't have to have a formal leadership position.**
- **If job-related, must go over and above normal responsibilities.**
- **Try to stick to examples in the recent past.**

LEADERSHIP IDEA 1: You made an impact as the actual leader of a team, group, or project.

What did you learn about leadership through this experience? _____

_____

_____

_____

_____

_____

LEADERSHIP IDEA 2: You had to assume a leadership position without formal authority.

What did you learn about leadership through this experience?

_____

_____

_____

_____

_____

_____

LEADERSHIP IDEA 3: You had to lead change in an individual or group during crisis.

What did you learn about leadership through this experience?

_____

_____

_____

_____

_____

_____

Workbook 6:
The Accomplishments Essay

While all good leadership essays include an accomplishment (the impact you had), accomplishments in and of themselves do not require the involvement of other people: You could do it on your own, but you don't *have* to.

Accomplishments (also called "achievements") fall into three categories: personal, professional, and extracurricular. A personal achievement could be attaining financial independence; a professional accomplishment could be working after hours, unasked, to write the first training manual for new interns; an extracurricular achievement could be creating a personal-finance training workshop for new owners of Habitat for Humanity homes.

Accomplishments must include the following elements:

- **A clear obstacle**

- **The risk you took (to your reputation/ego/career/relationship)**

- **Description of event before you stepped in (point A), how everything turned out (point B), and most important, *how you got from point A to point B***

- **The effect the accomplishment had on yourself or others**

ACCOMPLISHMENT 1: A "first" or a "best" (first in family to go to college; best analyst in class)

_____

_____

_____

_____

_____

_____

ACCOMPLISHMENT 2: A personal achievement

_____

_____

_____

_____

_____

_____

ACCOMPLISHMENT 3: A professional achievement (going over and above your job description)

_____

_____

_____

_____

_____

_____

ACCOMPLISHMENT 4: An extracurricular achievement

_____

_____

_____

_____

_____

_____

Workbook 7:
The Background/Diversity Essay

What makes you unique? That question is a potential minefield for so many reasons. Most people who truly believe they are unique come off as naïve, sheltered, provincial, or all of the above. We instinctively define ourselves by the most memorable or unusual experiences in our lives, especially when no one else we know can relate to such moments.

However, keep in mind that an admissions officer who reads ten thousand applications a year has, as they say, "seen it all." You're not the only child of divorce, or victim of stalking, or Rwandan refugee, or suburban kid whose world was shattered by a move to the inner city.

What makes you unique—what you bring to the table as a member of an MBA community—is not defined by your "greatest hits" collection of experiences, but rather by how all these experiences have uniquely shaped your perspective on life, your insight into your own and others' behavior, and your role in a team, your community, and the world.

In that light, the biggest mistake MBA candidates make when writing about their background or "uniqueness" is focusing on *what* they have done or *what* they have experienced. Instead, choose a few defining moments in your personal history and describe how each one has added value to you in some way. If you can communicate that, you'll find it much easier to demonstrate how you can add value to your MBA community.

This is a popular question because b-schools truly value diversity—and their definition goes far beyond demographics. They want to assemble an MBA class with diversity of experiences, opinions, perspectives, beliefs, academics, interests, and professions. Two white male bankers may seem similar, but when you factor in that one was a history major at a small liberal-arts school while the other was a statistics major at a large state university, their potential for bringing very different worldviews to the table becomes immediately obvious.

This essay can give you candidacy a considerable edge if you thoughtfully articulate—using specific examples from your personal history—the kind of classmate you will be.

- **Which student organizations will you join, and what role has your background prepared you to play in them? As president of your fraternity, you're eager to take a leadership role in a social-service group, but as a banker who wants to learn marketing, you'll be a good foot soldier in that group, eager to soak up more-experienced classmates' wisdom.**

- **Given your personal, academic, and professional background, what can you contribute to class discussions?**

- **In what ways are you suited to support your classmates, and which kind of classmates will benefit most from your particular skill sets and strengths? How will you avail yourself?**

- **Describe how your personality and interests make you a "fit" for the school, in light of its learning environment, mission, and your firsthand research.**

BACKGROUND 1: What are your three most defining moments?

_____

_____

_____

_____

BACKGROUND 2: What picture does your extracurricular activities paint about your interests, perspectives, and commitment to others?

_____

_____

_____

_____

Workbook 8:
The Failure Essay

Business schools are looking for visionaries and leaders, not functionaries. A good leader is someone who understands himself. This means he is not only able to spot and champion his own strengths, but he can also recognize his mistakes, admit to them—and grow from them.

Rule of thumb: If you think of a story you've never told anyone, you probably have a powerful essay in the making. "Almost" failures—where you managed to save everything at the last minute—is the worst mistake you can make. If Humpty Dumpty could have been put back together again, then leaving him on the wall was an "almost" failure.

And that's what makes this essay so difficult. You must be willing to discuss something that will not make you look good—at least not in the short term. It will, however, reveal your ability to have insight about yourself. To know who you are. And the more you know about yourself, the better equipped you are to lead a team, a company, a country.

So, a failure essay is an opportunity to express how clearly you see the world around you and how your actions have consequences. In short, a good failure essay proves that you are in a constant state of evolution, nimbly responding to the unexpected and moving forward instead of breaking down.

Other things to consider:

- **In team failures, make sure you own your share of the blame: Don't point fingers.**

- **The failure can be part of a process, rather than the end result.**

- **Don't dance around your mistakes: Be direct and quantify when appropriate.**

- **When stating what you learned, go one or two steps beyond the obvious—show sophistication in your insights, and give a brief example of how you acted differently when confronted with a similar situation later.**

FAILURE 1: A failure you did not see coming until it was too late.

_____

_____

_____

_____

_____

FAILURE 2: A failure you saw coming but did not act to prevent because of fear or inertia.

_____

_____

_____

_____

FAILURE 3: Someone else's failure you could have helped prevent, thus becoming an accomplice.

_____

_____

_____

_____

_____

Workbook 9:
The Ethical Dilemma Essay

Please, if you learn only one thing through this workbook, let it be the following: Essays that include the words "ethics," "values," or "beliefs" are not trick questions designed to test your moral code. Still, they are trick questions in a sense: They are sly ways of asking how you go about solving problems.

When thinking of stories for ethical dilemma essays, you should immediately discard ideas where there is a clear difference between right and wrong: If the choice you should make seems obvious, then it's not a good story, even if that choice is actually very difficult to make. For example, your boss tells you to fudge numbers in a report; you know it's wrong, but if you disobey, you could be fired—and lose your house. This is a bummer, but not an ethical dilemma, because you never question whether fudging numbers is actually the *right* thing to do.

A good ethical dilemma is when you have to choose between *right* and *right* (or sometimes between wrong and wrong). When stuck between a rock and a hard place, how do you go about extricating yourself?

A common mistake is devoting too many words to the nature of the dilemma rather than the thought process you underwent to come to a resolution. Consider this structure:

- **Devote the first 25 percent of the essay to describing the situation. End with a clear statement of the two values that are in conflict (or how one value has made you question another).**

- **Split the next 50 percent of the essay weighing the pros and cons of each choice.**

- **End with how you came to your decision and what the outcome was.**

ETHICAL DILEMMA 1: Two long-held beliefs come into conflict (e.g., keeping a promise vs. getting help for a friend who pledged you to secrecy)

_____

_____

_____

_____

_____

_____

_____

_____

ETHICAL DILEMMA 2: A core belief contradicts an untested belief (e.g., you never talk back to your elders yet your grandfather makes a racist comment)

_____

_____

_____

_____

_____

_____

_____

_____

Glossary of Auntie Evan-isms

You're only in competition with yourself.

Leadership is something you create, something you take hold of, something you're entitled to—not something you're granted.

Leaders aren't worried about résumés. They're worried about results.

Don't confuse sexy players with sexy essays.

When you're committed, you're passionate, and when you're passionate, you're transformational.

Create your own mandate and from that, authority will be created in you.

If you don't know *how* you succeed, that makes your success accidental instead of intentional.

If one of your alternatives is dressed in white and the other in black, you've got a melodrama—and the situation you are put in is called a "bummer," not a dilemma.

Being a White Boy is a mind-set, a way of life. Not to be confused with "enlightenment," it's something called "entitlement."

Claim more than your share of White Boyness, and you risk crossing the line from "person who has the strength, awareness, and resources to get things done" to "person who thinks all things should be done his way."

You don't get some credit for winning if you're not willing to take credit for losing.

on recommendations, 71
on support letters, 64
Diarte-Edwards, Caroline (INSEAD)
  on extracurriculars, 31
  on recommendations, 76, 77
Dilemmas, 156–66
Divergent thinking, 84
Dowden, Patty
  on bottom ten percent, 264
  on transformation, 4
Duke University (Fuqua), 33, 73

EAP. *See* Extracurricular Action Plan
Educational consultant
  IECA and, 73
  vs. interview consultant, 205–6, 212
  on well-rounded class, 187
Ego, vs. mission, 24–26
Embracing who you are, 85–86, 183–84, 189–87
Entitlement, 172
Entrepreneurial mind-set essay
  details and, 152
  example, 153–55
  lesson, 153
  overview of, 149–50
  process dissection in, 150, 154
Erin Brockovich (movie), 160
Essay(s)
  accomplishments, 120–35
  admissions process and, 16–17
  background, 182–90
  career goals, 91–119
  by committee-no!, 93, 99–100
  creative/slide show, 217–22
  culture shock, 223–29
  ethical dilemma, 156–66
  failure, 167–81
  general advise on, 89–90
  impact/opportunity, 149–55
  leadership, 136–48
  open, 201–4
  optional, 230–39

passion, 198–201
purpose of, 17
random topic, 192–97
résumés vs., 132–33
structure, 102–5
tight parameters and, 218–19
what matters most, 205–16
Whimsical, 191–204
Ethical dilemma essay, 156–66
  bottom line of, 160
  bummer or dilemma?, 157–59
  example, 164–66
  HBS and, 164
  lesson, 163–64
  purpose of, 157–60
  values choice in, 158–60
Exceptions to the rule, 17–18
Excuses, 28, 234–35
Experience
  2+2 program and, 13
  admissions process and, 16
  candidacy and, 12–14
  expectations surrounding, 14
  professional background and, 13–14
  purpose of, 12–13
  recommenders', 60, 62–63
Extracurricular Action Plan (EAP), 23, 268
Extracurriculars, 27–42
  admissions directors on, 30–35
  application and, 30
  choose something you care about step, 45–46, 48
  Clarke on, 34
  commitment and, 28, 29–30, 35–37
  Diarte-Edwards on, 31
  don'ts of, 31
  equation of, 29
  excuses regarding, 28
  Hargrove on, 33
  isolate "so what!" step, 46, 48

Panic, interview, 250
Passion,
    essay, 198–201
    in extracurriculars, 43–49
    goals essay and, 100–104, 105–8,
        108–13
    leadership and, 43
    lessons on, 108, 118–19, 199–200
Passion essay, 198–201
    example, 200–201
    lesson on, 199–200
Peeling onion back, 211–12
Peer recommenders, 53
Personal accomplishments essay,
    130–35
    best qualities included in, 131–32
    example, 135
    lesson regarding, 134–35
    nature of, 130–31
    résumé vs., 132–33
    should and, 131, 133
    subjects to avoid, 131, 132
Phelps, Michael, 20
Ping email, 258, 259
Platitudes, 69–70
PowerPoint. *See* Slideshow essay
Pratt, Anika Davis (NYU), 30
Primary recommenders, 52–53
Primer, telecom industry, 123–24
Process management, 139
Professional accomplishments, 122–25
    contribution and, 122
    essay, 125
    lesson on, 124–25

Questions, interview
    intimidating, 249
    preparing for, 248–49
    sample, 247–48
Quinlan, Sue, 81
Quiz, Wall Street myth, 34

Random topic essay, 192–97
    example, 196–97

example questions for, 192, 195
    lesson on, 195
Reading, 79
Reapplications
    differentiate yourself, 271–73
    Forster-Thomas triangle and,
        266
    lesson on, 273
    overview of, 265–66
    profiles of, 266–73
    quantitative proficiency and,
        266–67
    weak leadership/extracurriculars
        and, 267–69
    wrong recommenders, 271
    wrong story told, 269–70
Recommendations
    ABCs of, 51
    admissions directors on, 70–77
    anecdotes in, 70–72, 74
    choosing recommenders and,
        52–54, 271
    Clarke on, 74
    Cutler on, 52, 75
    DelMonico on, 71
    Diarte-Edwards on, 76
    Garcia on, 70
    Hargrove on, 73
    illustrated, 69–72
    involvement in, 51–52
    Johnson, Peter, on, 72
    killers of, 57–59, 76
    vs. letters of support, 64
    Mabley on, 52
    Meehan on, 73
    overview of, 50–52
    platitudes in, 69–70
    seeing, 62–63, 65
    Shores on, 76
    talking points for, 54–57, 59
    waitlist and, 257–58
    waiver, 62
    Wilson on, 77
    writing your own, 61–62

Recommenders
  alma mater, 66–68
  to avoid, 65–68
  bullshit weakness given by, 57–58
  choosing, 52–54, 65–68
  cutting-and-pasting by, 59
  experience of, 60, 62–63
  family, 55
  making it easy for, 61
  from nonprofits, 63
  options for different professions,
    54–55
  peer, 53
  prepping/meeting with, 59–61, 71, 72
  primary, 52–53
  reapplication and, 271
  relationship to you, 57, 65–66
  secondary, 53, 54–55
  seeing what's written by, 62–63, 65
  status regarding, 65–66
  talking points for, 54–57, 59
  tech oriented, 63, 65
  track record of, 62–63
  weakness/growth opportunity
    and, 58
Rejection
  differentiate yourself, 271–73
  Forster-Thomas triangle and, 266
  lesson on, 273
  overview regarding, 265–66
  profiles of, 266–73
  quantitative proficiency and,
    266–67
  weak leadership/extracurriculars
    and, 267–69
  wrong recommenders, 271
  wrong story told, 269–70
Research checklist, 112–15
Résumés , essays vs., 132–33
Roberts, Julia, 160

Sawyer, Randall (Cornell)
  on cutting-and-pasting talking
    points, 59

  on extracurriculars, 33, 40
  on interview clothing, 253
  on recommender/applicant
    relationship, 66
School guide, 112
Secondary recommenders, 53,
  54–55
Self-awareness, 168
Service accomplishments, 126–30
  essay on, 130
  failure and, 127–28
  finding, 126–29
  lesson regarding, 129
Shores, Mae Jennifer (UCLA)
  on extracurriculars, 34
  on recommendations, 76
Significant moments, 121–22
Slideshow essay, 217–22
  approaches to, 218
  clever vs. creative and, 218, 220
  examples of, 222
  lesson, 221–22
  overview of, 217–19
  tight parameters and, 218–19
Soros, George, 193, 196
Stanford, 246–47
Stats
  admissions committees use of,
    10–11, 12, 16
  admissions process and, 16
  bottom line, 12
  candidacy and, 10–12
  GMAT, 11–12
  GPA, 11, 12
  purpose of, 10
Support letters
  vs. recommendations, 64
  waitlist and, 258

Talking points
  content, 56
  cutting-and-pasting of, 59
  integration and, 56–57
  for recommenders, 54–57, 59

Testing, 79
Three Blind Mice, 96–97
Time, Wall Street Myth of, 31–33
Tip sheet, school research, 112–17
Toastmasters, 29–30
Tuck, 188, 260
2+2 program, 13

Uniqueness essay, 182–90
  embracing who you are in, 183–84,
    189–87
  example, 188–90
  lesson on, 186–87
  overview of, 182–83
University of California Berkeley
    (Haas), 32, 72, 192
University of California Los Angeles
    (Anderson), 34, 76
University of Chicago (Booth), 15, 35,
    218
University of Pennsylvania (Wharton),
    52, 75
University of Texas Austin
    (McCombs), 35, 52, 85
Update letter, writing, 256–57,
    260–61
Up-management, 146

Values
  accomplishments essays and, 121
  choosing between two, 158–60
Verbal tests, GMAT, 12
Vision
  barometer of, 92
  centrality of, 91
  lacking, 93–95
Visits, campus, 116–17, 258

Waitlist
  actions to get off, 255–59
  application review and, 255–56
  campus visits and, 258, 263
  conclusions regarding, 263–64
  getting off, 259–61, 261–63

GMAT retaking and, 258, 261–62
GPA/GMAT deficiencies and,
    261–62
new recommendation and,
    257–58
overview regarding, 254–55,
    263–64
ping email and, 258, 259
profiles, 259–63
significance of, 255
taking classes and, 258, 262–63
update letter and, 256–57,
    260–61
yield increased via, 261
Waiver, recommendations, 62
Wall Street myth
  analysts example of, 31–33
  quiz, 34
Weakness
  bullshit, 57–58
  fatal, 58
What makes you unique essay. See
    Uniqueness essay
What matters most essay,
    205–16
  Bolton and, 206, 207, 209
  connecting life themes in,
    207–12
  example, 213–16
  Obama regarding, 212
  overview of, 205–6
  pitfalls of, 206
  thinking levels regarding,
    211–12
Whimsical essay, 191–204
  example, 196–97
  example questions for, 192, 195
  Johnson, Peter, and, 192
  lessons, 195, 199–200, 203
  open, 201–4
  overview of, 191–92
  passion, 198–200
  random topic, 192–97
  what to avoid in, 194–97

www.forsterthomas.com
www.thembarealitycheck.com

About the Authors

Evan Forster is the founder of Forster-Thomas Inc., a premier educational consulting firm serving b-school candidates across North America, as well as foreign candidates from Beijing to Brazil. He is also a regular speaker at Wall Street investment banks, private equity shops, and management consulting firms. Forster came to educational consulting through his work as a writer, beginning as an admissions essay specialist. As a journalist, Forster has captured personalities for *New York*, *Jane*, and *Biography*; written features for *Details*, *Cosmopolitan*, *The Utne Reader*, and *POZ*; and covered service pieces from every angle in magazines as diverse as *Men's Health*, *Mademoiselle*, and *American Baby*. He was the college editor for *Seventeen* for five years. Forster also works extensively with college, law, clinical psychology, education, film, medical, and international relations candidates. He is a member of the Independent Educational Consultants Association, the National Association for College Admissions Counseling, and the Higher Education Consultants Association. Forster earned his BS in speech from Northwestern University and two MFAs from UCLA's film school.

David Thomas's encyclopedic collection of admissions trends and stats could fill a book in itself. He brings twelve years of experience as a magazine editor, including senior positions at *Yahoo! Internet Life*, *Individual Investor*, and *POZ* (which was nominated for a 1997 National Magazine Award for General Excellence during his term as editor in chief). He spent the obligatory late-'90s dot-com stint at Deja.com, where he produced the politics channel and buyers guides. He has published freelance articles in magazines including *Men's Health*, *Seventeen*, *Music Choice*, and *The New Physician*. As a financial journalist, Thomas interviewed such well-known players as Lou Dobbs, Richard Grasso, James Grant, and Henry Blodgett. Thomas received his BA in Asian studies from the University of Texas at Austin and a master's in magazine publishing from Northwestern University.

Business and life partners, Forster and Thomas currently reside in Brooklyn, New York.